GREAT MYTHS OF
ADOLESCENCE

Great Myths of Psychology

Series Editors
Scott O. Lilienfeld
Steven Jay Lynn

This superb series of books tackles a host of fascinating myths and misconceptions regarding specific domains of psychology, including child development, aging, marriage, brain science, and mental illness, among many others. Each book not only dispels multiple erroneous but widespread psychological beliefs, but provides readers with accurate and up-to-date scientific information to counter them. Written in engaging, upbeat, and user-friendly language, the books in the myths series are replete with scores of intriguing examples drawn from everyday psychology. As a result, readers will emerge from each book entertained and enlightened. These unique volumes will be invaluable additions to the bookshelves of educated laypersons interested in human nature, as well as of students, instructors, researchers, journalists, and mental health professionals of all stripes.

www.wiley.com/go/psychmyths

Published

50 Great Myths of Popular Psychology
Scott O. Lilienfeld, Steven Jay Lynn, John Ruscio, and Barry L. Beyerstein

Great Myths of Aging
Joan T. Erber and Lenore T. Szuchman

Great Myths of the Brain
Christian Jarrett

Great Myths of Child Development
Stephen Hupp and Jeremy Jewell

Great Myths of Intimate Relationships
Matthew D. Johnson

Great Myths of Education and Learning
Jeffrey D. Holmes

Great Myths of Adolescence
Jeremy D. Jewell, Michael I. Axelrod, Mitchell J. Prinstein, and Stephen Hupp

Forthcoming

Great Myths of Personality
M. Brent Donnellan and Richard E. Lucas

Great Myths of Autism
James D. Herbert

50 Great Myths of Popular Psychology, Second Edition
Scott O. Lilienfeld, Steven Jay Lynn, John Ruscio, and Barry L. Beyerstein

GREAT MYTHS OF ADOLESCENCE

Jeremy D. Jewell, Michael I.
Axelrod, Mitchell J. Prinstein,
and Stephen Hupp

WILEY Blackwell

This edition first published 2019
© 2019 John Wiley & Sons Ltd

The right of Jeremy D. Jewell, Michael I. Axelrod, Mitchell J. Prinstein, and Stephen Hupp to be identified as the authors of this work has been asserted in accordance with law.

Registered Offices
John Wiley & Sons, Inc., 111 River Street, Hoboken, NJ 07030, USA

John Wiley & Sons Ltd, The Atrium, Southern Gate, Chichester, West Sussex, PO19 8SQ, UK

Editorial Office
111 River Street, Hoboken, NJ 07030, USA

For details of our global editorial offices, customer services, and more information about Wiley products visit us at www.wiley.com.

Wiley also publishes its books in a variety of electronic formats and by print-on-demand. Some content that appears in standard print versions of this book may not be available in other formats.

Library of Congress Cataloging-in-Publication Data

Names: Jewell, Jeremy D., 1970– author. | Axelrod, Michael I., author. | Prinstein, Mitchell J., 1970– author. | Hupp, Stephen., author.
Title: Great myths of adolescence / Jeremy D. Jewell, Michael I. Axelrod, Mitchell J. Prinstein, and Stephen Hupp.
Description: First Edition. | Hoboken : Wiley, [2019] | Series: Great myths of psychology | Includes bibliographical references and index. |
Identifiers: LCCN 2018024850 (print) | LCCN 2018026691 (ebook) | ISBN 9781119248781 (Adobe PDF) | ISBN 9781119248798 (ePub) | ISBN 9781119248767 (hardcover) | ISBN 9781119248774 (pbk.)
Subjects: LCSH: Adolescence. | Adolescent psychology.
Classification: LCC HQ796 (ebook) | LCC HQ796 .J539 2019 (print) | DDC 305.235–dc23
LC record available at https://lccn.loc.gov/2018024850

Cover Design by Wiley
Cover Image: © A-Digit/Getty Images-School Kids Silhouettes;
© A-Digit/Getty Images-Cell Addiction

Set in 10/12.5pt Sabon by SPi Global, Pondicherry, India

Printed in Singapore by C.O.S. Printers Pte Ltd

10   9   8   7   6   5   4   3   2   1

This book is dedicated to teens everywhere who are
working to understand who
they are and how they fit in the world.
and

To Kelly, Brea, and Chaney
(J.J.)

To Henry, George, and Angela
(M.A.)

To Tina, Samara, and Max
(M.P.)

To Henry, Vyla, Evan, and Farrah
(S.H.)

CONTENTS

FOREWORD

Jeffrey Jensen Arnett

As monkeys go, we are a remarkably clever species in some ways. Alone among monkeys—alone among all creatures, in fact—we tamed fire many thousands of years ago and began to use it for our purposes. From the taming of fire to the creation of smartphones and their myriad apps, we have used our exceptional cognitive abilities to bend the world to our purposes, and to make our lives more comfortable and abundant.

Yet, at the same time, alone among all creatures, we have a special proclivity for believing nonsense. From the beginning of our recorded history, and no doubt for many millennia before, we have held a fabulous array of beliefs that are simply not true. From the belief that the sun is transported across the sky each day by a chariot pulled by heavenly horses, to the belief that misfortunes are a consequence of the malevolent "evil eye" of one's enemies, to the belief that the individual's personality is determined by the balance of four "humors" in the body—blood, phlegm, yellow bile, and black bile—and many, many more, we show an astonishing level of creativity for explaining how the world works and why things happen and why we behave the way we do, all of which is entirely fabricated. What other monkey would be so foolish?

The rise of science about 500 years ago was a brilliant and world-changing innovation which, for the first time ever—yes, including the ancient Greeks, who may have been wise in some ways but were also enthusiastic purveyors of nonsense—put a systematic check on the human tendency to believe in things that are not true. Science requires evidence, and has rules for judging the validity of proffered evidence that everyone who engages in the scientific enterprise commits to following. The establishment of systems of scientific evaluation led to an explosion of fact-based knowledge that changed everything about how we live, and that revolution continues today.

Nevertheless, the rise of science did not extinguish the human proclivity for believing nonsense. Science only muted this tendency, and provided rules and standards to expose it and correct it. Humans, including scientists themselves, have a persistent, immutable attraction to appealing stories that seem to explain things in a comforting and familiar way, regardless of whether the stories are fact-based. Hence, there is a perpetual need for important works like this one, to draw our attention to the things we believe that are not correct.

This book focuses on adolescence, and follows other "Great Myths" books including the original work on myths of popular psychology (Lilienfeld, Lynn, Ruscio, & Beyerstein, 2010) as well as a book that focused on "Great Myths of Child Development" (Hupp & Jewell, 2015). It covers a wide range of myths, 50 in all, and many of them will seem familiar to any reader. Some of the "Mini-Myths" are disposed of in a paragraph or two, whereas others receive more extended treatment. The latter include a useful "What you need to know" capsule summary at the end.

Almost everyone will discover here at least one myth they will have to give up in the face of the evidence. For me, it was "Greek life has a negative effect on college students academically." I was also surprised by the myth that "High school football players are more likely to become seriously injured than cheerleaders," given all the public attention to concussion risks among football players. I hope other readers will find, as I did, that even though it is never pleasant to have to admit you were wrong, there is satisfaction to be had in discarding false beliefs in favor of the facts.

But back to the original question of my Foreword, why do people have a tendency to believe nonsense? There are, no doubt, inherent cognitive tendencies we all share that lead us to misunderstand what we observe or experience, for example the tendency to interpret correlation as causation. However, with regard to adolescents in particular, many years of my own research and reading, as well as reading the present book, lead me to propose five factors that contribute to our beliefs in myths about adolescents.

1. Despising the young is arguably the last respectable prejudice, and believing the myths allows people to feel superior to them.
2. Some myths seem to be verified by the extensive media coverage they receive.
3. Many of the myths are portrayed in popular culture, particularly films and television.

4. Myths may be embraced because they are part of a broader political worldview.
5. Some myths seem logical, like they *should* be true.

Let's consider each of these explanations briefly.

The last respectable prejudice

The authors recognize that contempt for the young has been around for a long time, going back at least to Aristotle, and can be found in many different times and places (also see Arnett, 1999). The present book contains some potent examples of such myths, including that "Teens these days are worse behaved compared to previous generations" and that "The millennial generation is lazy."

But why? Why does each generation tend to find the generation on the rise to be deficient in some ways? Books can and probably have been written to explain why, but one simple explanation is that adolescents are always a low-status group because they have little power, and low-status groups always receive contempt from high-status groups (Cheng, Tracy, & Anderson, 2014). Adolescents have little power because they are young; they are economically dependent on their parents, and they have not yet had a chance to accrue the knowledge and skills that may translate later into power.

This explanation, however, is no excuse. In recent decades, Western societies have come to view numerous traditions of contempt toward low-status groups as unacceptable: slurs against women, ethnic minorities, or sexual minorities were once not just accepted but celebrated with zeal and mirth by those in high-status groups. Times have changed, for the better, but the prejudice against the young remains. The authors here state that "most of all we want to debunk the idea that teens these days are worse than previous generations," because they recognize how unfair that prejudice is and how destructive it is. It's time that bashing the young went the way of other formerly accepted prejudices. This book will help.

Media coverage distorts perceptions of frequency

Some myths flourish because they represent shocking events that draw media attention, and the media attention has the effect of leading us to believe the events are more common than they really are. Two examples of this would be "Teens have the highest suicide rate" and "School violence is on the rise."

Psychologists have identified what they call the "availability heuristic," meaning that when we try to judge the probability of an event, we think of "available" examples, things we have witnessed or heard about (Tversky & Kahneman, 1974). Media coverage makes events like teen suicide and school violence more available. This is not the media's fault, exactly. Suicide is less, not more, common in the teen years than in older age groups, but often more shocking because of the youth of the victim. If someone commits suicide at age 16 or 17, we not unreasonably think of it as a tragic waste of a potential life, because there is so much life yet to come, so much more opportunity to correct whatever is causing distress, compared to a suicide in the later years of life. In the case of school violence, we can hardly expect the media not to cover an event in which someone enters a school and commits mass murder, even if it is true that adolescents are at far more risk when they enter an automobile than when they enter a school.

However, this is not to let the media entirely off the hook. Spectacular coverage of teen suicides or school violence has the potential, at least, of generating more such events. Suicide contagion has been documented (Sisask & Värnik, 2012), and a motivation of at least some school shooters is to obtain a perverse kind of fame.

Myths of adolescence flourish in popular culture

A related reason for the prevalence of beliefs in myths of adolescence is that many of them are staples of the plot lines of popular culture, particularly films and TV shows. The authors do an excellent job in this book of providing many such examples.

This is unsurprising if you think about it a bit. It may not be true that "Popular teens are usually mean," but there's not much dramatic potential in popular teens being nice to the nerds and rejected kids. It's not true that "Most teens have strained relationships with their parents," but a movie about teens and parents getting along harmoniously would probably be short and not very compelling.

To some extent, these kinds of distortions and extremes are inherent in dramatic story lines, and not just for adolescents. It's not common, either, for a short-tempered man to kill his father unwittingly and then unwittingly marry his mother, but that's how you get the story of Oedipus Rex that has fascinated and appalled audiences for millennia. It's just that, given the above-discussed tendency to heap abuse on the young, it is important to remind people (as this book does) that films and TV plots about adolescents don't represent all adolescents or even most of them. It's just a movie, after all.

Myths can be part of a political worldview

It is also important to recognize that some false beliefs about adolescents are not isolated myths but part of a fabric of political beliefs into which the myth conveniently fits. For example, the myth that "Abstinence-only sex education programs are effective at keeping teens abstinent" fits neatly into a conservative worldview that premarital sex is wrong. Similarly, on the liberal side, the myth that "College placement tests are ineffective at predicting academic success in college" fits into a larger worldview that people can become whatever they wish to be and are not limited by the extent of inherited abilities or past experiences.

Myths that support a political worldview are likely to be especially hard to dispel. Mere facts may be of little use. The myth may be emotionally comforting, and acknowledging that it is wrong may mean casting doubt on the entire worldview, or creating cognitive dissonance, which people generally find unpleasant and try to avoid. On the other hand, it may be especially important to speak up loudly against this kind of myth, as these myths are often the basis of public policies that are useless or harmful, such as devoting government funding to "abstinence-only" sex education programs that do not reduce unintended pregnancies rather than to comprehensive sexuality education programs that do (Haberland & Rognow, 2015).

Myths sometimes seem logical and therefore plausible

Finally, some myths seem to make sense, so people embrace them without knowing about or caring about what research may say. In this vein, it is understandable that, for example, most people believe that "Traditional high school 'Driver Education' courses have a strong record of making teens safe drivers." How could it be otherwise? Isn't it obvious that being taught how to drive in a certified program would make you better prepared to begin driving? Sure it is, until you learn that research leads to the opposite conclusion, and this counterintuitive result is explained by adolescents who have taken driver education having a misplaced confidence in their driving abilities following the course, which raises their risk of accidents. Several other myths seem to fall into this category, including "Teens should have a job in high school to build character," "College students gain 15 pounds their freshman year," and "Teens can be 'scared straight.'"

One reason research is so important is precisely that many of the things we take for granted as true turn out not to be. Here as with the previous point, the consequences of false beliefs have important public policy implications. Once you know that traditional driver education programs predict greater risk of involvement in accidents, you can change their content to try to find more effective methods. Once you know there's no evidence that "Teens can be scared straight," you can shift public money from those kinds of programs to programs that research supports as more effective. And so on.

Conclusion: More empathy, fewer stereotypes

All in all, this provocative, informative, and entertaining book is a testimony to the value and importance of high-quality research. Because we have many cognitive tendencies that lead us to embrace nonsense, we are in perpetual need of the bracing tonic of science to steer us back toward the way things really are. The essays in the present book deepen our understanding of how adolescents really are in the twenty-first century. The book also subtly encourages us to be less harsh in our judgments of the young. Being young can be exciting, but it is not easy to find your way in the world. Dodging the opprobrium, ridicule, and nasty stereotypes of older folks does not help. It never has. By shattering many of these stereotypes, this book offers a sympathetic, encouraging, and—most important of all—reality-based portrayal of today's adolescents.

References

Arnett, J. J. (1999). Adolescent storm and stress, reconsidered. *American Psychologist*, 54(5), 317–326.

Cheng, J. T., Tracy, J. L., & Anderson, C. A. (2014). *The psychology of social status*. New York, NY: Springer.

Haberland, N., & Rogow, D. (2015). Sexuality education: Emerging trends in evidence and practice. *Journal of Adolescent Health*, 56(1), S15–S21.

Hupp, S., & Jewell, J. (2015). *Great myths of child development*. New York, NY: Wiley.

Lilienfeld, S. O., Lynn, S. J., Ruscio, J., & Beyerstein, B. L. (2010). *50 great myths of popular psychology: Shattering widespread misconceptions about human behavior*. Malden, MA: Wiley-Blackwell.

Sisask, M., & Värnik, A. (2012). Media roles in suicide prevention: A systematic review. *International Journal of Environmental Research and Public Health, 9*(1), 123–138.

Tversky, A., & Kahneman, D. (1974). Judgment under uncertainty: Heuristics and biases. *Science, 185*(4157), 1124–1131.

PREFACE

As with any book, *Great Myths of Adolescence* is the product of the hard work of a number of individuals, to whom would we like to give credit and thanks. First, we would like to extend our gratitude to Scott Lilienfeld and Steven Jay Lynn who wrote the founding book in this series, *50 Great Myths of Popular Psychology*. We especially appreciate their mentorship and guidance. We've used this founding book as a guide in many ways while writing *Great Myths of Child Development* and now *Great Myths of Adolescence*. We would also like to thank Darren Reed and Danielle Descoteaux from Wiley Publishing. Their encouragement and assistance during the early conceptual stages of this book were invaluable. We are also appreciative of Liz Wingett, Monica Rogers, and Elisha Benjamin for helping us carry this book over the finish line. There have also been a number of students who have helped with some of the research required for this book. In particular, we would like to give special thanks to several research assistants—Hannah Dahms, Madison Schoen, Bethany Myszka, Molly Logic, and Katie Paulich—for their important contributions to the development and investigation of some of the myths.

INTRODUCTION

Someone famous once described the youth of society in the following way:

> Young men have strong passions, and tend to gratify them indiscriminately. Of the bodily desires, it is the sexual by which they are most swayed and in which they show absence of self-control. They are changeable and fickle in their desires, which are violent while they last, but quickly over…They are hot-tempered, and quick-tempered, and apt to give way to their anger; bad temper often gets the better of them, for owing to their love of honour they cannot bear being slighted and are indignant if they imagine themselves unfairly treated.

In other words, "teens these days" are sex-starved, hot-headed, and become angry when they think they're being disrespected. And who is the mysterious writer? It was Aristotle, the famous Greek philosopher who lived more than 2,400 years ago (Aristotle, Rhetoric Book II Chapter 12 as translated in Barnes, 2014). And it seems that the cynical view of "teens these days" has continued throughout the centuries, as exemplified in the first season of the Emmy-nominated show *True Detective* (Fukunaga, 2014), starring Matthew McConaughey and Woody Harrelson. In the show, Harrelson's father-in-law echoes Aristotle:

> *So you're telling me the world isn't getting worse? I've seen kids today, all in black, wearing makeup, sh*t on their faces; everything is sex.*

Great Myths of Adolescence, First Edition. Jeremy D. Jewell, Michael I. Axelrod, Mitchell J. Prinstein, and Stephen Hupp.
© 2019 John Wiley & Sons Ltd. Published 2019 by John Wiley & Sons Ltd.

While negative stereotypes of teens and young adults have existed for millennia, some of these stereotypes hold true when scrutinized under the lens of science while other stereotypes do not. For example, the stereotype that risky behavior generally declines over time when one moves from the teen years into middle adulthood is quite true. However, the often-held notion that most teens routinely get drunk on the weekends is not true. In fact, research shows that half of high school seniors report that they have never been drunk.

Format of the book and target audiences

Myths related to sex, drugs, and self-control, as well as many others, will be tackled in this book, which could be considered a sequel to our first published book *Great Myths of Child Development* (Hupp & Jewell, 2015), and will share many of the features of that first book. For example, in the current book we define each myth, identify each myth's prevalence, and present the latest and most significant research debunking the myth. We also conduct our own research on the prevalence of belief in each myth, from the perspective of college students, and present those findings throughout the book. Additionally, we link each myth to various pop culture icons that have helped propagate the myths. For example, in the *Great Myths of Child Development* (Hupp & Jewell, 2015), we reference television shows such as *Moonshiners, Duck Dynasty, The Simpsons, Mad Men, Sex in the City,* and many more. In the current book we reference movies such as *Mean Girls, House Party, Superbad, Project X,* as well as the *Twilight* and *Hunger Games* movie series. Other television series that we also cite include *Stranger Things, South Park, Jackass, Degrassi, Glee, Two and a Half Men,* and *Gossip Girl.* We also give mention to a few well-known doctors such as Dr. Phil and Dr. Oz. At the end of each major myth, we conclude with a discussion about why the myth is harmful and best practices related to the topic in the "What you need to know" section. For example, the myth that most teens routinely get drunk on the weekends is harmful because the communication of that myth has the potential to actually increase teen alcohol use. Specifically, teens may be more likely to get drunk if the myth leads them to think that "everyone is doing it—so it's OK if I do too" or "everyone expects me to, so I guess I will."

Similar to our first book, we believe that *Great Myths of Adolescence* has two primary audiences. The first audience is teachers and college students who may use this book as an ancillary text to their primary textbook for Adolescent Development or Lifespan Development courses. We believe that the content of this book is complementary to information found in traditional textbooks. For example, as college students learn and read about physical and brain development in adolescence and emerging adulthood, myths in this book such as "The Teen Brain is Fully Developed by Age 18" present concepts and research that deepen the reader's understanding on brain development during adolescence. The second audience for this book is the broader public who is interested in myths of psychology, and in particular, parents of teens will likely find that considering these myths is helpful. Our society's stigma towards adolescents and the tumultuous "teen years" has made parents particularly intimidated by what are likely typical problems that teens face. We hope that the ideas presented in this book will help those parents perceive their teenager in a new light, seeing them as human beings that are on a path to become adults but faced with uncertainty as they make a host of important decisions in just a few short years.

Our research on prevalence of myths

Again similar to our first book *Great Myths of Child Development* (Hupp & Jewell, 2015), we strive to include data regarding the prevalence of belief in the myths. As before, we believe that for a myth to be a "great myth" it needs to be widely held. Unfortunately, despite our tireless searching, there are often gaps in the literature regarding the prevalence of a particular myth. Therefore, we cite current opinion polls from typical research centers such as Gallup and the Pew Research Center when we can. However, we also conducted our own research on the prevalence of the myths in this book with a sample of college students from a university in the Midwest. Specifically, we created the Opinions About Teens Scales (OATS) that had approximately 50 statements that were usually the precisely phrased myths from this book. We asked college student participants to respond as to whether they had heard of this myth, and they then rated their belief in the myth on a four-point scale ranging from "agree" to "disagree." Participants were considered to have endorsed a myth if they responded "agree" or "somewhat agree" to the item. In order to increase validity of the measure, we also mixed in several facts about adolescent development (e.g., "Developing a sense of self-identity is important for most teens") throughout the OATS. Data from 76 college student participants were gathered at the beginning of a Child Psychology course. Data from a second sample consisting of 170 students from a different Child Psychology course were gathered a few months later. When the prevalence rate for a particular myth is discussed from this study, it is often reported in terms of a range, which reflects the rate for the two samples (Jewell & Hupp, 2018).

Emphasis on evidence

A few guiding principles drove the collection of evidence for this book. Specifically, wherever possible we relied on meta-analyses or reviews, which accumulated results from several studies, rather than relying on individual studies. Although, we often described a single study as an example of the type of research on a given topic, in most cases many other studies arrived at similar conclusions. We also gave a lot of weight to well-designed studies and findings that were supported by more than one research team. Relatedly, in the "What you need to know" sections we often included reviews that identify evidence-based treatments (EBTs) as defined by the Society for Clinical Child and Adolescent Psychology (Southam-Gerow & Prinstein, 2014). Here's a brief summary of their definition of different levels of EBTs:

Level 1: Well-established treatments. Treatments in this category have at least two well-designed studies showing the treatment was more effective than another treatment or placebo, and at least two of the studies were conducted by different research teams.

Level 2: Probably efficacious treatments. There are two options for this category. One is that the treatment has at least two well-designed studies, but instead of comparing the treatment with another treatment it is compared with a waitlist group and thus unable to control for placebo effects. The other is that the study meets the full criteria for the well-established level, but there is only one study or only one team doing more than one study.

Level 3: Possibly efficacious treatments. This level only requires one well-done randomized control trial where the treatment is compared with a waitlist group.

Level 4: Experimental treatments. The treatment has not yet been tested or, if tested, still does not meet the above criteria.

Level 5: Treatment of questionable efficacy. Treatments in which the "only evidence available from experimental studies suggests the treatment produces no beneficial effect" (Southam-Gerow & Prinstein, 2014, p. 2).

Many of the topics in this book do not relate to treatments for disorders; however, the above definitions of EBTs are consistent with the type of research we used to present information about the myths.

Primary theme of the book

In our first book *Great Myths of Child Development* (Hupp & Jewell, 2015), we discussed a number of myths. However, if there was one main theme of that book, it would probably be that many myths held by society induce a lot of unnecessary guilt in parents. For example, the myth that only children are selfish and spoiled may lead couples to have a second child out of guilt when actually they would be quite satisfied with only one child. Or the myth that divorce ruins most kids' lives may cause a parent to remain in a highly conflictual or abusive relationship when in fact their child may thrive after divorce due to the decrease in family conflict. And finally, the myth that daycare damages the parent–child attachment may cause guilt and mood problems in parents who are forced to work and place their child in daycare for financial reasons.

With this in mind, the primary theme of the current book is something quite different. Going back to the quote from Aristotle, we believe that the idea that "teens these days" are quite different—and worse—than previous generations of adolescents is harmful to society as a whole for several reasons. For example, when adults believe that "teens these days" exhibit problematic behavior at a greater rate than when they were teenagers, this idea creates an attitude of "us" versus "them." This, somewhat artificial, generational divide makes it more difficult for adults to communicate with, and relate to, teenagers. Secondly, similar to a self-fulfilling prophecy, when adults expect to have problems connecting with teenagers, they will actually have more of the problems that they expected. This idea is exemplified and explored in the two myths that "Most teens have a strained relationship with their parents" and "Successful transition into adulthood requires that teens detach from parents." Finally, it is important to understand that what society believes is mostly a "teen problem" is actually experienced in adults much more than many would like to admit. For example, a recent review found that the average prevalence rate for teen sexting ranged from 10% to 15% while sexting in adult samples was about three times higher, ranging from 33% to 53% (Klettke, Hallford, & Mellor, 2014). And regarding drug use, the United States Centers for Disease Control (CDC) found that in 2014, 7.4% of teens (ages 12–17) used marijuana in the last month (Azofeifa et al., 2016).

However, the same report found that 8.0% of adults ages 35–44 also used marijuana in the last month. This finding led to the headline by the *Washington Post* that "Middle-aged parents are now more likely to smoke weed than their teenage kids" (Ingraham, 2016). Thus, most of all we want to debunk the idea that teens these days are worse than in previous generations. Because the truth is that the developmental period of adolescence today is more similar than different compared with the days of Aristotle. And teens' shortcomings are rarely confined to the teenage years, with many adults exhibiting similar flaws. So in a nutshell, let's cut teens a little more slack.

References

Azofeifa, A., Mattson, M. E., Schauer, G., McAfee, T., Grant, A., & Lyerla, R. (2016, December). National estimates of marijuana use and related indicators—National Survey on Drug Use and National Center for Statistics and Analysis. Alcohol impaired driving: 2015 data. *Traffic Safety Facts. DOT HS 812 350*. Washington, DC: National Highway Traffic Safety Administration.

Barnes, J. (Ed.) (2014). *Complete works of Aristotle, Volume 1: The revised Oxford translation*. Princeton, NJ: Princeton University Press.

Fukunaga, C. (Director). (2014). Seeing things. [Television series episode]. In N. Pizzolato (Creator), *True detective*. New York City, NY: HBO.

Hupp, S., & Jewell, J. (2015). *Great myths of child development*. Malden, MA: Wiley.

Ingraham, C. (2016, September). Middle-aged parents are now more likely to smoke weed than their teenage kids. *Washington Post*. Retrieved from https://www.washingtonpost.com/news/wonk/wp/2016/09/02/middle-aged-parents-are-now-more-likely-to-smoke-weed-than-their-teenaged-kids/?utm_term=.2796e78ac918.

Jewell, J. D., & Hupp, S. D. A. (2018). Prevalence of myths about adolescence [Manuscript in preparation].

Klettke, B., Hallford, D. J., & Mellor, D. J. (2014). Sexting prevalence and correlates: A systematic literature review. *Clinical Psychology Review, 34*(1), 44–53.

Southam-Gerow, M. A., & Prinstein, M. J. (2014). Evidence base updates: The evolution of the evaluation of psychological treatments for children and adolescents. *Journal of Clinical Child & Adolescent Psychology, 43*(1), 1–6.

1 DEVELOPMENT OF THE BODY, BRAIN, AND MIND

Great Myths of Adolescence, First Edition. Jeremy D. Jewell, Michael I. Axelrod,
Mitchell J. Prinstein, and Stephen Hupp.
© 2019 John Wiley & Sons Ltd. Published 2019 by John Wiley & Sons Ltd.

Myth #1

Adolescence ends at 18 years old

Disney built an animated film empire by telling coming of age stories about princesses and female heroines. Take Rapunzel from the movie *Tangled* (Conli, Greno, & Howard, 2010), who, on the eve of her 18th birthday, leaves her sheltered tower to enter a world that is both dangerous and enchanting. "Venture outside your comfort zone. The rewards are worth it," she says as she lowers herself out of the tower using her long, blond hair (Conli et al., 2010). What follows is the story of Rapunzel's journey from childhood to adulthood. Jasmine from *Aladdin* (Clements & Musker, 1992) was 15. Ariel from *The Little Mermaid* (Musker, Ashman, & Clements, 1989) was 16. Belle from *Beauty and the Beast* (Hahn, Trousdale, & Wise, 1991) was 17. Aurora from *Sleeping Beauty* (Disney & Geronimi, 1959) was 16. Merida from *Brave* (Sarafian, Andrews, & Chapman, 2012) was 16, and Snow White (Disney & Hand, 1937) was 14 when they had their coming-of-age experiences or events marking the transition from childhood to adulthood. For these Disney characters, the transition involved becoming mature, independent, and self-assured.

Disney's depiction of these characters' coming-of-age happening at or slightly before 18 coincides with the age at which many cultural and religious traditions honor the adolescent becoming an adult. In Spanish-speaking Latin America, families and friends celebrate a girl's 15th birthday by throwing a large party, or Quinceanera, marking the transition from childhood to young womanhood. The Jewish coming-of-age takes place when boys celebrate their Bar Mitzvahs and girls celebrate their Bat Mitzvahs at age 13 and 12 respectively, a demonstration of their religious commitment, recognition of the responsibilities associated with Jewish law, and acknowledgment of adulthood. On North Baffin Island, the Inuit coming-of-age for boys occurs between the ages of 11 and 12 when they're expected to demonstrate their hunting skills and ability to survive the harsh Arctic weather.

Scholars have traditionally viewed high school graduation as marking the end of the coming of age for most contemporary teenagers in industrialized societies (see Delaney, 1995). The culmination of 4 years of supervised education by adults concluding in the graduation ceremony resembles many religious and tribal coming-of-age rituals. What follows for the majority of American high school graduates is higher education (i.e., 2- or 4-year college) or a place in the workforce (Bureau of Labor Statistics, 2016), both traditionally considered a time when an individual is expected to behave in an adult-like manner. The public generally views

18 to be the start of adulthood. For example, *The Escapist*, an online magazine, conducted an online poll and found 18 years to be the most often selected age to the question "when does adolescence end?" (*The Escapist*, 2015).

It shouldn't be surprising that people believe 18 to be the end of adolescence. Many of the freedoms and responsibilities of adulthood are legally permitted by the age of 18. For example, in most countries, boys and girls can marry, enlist in the military, purchase alcohol and tobacco products, drive a tractor trailer, get a tattoo, and skydive on their 18th birthday. In the US, the Fair Standards Labor Act sets 14 years as the minimum age for employment. Fourteen is also the minimum age in most states when juveniles may be tried in criminal (i.e., adult) court (Office of Juvenile Justice and Delinquency Prevention, 2003). So it seems that the myth that adolescence ends at 18 years is promoted by both distorted popular culture references, like the Disney princesses and heroines, as well as state and federal governmental statutes.

Another source for this myth is the desire for easy answers. Human beings want to believe that answers to important questions are straightforward and void of gray areas. For human and nonhuman primates, the purpose of adolescence is clear. It's a time of physical and sexual maturity, acquisition of skills necessary for adulthood, establishing independence from parents, and modifying social relationships with same and opposite gender peers. What is much less clear is when the developmental period of adolescence ends and adulthood begins. Such uncertainty can be problematic, as behavioral research has found human beings avoid ambiguity or individuals' subjective experiences with uncertainty (Frisch & Baron, 1988). Perhaps it's more comforting to believe that adulthood begins at or shortly after 18 years of age rather than consider the complexity of the question or admit that there is no straightforward answer.

So, when does adolescence end? At one time, the boundaries of adolescence were the teenage years, beginning at 13 and ending at 19 (Steinberg, 2011). During the 20th century, the span of adolescence increased substantially following research suggesting physical maturity (e.g., puberty) begins earlier (Settersten, Furstenberg, & Rumbaut, 2005), as science has learned, for example, that the average age of menarche has dropped since data were first collected almost 200 years ago (Steinberg, 2011). However, many contemporary adolescent development scholars now recommend understanding the end of adolescence by examining specific biological and societal markers that represent the transition from adolescence to adulthood rather than simply considering age (e.g., Arnett, 2000).

Biologically, three hormonal events mark the start of puberty (see Blakemore, Burnett, & Dahl, 2010). Gonadarche begins with the activation of the hypothalamus-pituitary-gland gonadal gland system, triggering the production of estrogen and testosterone, and marking the beginning of puberty. Adrenache, which often occurs before gonadarche, begins with the secretion of increased levels of androgens leading to the development of secondary sex characteristics. The third hormonal event involves a growth spurt that results in body size and composition changes. Only gonadarche has a clear end, developing the ability to reproduce, which can vary considerably among individuals making it difficult to assign a specific age to the official end of puberty and adolescence.

A different biological marker might provide a more exact answer to the question of when adolescence ends. Researchers have found that the chronotypes, or the behavioral expression of circadian rhythms (i.e., biological sleeping patterns), of humans increase until 19.5 years for females and 20.9 years for males, and then begin decreasing across the remainder of the lifespan (Roenneberg, Wirz-Justice, & Merrow, 2003). Put slightly differently, humans start becoming night owls at about the age of 10 until about the age of 20, when they gradually shift, over time, to becoming early risers. The amount of time asleep might not change much, but the general tendency for someone to fall sleep later (and wake later) or fall asleep earlier (and wake earlier) seems to vary between different developmental periods. Interestingly, and perhaps not surprisingly, given both are related to biology, changes in chronotype correspond to pubertal changes. There is a general propensity for girls to develop before boys, which is also observed in chronotype. While research hasn't yet ruled out other factors related to chronotype (e.g., behavioral, environmental), convincing data suggest the changes in sleep patterns might signify a biological endpoint to adolescence at about 20 years of age (Roenneberg et al., 2004).

Societal markers that represent the transition from adolescence to adulthood are much more subjective than biological markers but equally important in the developmental literature. A social perspective suggests the conclusion of adolescence coincides with an individual's realization of a stable adult role (Choudhury, 2010). Specifically, societal transitions have involved becoming economically independent, leaving home, completing formal education, working full time, getting married, and having a child (Melgar & Rossi, 2012). Research is finding that these transitions are occurring later for young people today. For example, the median age of marriage 50 years ago was 22 for men and 20 for women (Arnett, 2000). In 2016, the median age of marriage for men and women was almost 30 and 28, respectively (U.S. Census Bureau, 2017). In addition, the mean age of first-time mothers has increased from just over 21 years of age in 1970 to just over 26 years in 2014 (Mathews & Hamilton, 2002, 2016). To summarize, people are marrying later and having children later, possibly changing the societal marker for when adolescence ends and adulthood begins.

Other research paints, perhaps, a more striking difference between young people today and those of previous generations. Large-scale surveys spanning multiple decades and comparing generations of 23-year-olds on economic independence indicators such as full-time employment, still in school, leaving home, and receiving financial support have uncovered some interesting and, perhaps, not surprising findings. Specifically, all indicators decreased in favor of less financial independence in the younger generation (Steinberg, 2014). For example, more 23-year-olds from the high school graduating classes of 2002 and 2003 were in school compared with the graduating classes of 1976 and 1977 (33% vs. 20%), more were receiving financial support from parents (67% vs. 30%), fewer were living on their own (50% vs. 67%), and fewer were working more than 35 h a week (60% vs. 75%). These differences were just as noticeable when considering 25-year-olds. Fewer from the younger generation (i.e., graduating classes of 2002 and 2003) were financially independent from their parents (67% vs. 75%), living on their own (less than 67% vs. more than 75%), and working full time (70% vs. 80%) when compared with those from the older generation (i.e., graduating classes of 1976–1977).

These data are consistent with other data indicating many young adults remain unsettled after the age of 18. For example, young people between the ages of 20 and 29 are four times more likely than 15- to 19-year-olds and three times more likely than 30- to 34-year-olds to change where they live (Arnett, 2000). A common societal feature of adulthood is establishing a permanent residence, and it appears from the data that fewer young adults are settling down, at least in terms of where they reside. In addition, young people are changing jobs more now than ever before, as loyalty towards employers has decreased with each generation since World War II (Tolbize, 2008). A recent LinkedIn report (Berger, 2016) found that those graduating college between 2006 and 2016 worked, on average, for three companies within 5 years of graduating college. College graduates between 1986 and 1990 worked, on average, for about 2.5 companies within 10 years of graduating college. Scholars contend that the period between 19 and 30 years represents many demographic changes, including where one lives and works (Arnett, 2000).

These data suggest that individuals are transitioning later in life to roles and responsibility generally associated with adulthood. Furthermore, individuals are achieving financial independence from their parents later in life, including completing higher education, holding a full-time job, and living away from mom and dad. Taken together, it doesn't seem appropriate to label 18 as the end of adolescence when considering these generally agreed-upon social markers. However, it is also possible these social markers are either outdated or considered less important by today's standards. To investigate this issue, developmental psychologist Jeffrey Jensen Arnett (2001) asked adolescents (age 13–19), young adults (age 20–29), and midlife adults (age 30–55) about their conceptions of the transition from the adolescent years to adulthood. Arnett found that accepting responsibility and the consequences for one's behavior, identifying personal beliefs and values independent of parental or others' influences, and establishing a relationship with parents based on equality were most important across all three groups. He also found that, while being financially independent from parents was rated high among the groups, other social markers described above (e.g., full-time employment, completed education, purchase of a house, marriage, having at least one child) were rated lower than biological (e.g., able to father or bear children) and legal/chronological (reached age 18 or 21) transitions. In summarizing his findings, Arnett said, "individualistic criteria rank highest in importance, especially character qualities of accepting responsibility for one's own actions and deciding on one's own beliefs and values" (p. 142). And do young people feel as if they've achieved or reached adulthood? Arnett, in the same study, found that 86% of midlife adults (age 30–55) endorsed feeling they had reached adulthood compared to 46% of the young adults and 19% of the adolescents. Most notable, however, was the finding that 50% of the young adults endorsed the item "in some respects yes, in some respects no" when reporting on their beliefs about reaching adulthood.

What you need to know

A single, universal age boundary cannot be drawn between adolescence and adulthood. Rather, it might be best to think about the transition as occurring gradually over time, which is, in theory, what adolescence represents. The word *adolescence* comes from the Latin verb *adolescere*, which means "to grow into adulthood." Adolescence is the period in which a child becomes an adult. Placing an age on that process misses the point of what this developmental period signifies, a period influenced by many variables. Moreover, individual differences exist in when the process begins and ends. However, there are other frameworks to consider. For example, it might be best, as Arnett (2001) suggests, to consider the period following adolescence (i.e., 19–25 years) as *emerging adulthood*. He argues that this period is distinct from both adolescence and adulthood. Adolescence might no longer be conceptualized as a transition period from childhood to adulthood but, rather, a developmental period characterized by dramatic biological, cognitive, and social changes resulting in a preparedness to enter emerging adulthood. Emerging adulthood, then, describes the period after adolescence and before mid-adulthood. As author Jacqueline Arnone (2014) wrote, it seems that "25 is the new 18."

Research is clear that fewer young adults are taking on adult responsibilities (e.g., financial independence, marriage, parenthood) at the same age that their parents did. But why? To answer this question it might be important to understand the reasons young people are transitioning to adulthood later in life compared with just a few generations ago. Laurence Steinberg (2014), an expert on adolescent development, espoused several commonly held assumptions regarding this question that might not necessarily be supported by solid scientific research. For example, adults see young people today as "lazy, self-absorbed, and spoiled" (p. 60). Moreover, the media has labeled today's youth as entitled, believing they inherently deserve a life of privilege and special treatment (Greenbergerm, Lessard, Chen, & Farruggia, 2008). However, youth today are no more entitled than those of previous generations, as research over the last 30 years has found that changes in selfishness are related more to age than generation. For example, college students today are no less self-centered than college students 10 or 20 years ago; they are, however, more self-centered than their parents and grandparents when examining differences across generations (see Roberts, Edmonds, & Grijalva, 2010).

So, attempts at answering the question why are young people making the transition to adulthood later have been met with unsupported theories. What about theories supported by evidence? Steinberg (2014) offers one that considers recent research on brain development. Studies examining adolescent brain structure confirm that brain regions underlying attention, evaluation of risk and reward, and self-control continue to develop beyond age 18 (see Yurgelun-Todd, 2007). Furthermore, changes in cognitive ability, as a result of changes in the brain, gradually improve problem-solving during this time. Taken together, the lengthening of adolescence or the appearance of a new development period (i.e., emerging adulthood) might have something to do with brain development and the emergence of skills important for success in adulthood.

For those individuals transitioning from adolescence to adulthood and for the parents of those transitioning from adolescence to adulthood, understanding research and current scientific thinking about this developmental period is important for two reasons. First, it might alleviate worries or concerns about a failed adolescence. That is, those who are late transitioning from adolescence to adulthood aren't necessarily unsuccessful but, rather, more typical of their peers. For example, it's more acceptable now, versus 30 years ago, to settle down with a career and family after age 25. Thinking back to Disney princesses and heroines, Elsa from the movie *Frozen* (Del Vecho, Buck, & Lee, 2013), who was coroneted at 21, might represent a more typical picture of when emerging adulthood begins (at least from the viewpoint of a Disney princess). Second, no one should expect an overnight transformation. Experiences and learning opportunities occurring during adolescence are critical to helping an individual acquire skills important for success in adulthood. This, coupled with dramatic changes in the brain occurring simultaneously, marks a transitional period covering many years and not several days, making Rapunzel's one-day coming-of-age story seem as unrealistic as her using her long hair to escape a castle tower.

References

Arnett, J. J. (2000). A theory of development from the late teens through the twenties. *American Psychologist, 55*, 469–480.

Arnett, J. J. (2001). Conceptions of the transition to adulthood: Perspectives from adolescence through midlife. *Journal of Adult Development, 8*, 133–143.

Arnone, J. M. (2014). Adolescents may be older than we think: Today 25 is the new 18, or is it? *International Journal of Celiac Disease, 2*, 47–48.

Berger, G. (2016, April 12). Will this year's college grads job-hop more than previous grads? [Blog]. Retrieved from https://blog.linkedin.com/2016/04/12/will-this-year_s-college-grads-job-hop-more-than-previous-grads

Blakemore, S. J., Burnett, S., & Dahl, R. E. (2010). The role of puberty in the developing adolescent brain. *Human Brain Mapping, 31*, 926–933.

Bureau of Labor Statistics. (2016, April 28). College enrollment and work activity of 2015 high school graduates. Retrieved from https://www.bls.gov/news.release/hsgec.nr0.htm

Choudhury, S. (2010). Culturing the adolescent brain: What can neuroscience learn from anthropology? *Social Cognitive and Affective Neuroscience, 5,* 159–167.

Clements, R. (Producer & Director), & Musker, J. (Producer & Director). (1992). *Aladdin* [Motion picture]. United States: Walt Disney Pictures.

Conli, R. (Producer), Greno, N. (Director), & Howard, B. (Director). (2010). *Tangled* [Motion picture]. United States: Walt Disney Pictures.

Del Vecho, P. (Producer), Buck, C. (Director), & Lee, J. (Director). (2013). *Frozen* [Motion picture]. United States: Walt Disney Pictures.

Delaney, C. H. (1995). Rites of passage in adolescence. *Adolescence, 30,* 891–897.

Disney, W. (Producer), & Geronimi, C. (Director). (1959). *Sleeping Beauty* [Motion picture]. United States: Walt Disney Productions.

Disney, W. (Producer), & Hand, D. (Director). (1937). *Snow White and the Seven Dwarfs* [Motion picture]. United States: Walt Disney Productions.

Frisch, D., & Baron, J. (1988). Ambiguity and rationality. *Journal of Behavioral Decision Making, 1,* 149–157.

Greenbergerm, E., Lessard, J., Chen, C., & Farruggia, S. P. (2008). Self-entitled college students: Contributions of personality, parenting, and motivational factors. *Journal of Youth and Adolescence, 37,* 1193–1204.

Hahn, D. (Producer), Trousdale, G. (Director), & Wise, K. (Director). (1991). *Beauty and the Beast* [Motion picture]. United States: Walt Disney Pictures.

Mathews, T. J., & Hamilton, B. E. (2002, December 11). Mean age of mother, 1970–2000. *National Vital Statistics Report,* vol. 51, no. 1. Hyattsville, MD: National Center for Health Statistics.

Mathews, T. J., & Hamilton, B. E. (2016, January). Mean age of mother is on the rise: United States, 2000–2014. *National center for health statistics data brief, no.* 232. Hyattsville, MD: National Center for Health Statistics.

Melgar, N., & Rossi, M. (2012). When do people become adults? The Uruguayan case. *International Journal of Population Research, 2012,* 1–6.

Musker, J. (Producer), Ashman, H. (Producer & Director), & Clements, R. (1989). *The Little Mermaid* [Motion picture]. United States: Walt Disney Pictures.

Office of Juvenile Justice and Delinquency Prevention. (2003, June). All states allow juveniles to be tried as adults in criminal court under certain circumstances. *Juvenile Offenders and Victims National Report Series: Bulletin.* Retrieved from https://www.ncjrs.gov/html/ojjdp/195420/contents.html

Roberts, B. W., Edmonds, G., & Grijalva, E. (2010). It is developmental me, not generational me: Developmental changes are more important than generational changes in narcissism – commentary on Trzesniewski & Nonnellan (2010). *Perspectives on Psychological Science, 5,* 97–102.

Roenneberg, T., Kuehnle, T., Pramstaller, P. P., Ricken, J., Havel, M., Guth, A., & Merrow, M. (2004). A marker for the end of adolescence. *Current Biology, 14,* R1038–R1039.

Roenneberg, T., Wirz-Justice, A., & Merrow, M. (2003). Life between clocks-daily temporal patterns of human chronotypes. *Journal of Biological Rhythms, 18*, 80–90.

Sarafian, K. (Producer), Andrews, M. (Director), & Chapman, B. (Director). (2012). *Brave* [Motion picture]. United States: Walt Disney Pictures.

Settersten, R., Furstenberg, F., & Rumbaut, R. (2005). *On the frontier of adulthood*. Chicago, IL: University of Chicago Press.

Steinberg, L. (2011). *Adolescence* (9th ed.). New York, NY: McGraw-Hill.

Steinberg, L. (2014). *Age of opportunity: Lessons from the new science of adolescence*. New York, NY: Houghton Mifflin Harcourt.

The Escapist. (2015). Poll: When are you an adult? Retrieved from http://www.escapistmagazine.com/forums/read/18.870668-Poll-When-are-you-an-adult

Tolbize, A. (2008). *Generational differences in the workplace*. Minneapolis, MN: University of Minnesota, Research and Training Center on Community Living.

United States Census Bureau. (2017, November). Figure MS-2: Median age of first marriage: 1890 to present. *Historical Marital Status Tables*. Retrieved from https://www.census.gov/content/dam/Census/library/visualizations/time-series/demo/families-and-households/ms-2.pdf

Yurgelun-Todd, D. (2007). Emotional and cognitive changes during adolescence. *Current Opinion in Neurobiology, 17*, 251–257.

Myth #2 Girls are universally experiencing puberty sooner in recent years

The *New York Times Magazine*, in a headline, asked if puberty before the age of 10 was the new normal (Weil, 2012). Citing historical data, the article suggested that girls were experiencing puberty much earlier today when compared with girls a decade ago. The article complemented the data with stories of young girls, as young as 4 years of age, growing pubic hair, developing breasts, and sprouting to heights well above their classmates.

Puberty refers to "the period during which an individual becomes capable of sexual reproduction" (Steinberg, 2011, p. 24). More generally, puberty represents a time when significant biological and physical changes occur in developing boys and girls. Biologically, hormonal events mark the start of puberty. These hormonal events trigger physical changes that occur during puberty. Physically, puberty is marked by an acceleration in growth prompting noteworthy increases in height and weight. Puberty is also indicated by the development of primary sex characteristics, including sex glands that enable sexual reproduction, and secondary sex characteristics that include changes in the genitals and breasts, and the growth of pubic and body hair.

Stories about young children showing signs of puberty are alarming, especially to parents who might be concerned that their young daughter could become capable of sexual reproduction at such an early age. Perhaps even more alarming, the data are, in fact, indicating girls experience aspects of puberty earlier now than ever before. For example, trends over time show statistically significant declines over the last two decades in the mean age at onset of breast development (also called breast budding; see Euling et al., 2008). Specifically, the mean age at onset of breast development has dropped from approximately 11 years of age for American and European girls in studies published prior to 1980 to below 10 years of age in studies published since 2000 (Aksglaede, Sorensen, Petersen, Skakkebaek, & Juul, 2009; Sorensen et al., 2012). For example, a 2009 study of Danish girls estimated the mean age to be 9.86 years (Aksglaede et al., 2009). Research also indicates a downward trend over time. The Danish study reported data from a 1991 cohort (i.e., girls assessed 15 years earlier) estimating the mean age at onset of breast development to be 10.88 years or a whole year later than the 2006 Danish cohort. Studies of American women born between 1959 and 1965 placed the mean age at onset between 11.2 and 12.8 years (Harlan, Harlan, & Grillo, 1980; Marshall & Tanner, 1969). In a more recent study conducted in the United States, the average age at onset of breast development of women born between 1996 and 1998 estimates the age of onset of breast development to be approximately 8.8 and 9.7 years for African American and non-Hispanic white girls, respectively (Biro et al., 2013). Breast development, or the first appearance of breast tissue, is generally considered one marker used for identifying the onset of puberty in girls.

So, given the data presented above, wouldn't it be true that girls are experiencing puberty earlier in recent years? Well, herein lies one likely source of this myth—confusion over terminology. While it's true the mean age at which girls begin developing breasts has declined, other indications of puberty's onset, such as the mean age of menarche (i.e., first time of menstruation), have stabilized (Harris, Prior, & Koehoorn, 2008; McDowell, Brody, & Hughes, 2007). Furthermore, data on trends associated with the onset of pubic hair growth of girls, another marker of puberty, are inconclusive (Euling et al., 2008). Specifically, studies using Tanner stages (i.e., a common system for describing the five physical stages of pubertal development) show considerable inter-individual and interracial/ethnicity variability in the onset of female pubic hair growth making it difficult to establish secular trends in either direction. Consequently, the claim that girls are universally experiencing puberty earlier is largely dependent on how "experiencing puberty" is defined and if "universally experiencing puberty earlier" means all aspects of puberty, including menarche and pubic hair growth, then, no, the statement that girls are experiencing puberty earlier in recent years is not true.

The myth that girls are universally experiencing puberty earlier in recent years also provides an example of how a kernel of truth can be confused for a more complicated fact. Historical data since the mid-19th century indicate a downward trend in mean age of menarche. However, remember long-term trends in mean age of menarche in the United States and other developed countries have slowed or leveled off in recent decades (Papadimitriou, 2016a). For example, studies since the 1960s have found a slight increase in the average age of menarche in the United Kingdom, Sweden, and Belgium (+0.14, +0.05, and +0.03 years per decade, respectively) suggesting secular trends have, at least in these countries, stabilized (Parent et al., 2003). Other developed European countries have shown a deceleration in secular trends. For example, the mean age of menarche has declined no more than 44 days per decade since 1960 in the countries of Denmark, Finland, the Netherlands, Russia, and France (Parent et al., 2003). These data are similar to those reported in studies of samples from the United States (McDowell et al., 2007; Papadimitriou, 2016a). Illustrating the complex nature of this myth, data from Israel and certain studies from the United Kingdom indicate recent declines in average age of menarche after a period of stabilization (Flash-Luzzatti, Weil, Shalev, Oron, & Chodick, 2014; Morris, Jones, Schoemaker, Ashworth, & Swerdlow, 2011).

Research has found a four- to five-year range in age at onset of puberty, which observed in most human beings is unique among mammals (Parent et al., 2003). Menarche, another marker of puberty, is an important developmental milestone in a girl's life. Anthropologists frequently describe how menarche as a coming of age rite is celebrated in non-Western cultures (Rosewarne, 2012). Usually occurring between 2 and 2.5 years after the appearance of breast tissue, menarche marks the time when females achieve advanced sexual maturation (Papadimitriou, 2016b). In addition, there are differences in the age of menarche among girls of different ethnicities and races, geographical regions, and socioeconomic backgrounds. For example, a study of over 1,100 girls found the mean age of menarche for African American girls was half a year earlier than for non-Hispanic white girls (12.6 versus 12.0; Biro et al., 2006). Such variability appears to be a function of the interaction between genes and the environment (nature and nurture). That is, individual differences in the onset of menarche are accounted for by heritable predispositions to begin puberty at a certain time interacting with environmental variables, especially nutrition and health.

Understanding long-term trends in the mean age at onset of menarche requires the review of available data over long periods of time. Unfortunately, formal data collection of age at onset of menarche only started around the mid-1800s (Steinberg, 2011). However, broad long-term changes in age at onset of menarche date to Neolithic times. Obtaining estimates from skeletal remains, researchers have suggested menarche occurred for prehistoric girls between 7 and 13 years of age (Gluckman & Hanson, 2006). Ancient Sanskrit writings by Indian officials dating back 2,500 years reference upper-class girls first menstruating at 12 years (Papadimitriou, 2016b). Surprisingly, the mean age of 12 years didn't appear to change much in the thousand years between 500 BCE and 500 CE. During classical times (i.e., between 400 BCE and 400 CE), Greek and Roman writers, from Aristotle to the famous physician Galen, consistently marked the age of menarche at around 14 years (Papadimitriou, 2016b). A medical encyclopedia published during the Tang dynasty period (618–906 CE) in China placed the age of menarche also at 14 years, although this number might have had more to do with the influence of numbers in Chinese medicine (the number 7 held significance in the life of Chinese females) than accurate observations (Papadimitriou, 2016b). Writings in medieval Europe also suggested the age of menarche was 14 years, with a range between 12 and 15 years (Admundsen & Diers, 1973). Data on age of menarche during the modern era, especially after the industrial revolution, suggest a delay. Likely caused by disease spread by increasing population density, and poor hygiene and health conditions, the onset of menarche in industrialized nations across the second half of the 18th century ranged between about 15.5 and 17 years, slightly later than what was reported during the Middle Ages but much later than what has been reported in modern times (Papadimitriou, 2016a; Steinberg, 2011).

What's clear from the data described here is that stabilized long-term trends in average age of menarche have not followed decreasing long-term trends in average age at onset of breast development. For example, correlations between menarche and the onset of breast development for women born between 1977 and 1979 are low, suggesting a minimal relationship between the two events, whereas a strong relationship existed between menarche and the onset of breast development for women born between the 1930s and 1960s (Biro et al., 2006). Several researchers have theorized maturational changes in tempo (i.e., changes in the length of time of puberty) are responsible for this discrepancy (e.g., Papadimitriou,

2016a), whereas others have suggested the age at onset of breast development may be an early sign of the interaction between genes and the environment (e.g., Parent et al., 2003). Researchers have attributed improvements in health, nutrition, and general living conditions to the steady decline in age of menarche from the late 1800s to the mid-1900s (Euling et al., 2008). Researchers have also noted that recent health trends, such as the alarming rise of obesity among young girls in the United States, have likely contributed to the long-term trends noted above. Taken altogether, these findings only underscore the complexities associated with understanding trends about the age at onset of puberty for females.

It's also worth noting that varying research design characteristics cloud the long-term trend picture. According to an expert panel of researchers that examined data from 1940 to 1994, factors involving sample size, subject characteristics (e.g., race/ethnicity, socioeconomic status), assessment, and reporting methods make comparisons across studies difficult (Euling et al., 2008). For example, different methods of reporting age at menarche are used across studies, and each method has noteworthy design limitations that warrant caution when interpreting results. Retrospective reporting asks women to recall the first time of menstruation. This method is prone to recall bias and is impacted by the length of time between being asked about age at menarche and the actual event (Karapanou & Papadimitriou, 2010). Another common reporting method involves prospective inquiry or questioning a sample of nonmenstruating girls at fixed time intervals until menstruation occurs. Although this method is more accurate than retrospective reporting, attrition (i.e., subjects dropping out of the research study or otherwise being lost to the researchers) and other practical challenges with conducting research over several years are considered methodological limitations (Biro et al., 2006; Karapanou & Papadimitriou, 2010).

To summarize, there appears to be a kernel of truth to the statement that girls are universally experiencing puberty earlier. Yet, the data paint a complicated picture. Trends over time describing the onset of puberty differ depending on the markers used. Research using the initial appearance of breast tissue (i.e., onset of breast development) to mark puberty's onset clearly identifies a declining trend over time. Studies using age at menarche as the indicator of onset of puberty find secular trends are slowing down or leveling off. Menarche is most associated with sexual reproduction, which is when females are generally considered to have achieved advanced sexual development. Consequently, concerns over the early attainment of sexual maturity in girls might be overstated.

What you need to know

Although long-term trends in age at menarche have stabilized, there remains a population of girls whose first menstruation occurs early. This finding, coupled with research indicating the average girl begins to show breast tissue development at 9 years of age, has certain health implications. Premature sexual development and maturation, or precocious puberty, is a common source of pediatric referral (Leger & Carel, 2016). Precocious puberty describes a clinical condition in which the signs of puberty (e.g., appearance of secondary sexual characteristics including breast tissue and pubic hair, noted growth acceleration) appear before the age of 8 years in girls (Partsch & Sippell, 2001). Epidemiological estimates from the 1980s suggested approximately 1:5,000 to 1:10,000 children met clinical thresholds with a female to male ratio of about 10 to 1 (Gonzalez, 1982). Not surprisingly, given the decline in mean age of onset of breast development, more recent data indicate higher prevalence rates. For example, a recent large-scale study of Danish children found about eight per 10,000 girls aged 5 to 9 met criteria for precocious puberty (Teilmann, Pedersen, Jensen, Skakkebaek, & Juul, 2005). Also not surprisingly, the incidence of precocious puberty of children with conditions affecting the central nervous system, such as neurofibromatosis and encephalopathy, is much higher (Partsch & Sippell, 2001). Understanding etiologies and underlying mechanisms of precocious puberty is beyond the scope of this chapter. However, premature activation of the hormones by parts of the brain responsible for the initiation of puberty has been implicated as a likely cause.

Researchers note that normal developmental variations among girls when secondary sex characteristics appear are responsible for the many challenges that exist in accurately identifying precocious puberty. Specifically, "the distinction between early puberty and normal puberty is not clear-cut" (Leger & Carel, 2016, p. 147). Many experts contend that age-related norms for pubertal stages for breast growth have not been updated to account for downward secular trends and a redefinition of precocious puberty is necessary (see Sorensen et al., 2012).

What is clear is that early pubertal timing is related to negative developmental outcomes. For example, health implications of early menarche include obesity, cardiovascular risks, and increased risk of cancer (Karapanou & Papadimitriou, 2010). Early menarche is also associated with negative psychological outcomes including anxiety, depression, eating disorders, and delinquency (Marceau, Ram, Houts, Grimm, & Susman, 2011). Finally, early pubertal timing in girls has been linked to earlier sexual activity including sexual intercourse (Karapanou & Papadimitriou, 2010; Marceau et al., 2011). However, correlation (or linking two associated variables) should never be confused for causation. In the research described earlier, other variables might help explain the relationship between puberty onset and health and developmental outcomes. For example, exposure to carefully designed sexual education programming can reduce the risk of adolescent sexual activity (Steinberg, 2011).

Parents should make themselves aware of when their daughter might expect to begin developing secondary sex characteristics (e.g., appearance of breast tissue and pubic hair) and experience menarche. It's equally important for parents to recognize that the timing and tempo of puberty and sexual maturation can differ considerably among girls. Experts recommend maintaining an open parent–daughter dialogue about puberty and consulting health care professionals when concerns about the timing or tempo of puberty surface. Finally, for more excellent discussion of this myth, see Mercer (2016).

References

Admundsen, D. W., & Diers, C. J. (1973). The age of menarche in medieval Europe. *Human Biology, 45,* 605–612.

Aksglaede, L., Sorensen, K., Petersen, J., Skakkebaek, N. E., & Juul, A. (2009). Recent decline in age at breast development: The Copenhagen puberty study. *Pediatrics, 123,* e932–e939.

Biro, F. M., Greenspan, L. C., Galvez, M. P., Pinney, S. M., Teitelbaum, S., Windham, G. C., ... Wolff, M. S. (2013). Onset of breast development in a longitudinal cohort. *Pediatrics, 132,* 1019–1027.

Biro, F. M., Huang, B., Crawford, P. B., Lucky, A. W., Striegel-Moore, R., Barton, B. A., & Daniels, S. (2006). Pubertal correlates in black and white girls. *Journal of Pediatrics, 148,* 234–240.

Euling, S. Y., Herman-Giddens, M. E., Lee, P. A., Selevan, S. G., Juul, A., Sorensen, T. I., ... Swan, S. H. (2008). Examination of US puberty-timing data from 1940 to 1994 for secular trends: Panel findings. *Pediatrics, 121,* S172–S191.

Flash-Luzzatti, S., Weil, C., Shalev, V., Oron, T., & Chodick, G. (2014). Long-term secular trends in the age at menarche in Israel: A systematic literature review and pooled analysis. *Hormone Research in Paediatrics, 8,* 266–271.

Gluckman, P. D., & Hanson, M. A. (2006). Evolution, development and timing of puberty. *Trends in Endocronology & Metabolism, 17,* 7–12.

Gonzalez, E. R. (1982). For puberty that comes too soon, new treatment highly effective. *Journal of the American Medical Association, 248,* 1149–1152.

Harlan, W. R., Harlan, E. A., & Grillo, G. P. (1980). Secondary sex characteristics of girls 12 to 17 years of age The US Health Examination Survey. *Journal of Pediatrics, 96,* 1074–1078.

Harris, M. A., Prior, J. C., & Koehoorn, M. (2008). Age at menarche in the Canadian population: Secular trends and relationship to adulthood BMI. *Journal of Adolescent Health, 42,* 548–554.

Karapanou, O., & Papadimitriou, A. (2010). Determinants of menarche. *Reproductive Biology and Endocrinology, 8,* 115–122.

Leger, J., & Carel, J. (2016). Precocious puberty. In P. Kumanov & A. Agarwal (Eds.), *Puberty: Physiology and abnormalities* (pp. 137–154). New York, NY: Springer.

Marceau, K., Ram, N., Houts, R. M., Grimm, K. J., & Susman, E. J. (2011). Individual differences in boys' and girls' timing and tempo of puberty: Modeling development with nonlinear growth models. *Developmental Psychology, 47,* 1389–1409.

Marshall, W. A., & Tanner, J. M. (1969). Variations in pattern of pubertal changes in girls. *Archives of Disease in Childhood, 44,* 291–303.

McDowell, M. A., Brody, D. J., & Hughes, J. P. (2007). Has age of menarche changed? Results from the National Health and Nutrition Examination Survey (NHANES) 1999–2004. *Journal of Adolescent Health, 40,* 227–231.

Mercer, J. (2016). *Thinking critically about child development* (3rd ed.). Los Angeles, CA: Sage.

Morris, D. H., Jones, M. E., Schoemaker, M. J., Ashworth, A., & Swerdlow, A. J. (2011). Secular trends in age at menarche in women in the UK born 1908–93. Results from the breakthrough generations study. *Paediatric and Perinatal Epidemiology, 25,* 394–400.

Papadimitriou, A. (2016a). Timing of puberty and secular trend in human maturation. In P. Kumanov & A. Agarwal (Eds.), *Puberty: Physiology and abnormalities* (pp. 121–136). New York, NY: Springer.

Papadimitriou, A. (2016b). The evolution of the age at menarche from prehistorical to modern times. *Journal of Pediatric and Adolescent Gynecology, 29,* 527–530.

Parent, A., Teilmann, G., Juul, A., Skakkebaek, N. E., Toppari, J., & Bourguignon, J. (2003). The timing of normal puberty and the age limits of sexual precocity: Variations around the world, secular trends, and changes after migration. *Endocrine Reviews, 24,* 668–693.

Partsch, C. J., & Sippell, W. G. (2001). Pathogenesis and epidemiology of precocious puberty: Effects of exogenous oestrogens. *Human Reproduction Update, 7,* 292–302.

Rosewarne, L. (2012). *Periods in pop culture: Menstruation in film and television.* Lanham, MD: Lexington Books.

Sorensen, K., Mouritsen, A., Aksglaede, L., Hagen, C. P., Mogensen, S. S., & Juul, A. (2012). Recent secular trends in pubertal timing: Implications for evaluation and diagnosis of precocious puberty. *Hormone Research in Paediatrics, 77,* 137–145.

Steinberg, L. (2011). *Adolescence* (9th ed.). New York, NY: McGraw-Hill.

Teilmann, G., Pedersen, C. B., Jensen, T. K., Skakkebaek, N. E., & Juul, A. (2005). Prevalence and incidence of precocious pubertal development in Denmark: An epidemiologic study based on national registries. *Pediatrics, 116,* 1323–1328.

Weil, E. (2012, March 30). Puberty before age 10: A new "normal"? The New York Times Magazine. Retrieved from https://www.nytimes.com/2012/04/01/magazine/puberty-before-age-10-a-new-normal.html

Myth #3

The teen brain is fully developed by age 18

Mozart was said to have been a skilled pianist and violinist at the age of 5 and composed his first symphony at 8. Before turning 13, Pablo Picasso was well on his way to becoming a historically significant artist. At the 1990 United States Open, Serena Williams won her first tennis grand slam event two weeks before turning 18, besting Martina Hingis, who, herself, won a grand slam event at age 17. Akrit Jaswal, a boy from a small rural village in India, successfully performed surgery at the ripe old age of 7.

Using these youth as examples, it isn't surprising many believe the brain is fully, or at least mostly, developed by age 18. How else are these youth able to achieve such fantastic feats? And the idea of fully developed adolescent brains is commonplace in popular culture. Consider the brains of Bella of the *Twilight Saga Series* (Meyer, 2010) or Katniss from the *Hunger Games* (Collins, 2009). These teenage heroines were articulate, confident, independent, and thoughtful. They were also great problem-solvers, and acted responsibly and heroically. In Katniss's case, she started a revolution on par with the likes of John Adams and Thomas Jefferson. How could she not have a mature, adult-like brain?

Yes, Hollywood frequently portrays teenagers as sex-crazed, carefree, sensation-seekers who have no regard for anyone but themselves, and the news media mostly reports on teenagers making poor decisions. However, it's hard to ignore images of, or stories about, teenagers who are clearly well beyond their years.

A 2006 *New Yorker* cartoon showed two parents grounding their teenage son until his cerebral cortex fully matured (Smaller, 2006). This cartoon illustrates how many parents think of their adolescent and his or her brain as a work in progress until some magical day close to the 18th birthday. Dr. David Moshman (2011), professor emeritus of educational psychology wrote about the cartoon, suggesting it revealed several false assumptions about adolescents and their brains. For example, he noted that a common misconception about the adolescent brain is that the outcome of brain development in adolescence is a mature brain in adulthood at around the age of 18 years. However, this belief ignores a great deal of research indicating that the brain continues developing well beyond 18 years of age (see Johnson, Blum, & Giedd, 2009). Specifically, important parts of the brain responsible for decision-making and problem-solving are not fully developed until well into an individual's 20s. Moreover, a mature brain resulting from the completion of brain development at age 18 coincides with societal markers representing the end of adolescence and beginning of adulthood. For example, in most countries, many of the freedoms and responsibilities of being an adult (e.g., age of consent to marry, purchase alcohol and tobacco, enlist in the military) are legally permitted by the age of 18. Such legal standards might assume the brain is fully developed by this time, suggesting individuals are capable of advanced decision-making and problem-solving at this age. However, the notion that adolescence, as a distinct developmental period, ends at 18 years is also a myth, thus refuting this assumption.

People tend to accept some evidence as truth and fail to fully appreciate the complexity of the science behind a claim. For example, research indicates that sensation-seeking peaks at about age 18 (Romer & Hennessy, 2007). This trend is notably consistent with other age-related trends in risk-taking behavior (gun mortality, traffic fatalities, criminal behavior; see Males, 2009; Romer, 2010). Considering that risk-taking behavior is generally associated with areas of the prefrontal cortex, or the area of the brain responsible for planning, organizing, and weighing risks and benefits, it seems reasonable to conclude that the decline in sensation-seeking or delinquency that occurs at 18 years coincides with a fully developed or adult-like brain at that same age. However, research has found other risk-taking behaviors peak later. For instance, alcohol use peaks at about 21 years of age (see Romer, 2010). It's likely this peak has as much to do with when one can legally purchase alcohol in the US than when the brain stops developing. Furthermore, we forget that the brain is a highly complex organ and we make a mistake when assigning total blame to the brain for aberrant behavior, especially when establishing claims from brain scan research. We also falsely conclude a one-to-one correspondence between the brain and impulsivity, anxiety, depression, or any other behavior or mental health condition, appropriate or inappropriate, adaptive or maladaptive. Rather, a more complete conceptualization of the relationship between the brain and behavior suggests complex transactions among the brain, behavior, and the social environment (Dahl, 2004).

Myths are also promoted when research findings are misrepresented in the news media, such as a 2004 research study published in *The Journal of Neuroscience* (see Bjork et al., 2004). The researchers asked 12 healthy adolescents and 12 healthy young adults to engage in a task in which they were required to quickly press a button after a brief period (i.e., 2s) following the display of a symbol on a small mirror mounted in front of the eye. The symbols differentiated whether subjects could earn money or avoid losing money. Subjects' brains were monitored using magnetic resonance imaging (MRI) with the area of the brain thought to be associated with motivation scanned specifically. During high-payment trials, brain activity in the right nucleus accumbens, commonly described as the center of the brain's reward circuit, was slightly higher for adults than for adolescents. The authors of the study noted in the published article that similarities existed between adolescents and adults when performing the task and when most areas of the brain that were scanned. However, a New York newspaper led with the headline "scientists may have discovered a biological excuse for laziness" (Talan, 2004). James Bjork, lead author on the study, was quoted in the story as saying the research "tells us that teenagers love stuff, but aren't willing to get off the couch to get it as adults are." The study's findings support neither claim. Studying laziness and the adolescent brain would require conducting brain scans on a preidentified group of lazy teenagers and a preidentified group of hardworking teenagers. To understand how the teenage brain might differ from the adult brain, researchers would also have to include lazy and hardworking adults, and compare the four groups. Even such a research design wouldn't be able to conclude that certain types of brains *caused* laziness.

Laurence Steinberg (2010), author of a popular college textbook on adolescence, wrote in a commentary on the science of adolescent brain development that the adolescent brain is markedly different from both the child brain and adult brain. Perhaps more importantly, Steinberg noted that the changes in the brain occurring during adolescence are "among the most dramatic and important to occur during the human lifespan" (p. 161). For example, the prefrontal cortex is pruned during adolescence (see Spear, 2010). This synaptic pruning involves the elimination of unnecessary connections between brain cells, thus enhancing the brain's efficiency. Regarding brain function, research suggests that individuals begin using multiple parts of the brain concurrently during the adolescent developmental period. For instance, the prefrontal cortex works together with other areas, including the limbic system, when someone is required to organize thinking and feeling simultaneously (see Steinberg, 2011). This marks an important point in brain development, as the limbic system, which is partially responsible for the processing of emotions, experiences, social information, and rewards and punishment, is generally overactive during adolescence. Collaboration between the prefrontal cortex and the limbic system results in better emotional self-regulation or management of emotions and behavior. While it is known that adolescent brain development is significant and necessary for individuals to begin acquiring adult characteristics and skills, the question remains—when does the brain stop developing?

The study of the brain is generally divided into two areas: brain structure and brain function. Brain structure refers to the brain's physical form and shape, while brain function describes how the brain works. Considering brain structure first, researchers have discovered that the organization of the brain changes through childhood and adolescence, but also well into adulthood. That is, the brain that you're born with is markedly different from the brain you have as a teenager, and the brain you have as a teenager is markedly different from the brain you have as an adult. More to the point, the brain's physical structure does not stop developing once you turn 18 years of age.

Brain science has provided much in the way of support for the notion that brain structure continues to develop beyond an individual's transition from adolescence to adulthood. Jay Giedd (2008), a noted neuroscientist, concluded, in his review, that the brain's gray matter—the parts of the brain containing cell bodies—peaks at puberty and declines through adolescence. Specifically, the density of gray matter, which appears to correlate negatively with an individual's abilities and skills, is most pronounced during childhood with noticeable drop-offs into adulthood (i.e., up to the age of 30) because of continued synaptic pruning. What this means is that the adolescent brain continues to improve its efficiency well into adulthood. Conversely, white matter in the brain, or structures in the brain that extend from cell bodies and carry electrical signals across neurons, increases throughout adolescence, likely as a result of myelination, or the process by which a fatty substance surrounds part of the neuron, insulating it to ensure proper functioning of the nervous system. According to Giedd, increased myelination is noticeably apparent in the corpus callosum (the part of the brain associated with integration between the right and left hemisphere), rapidly increasing during adolescence and young adulthood, improving functions such as memory, attention, and language. Taken altogether, Giedd's review suggests the adolescent brain is rapidly developing and that this rapid development continues at least through early adulthood. Other reviews of the research have noted similar developmental trends in gray and white matter. Age-related increases in white matter coincided with gray matter decreases throughout adolescence, with an acceleration in the loss of prefrontal cortex gray matter occurring between the ages of 23 and 30 years, or well after the generally accepted end of adolescence (i.e., 18 years; see Paus, 2005). These findings offer insight into some of the changes that occur during and after adolescence. Remember, the prefrontal cortex is responsible, in part, for planning, organizing, and weighing risks and benefits. With these changes occurring through adolescence and not ending at adolescence, we should be cautious about expecting teenagers or even young adults to be completely autonomous or independent when planning, organizing, and weighing risks and benefits.

Many other studies examining brain structure confirm that the prefrontal cortex matures later than other brain regions. Specifically, research using MRI has found that brain regions underlying attention, evaluation of risks and rewards, and response inhibition continue to develop structurally beyond adolescence (see Yurgelun-Todd, 2007). In addition, MRI techniques show that the most noteworthy changes during adolescence and young adulthood involve regions of the brain responsible for abstract thought, organization, decision-making, and planning (Yurgelun-Todd, 2007). These studies have led researchers to conclude that structural changes in the brain correspond to improvements in cognitive functioning and efficiency, and emotional processing and regulation during adolescence and young adulthood.

Research on brain functioning across childhood, adolescence, and adulthood tells a similar story. That is, the brain's functions continue to mature long after adolescence. Researchers using functional magnetic resonance imaging (fMRI) techniques have found that the adolescent brain differs significantly from the adult brain when individuals are required to consider a speaker's intention (i.e., recognize whether the speaker was being sincere or ironic), comprehend one's own intentions (i.e., recognize the causality of events), and understand thoughts and emotions (see Blakemore, 2012). In one example, researchers scanned the brains of adolescent (aged 10–18) and adult (aged 22–32) participants while the participants read scenarios related to social emotions (e.g., embarrassment, guilt; see Burnett, Bird, Moll, Frith, & Blakemore, 2009). Different from basic emotions (e.g., fear, anger), social emotions necessitate an understanding of another person's emotional state (e.g., guilt requires you to understand how another person feels as a result of your behavior). The scans revealed several interesting findings. Adolescent brains were more active than adult brains in a region generally believed to be responsible for an individual's consideration of the mental state of others. However, a part of the brain thought to be associated with recognizing social concepts was more active for adults than adolescents. These results confirm findings from many studies over more than 30 years suggesting the relative functions of different parts of the brain change with age. That is, adolescents use different brain regions when engaging in cognitive and emotional processing tasks than adults, indicating noteworthy changes to how the brain functions between adolescence and the onset of adulthood (Yurgelun-Todd, 2007).

Other fMRI studies have found that, with age, activity in the prefrontal region of the brain "becomes more focal and specialized while irrelevant and diffuse activity in this region is reduced" (Yurgelun-Todd, 2007, p. 255). This change translates into improved cognitive performance (e.g., abstract reasoning, attention, memory) and emotional processing (e.g., understanding and managing emotional responses) not just from childhood into adolescence but from adolescence into adulthood. Steinberg (2010) noted that impulse control, effective decision-making, recognizing consequences, planning, and ignoring peer pressure all improve from preadolescence into early adulthood. However, impulsive and risk-taking behavior doesn't cease when adolescents turn 18 years of age. For example, longitudinal studies of alcohol, marijuana, and tobacco use show increased usage between 19 and 21 years of age with a slight decline at about 23 years of age (see Romer, 2010). This shouldn't come as a surprise, as brain functioning occurring in regions of the brain responsible for impulse control and risk-taking behavior appears to be in a state of constant change between adolescence and young adulthood.

What you need to know

Brain researchers use the terms "malleable" and "plastic" to describe the fact that the brain has the enormous potential to change. When considering the brain, and specifically the incredible structural and functional changes that occur, many authors and child development professionals only reference early childhood. However, the brain appears to be a work in progress across the lifespan. Such an understanding about the brain provides a hopeful perspective, one that suggests you might be able to teach an old dog new tricks. Specific to teenagers, the time between 10 and 20 years of age offers an array of psychological, physiological, and neurological changes, which can promote development in multiple domains (e.g., academic, behavioral, emotional, social; White, 2009). However, the teenage brain is not an incomplete brain. Adolescents come into possession of certain cognitive skills that allow for critical and thoughtful reasoning to occur. Taken altogether, adolescence might be best viewed as a time of opportunity.

Sheryl Feinstein (2009), an author on parenting, suggested the adolescent brain represented "a chance to learn something quickly and with more ease than at any other time of life" (p. 7). Just as the toddler brain prepares the child to learn language, the teenage brain primes the adolescent to learn impulse control skills (e.g., manage emotions and resist urges), reason more abstractly (e.g., morality isn't black and white), think more critically (e.g., "my parents can't always be right"), enhance communication skills (e.g., speaking to members of the opposite sex), and develop new social relationships (e.g., romantic relationships). Adolescence is also a time of discovery and changes in cognition associated with changes in the brain allowing teenagers to consider themselves and their lives in the future (Dahl, 2004).

Adults are encouraged to be sources of support for teenagers. They should facilitate opportunities for adolescents to establish autonomy and trust, work hard to maintain open lines of communication, model appropriate social behavior, and allow for a teenager's self-discovery. Feinstein (2009) recommends "understanding and tolerance" (p. 57) during the teen years. However, setting limits on teenage behavior and providing adequate supervision is also important (Friman, 2010). Research has found that parenting styles characterized by high levels of warmth and responsiveness, and high expectations often produce better outcomes for adolescents than parenting styles that are punitive (i.e., use harsh and punitive disciplinary practices), indulgent (i.e., responsive but with low expectations), or indifferent (i.e., low responsiveness with low expectations; Steinberg, 2011).

Changes occurring in the brain during adolescence may help explain many of the challenges of this developmental period. The developing amygdala, a part of the brain related to emotional control, may stimulate intense feelings that appear for no apparent reason. Furthermore, adolescents are prone to impulsivity and risk-taking behavior, show suspicion for adults and authority, and increase the amount of time spent with peers (White, 2009). These common features of adolescence might produce tension between teenagers and parents, and lead to intense conflicts. However, these challenges of adolescence, or the developmental changes that occur between childhood and adulthood, also represent opportunities. The trials and tribulations of adolescence "serve valuable purposes and allow adolescence to work as a stage of change" (Dahl, 2004, p. 81). Put slightly differently, overcoming challenges of adolescence prepares individuals for adulthood and the challenges that occur during adulthood.

As much as adolescence is a time of opportunity, it is also a time of risk. The phrases "natural tinderbox" and "hazard period" have been used by scholars to describe the liabilities that exist during adolescence (see Dahl, 2004; White, 2009). Specifically, entering adolescence can be a risk factor for the onset of psychological disorders including anxiety and depression. In addition, adolescents are susceptible to problems involving delinquency, substance use, and school failure. While there are obvious environmental contributors to these problems (e.g., increased unsupervised time, more intense social pressures), the developing brain is, at least partially, responsible for why adolescents are at risk for these problems. For example, areas of the brain responsible for risk-taking behavior are more active during adolescence (Steinberg, 2010). In addition, neural circuits applied to problem-solving during adolescence are likely to become established during adulthood (White, 2009). That's fine if the problem-solving leads to positive outcomes. Unfortunately, maladaptive problem-solving skills learned during adolescence can remain with an individual into adulthood. Perhaps equally important, parents and others must remember that the adolescent brain continues to develop beyond the age of 18 years. Consequently, maladaptive problem-solving happening the first few years after high school, for example during college, could influence an individual's functioning as an adult.

Coming back to the brilliant teenagers described at the beginning of this chapter, it's likely these wunderkinds represent outliers, exceptional individuals with exceptional talents. Moreover, it's likely their brains were in a state of change just like the brains of their more typical peers. As for Bella and Katniss, they, too, are unusual. When referencing archetypical adolescent brains from popular culture, perhaps it's best to consider Seth, Evan, and McLovin from the movie *Superbad* or the kids from *The Goldbergs, Modern Family*, or *The Middle*, contemporary sitcoms that feature common teenager experiences. These teens better exemplify the consequences of an overactive limbic system and a prefrontal cortex that is sometimes out for lunch.

References

Bjork, J. M., Knutson, B., Fong, G., Caggiano, D. M., Bennett, S. M., & Hommer, D. W. (2004). Incentive-elicited brain activation in adolescents: Similarities and differences from young adults. *The Journal of Neuroscience, 24,* 1793–1802.

Blakemore, S. J. (2012). Imaging brain development: The adolescent brain. *Neuroimage, 61,* 397–406.

Burnett, S., Bird, G., Moll, J., Frith, C., & Blakemore, S. J. (2009). Development during adolescence of the neuro processing of social emotions. *Journal of Cognitive Neuroscience, 21,* 1736–1750.

Collins, S. (2009). *The hunger games series. Catching fire.* Detroit, MI: Thorndike Press.

Dahl, R. E. (2004). Adolescent brain development: A period of vulnerabilities and opportunities. *Annual New York Academy of Science, 2021,* 1–22.

Feinstein, S. (2009). *Inside the teenage brain: Parenting that works.* Lanham, MD: Rowman & Littlefield.

Friman, P. (Writer). (2010). Adolescence and other temporary mental disorders: Why crazy teen behavior is more normal than you think and how you can deal with it without losing your mind [Motion picture on DVD]. *Boys Town.*

Giedd, J. N. (2008). The teen brain: Insights from neuroimaging. *Journal of Adolescent Health, 42,* 335–343.

Johnson, S. B., Blum, R. W., & Giedd, J. N. (2009). Adolescent maturity and the brain: The promise and pitfalls of neuroscience research in adolescent health policy. *Journal of Adolescent Health, 45,* 216–221.

Males, M. (2009). Does the adolescent brain make risk taking inevitable? *Journal of Adolescent Research, 24,* 3–20.

Meyer, S. (2010). *Twilight saga series.* London: Atom.

Moshman, D. (2011, May 17). The teenage brain: Debunking the 5 biggest myths [Blog post]. Retrieved from http://www.huffingtonpost.com/david-moshman/adolescents-and-their-tee_b_858360.html

Paus, T. (2005). Mapping brain maturation and cognitive development during adolescence. *Trends in Cognitive Sciences, 9,* 60–68.

Romer, D. (2010). Adolescent risk taking, impulsivity, and brain development: Implications for prevention. *Developmental Psychobiology, 52,* 263–276.

Romer, D., & Hennessy, M. (2007). A biosocial-affect model of adolescent sensation seeking: The role of affect evaluation and peer-group influences in adolescent drug use. *Prevention Science, 8,* 89–101.

Smaller, B. (2006, April 24). [Cartoon]. The New Yorker. Retrieved from www.art.com.

Spear, L. (2010). *The behavioral neuroscience of adolescence.* New York, NY: Norton.

Steinberg, L. (2010). Commentary: A behavioral scientist looks at the science of adolescent brain development. *Brain and Cognition, 72,* 160–164.

Steinberg, L. (2011). *Adolescence* (9th ed.). New York, NY: McGraw-Hill.

Talan, J. (2004, March 1). Lazy teens may have excuses, scientists say. *Newsday*. Retrieved from http://articles.latimes.com/2004/mar/01/health/he-teenbrains1

White, A. M. (2009). Understanding adolescent brain development and its implications for the clinician. *Adolescent Medicine, 20,* 73–90.

Yurgelun-Todd, D. (2007). Emotional and cognitive changes during adolescence. *Current Opinion in Neurobiology, 17,* 251–257.

Myth #4 Anorexia treatment usually requires teens to be separated from their parents

A tonsillectomy is the surgical practice of removing tonsils from a youth most commonly due to recurring tonsil infections or inflammation of the tonsils. Similarly, the term "parentectomy" has been applied to the therapeutic practice of removing parents from a youth who has been diagnosed with anorexia nervosa (Harper, 1983). Anorexia nervosa is an eating disorder characterized by a restriction of food intake that leads to significantly low weight. The disorder also commonly includes an intense fear of weight gain and a problematic perception of one's body (American Psychiatric Association, 2013).

Even the earliest documented interventions for anorexia included a recommendation to separate youth from their "anorexogenic" parents (Le Grange, Lock, Loeb, & Nicholls, 2009). For example, in his seminal 1874 work describing the disorder, after coining the term anorexia nervosa, Sir William Withey Gull (1874) also advocated the position that youth with anorexia should be separated from their family as part of the treatment. About a decade later, in the 1880s, Jean-Martin Charcot further advanced Gull's position by advocating the use of "isolation therapy" for anorexia in order to keep youth and their family separated during treatment (Silverman, 1997).

Charcot even describes a case in which a teenage girl was near death, and she only got better once he insisted to her hesitant parents that they must leave the city. The teen even recognized the value of her isolation as she reportedly told Charcot:

> As long as papa and mama had not gone...I was afraid that my illness was not serious, and as I had a horror of eating, I did not eat. But when I saw that you were determined to be master, I was afraid, and in spite of repugnance I tried to eat, and I was able to, little by little. (Silverman, 1997, p. 298)

Ever since these early descriptions of anorexia, the "anorectic family," also called the "psychosomatic family," has continued to receive considerable blame for the development and maintenance of anorexia due to family characteristics such as rigidity, overprotectiveness, and overly feeling each other's emotions (Minuchin et al., 1975; Minuchin, Rosman, & Baker, 1978). This persistent parent-blaming approach has led to the common practice of admitting youth with anorexia into hospital inpatient units, often with the goal of separating youth from their families for an extended period of time (Insel, 2012; Le Grange, n.d.).

More recently, news headlines such as "Pushy Parents 'to Blame for Anorexia in Sporty Teenagers'" reflect the notion that parents are a primary cause of anorexia (Wynne-Jones, 2006), and this level of parent-blaming may lead some to believe it is necessary for youth to be separated from their parents during treatment. The separation of parents from their youth with anorexia is also reflected in the recent movie *To the Bone* (Curtis, Miller, Lynn, & Noxon, 2017). In the movie, the 20-year-old main character, Ellen, is required to agree to at least six months of inpatient care in order to be treated by Dr. Beckham (played by a lightly bearded Keanu Reeves). During the movie, it's revealed that Ellen's parents have let her down in many ways, such as by going through a divorce and by being disengaged from Ellen's life. Toward the beginning of Ellen's inpatient stay, Dr. Beckham attempts one session of therapy with her parents, but it goes so badly he vows, "We're never doing family therapy again," also adding, "That was a sh*t show." The only other contact Ellen has with a parent is when she sneaks away to visit her mother. Taking blame for Ellen's anorexia, her mother admits "I didn't hold you enough; I didn't bond with you." Moreover, Ellen's mother had recently received some advice that prompted her to pull out a baby bottle filled with rice milk. Ellen initially rejected this attempt to make up for the lost bond, but moments later she let her mother cradle her, feed her, and sing "Hush, Little Baby." Overall, this movie sends the messages that parents are a primary cause of anorexia and that the treatment requires significant separation from the family.

Relatedly, two questions need to be considered that are to do with the role of parents in the development and treatment of anorexia. The first question is: Do parents cause anorexia? The answer is somewhat complicated because there is no way to conduct a randomized control study in which different children are randomly assigned to having different types of parents. Thus, we are left with adoption and correlational studies, which cannot be used to definitively determine causes. However, the existing research points toward many variables that have been associated with the development of anorexia in youth. Twin studies and other types of research point toward a strong genetic contribution (Bulik, Slof-Op't Landt, van Furth, & Sullivan, 2007) that may also interact with environmental variables. Some possible environmental variables include exposure to certain types of media, peer groups, and adverse life events (Mazzeo & Bulik, 2009). Parenting behaviors, such as parental modeling of problematic eating, parental teasing about weight, and parental psychopathology are also associated with anorexia (Mazzeo & Bulik, 2009). That is, for some youth with anorexia, their parents' behavior could have been one of several factors contributing to their eating history. However, for many youth with anorexia, no such problematic parenting behaviors are evident. In sum, after reviewing all of the evidence, the Academy for Eating Disorders concludes in a position paper that "whereas family factors can play a role in the genesis and maintenance of eating disorders, current knowledge refutes the idea that they're either the exclusive or even the primary mechanisms that underlie risk" (Le Grange et al., 2009, p. 1).

The second question to consider is: Do youth need to be separated from their parents for treatment to be successful? The answer to this question is more clear-cut. That is, most adolescents with anorexia do not need to be separated from their parents for a positive treatment outcome. In fact, quite the opposite is often true. Several randomized control studies have demonstrated that effective treatment often incorporates parents as a key part of the treatment process. For example, one such study compared a family-based treatment (in which parents were involved) to an adolescent-focused treatment (in which the parents were *not* involved). One year following treatment, 49% of the adolescents in the family-based treatment group experienced a full remission, which was significantly higher than the 23% of the adolescents in the adolescent-focused treatment group attaining full remission. Several other well-designed studies found similar results (Lock, 2015). Taken together, these studies indicate that the inclusion of parents in therapy was helpful for the long-term maintenance of improvements made during therapy.

One major reason that people may believe youth should routinely be separated from their parents as part of treatment for anorexia is that there is a kernel of truth to this idea. That is, a small minority of parents demonstrate such dysfunctional parenting behaviors that they may need to receive substantial treatment for themselves, and in some cases youth may need to be removed from their homes due to child abuse or neglect. However, this is not the case for the majority of parents with youth diagnosed with an eating disorder. Although some parents also may engage in some behaviors that contribute to their child's anorexia, it is likely more beneficial to include them in treatment so that they can help the treatment gains last over time. Another kernel of truth is that some adolescents have restricted their calorie consumption so severely that their life is in imminent danger, and they may need to be hospitalized. However, parents can still provide helpful support during and after the hospitalization.

There are a few reasons that this myth can be harmful. First, if parents are worried about being blamed for their child's anorexia, they may be less likely to bring their child to treatment (Bozsik, Bennett, Stefano, Whisenhunt, & Hudson, in press). Second, this myth may make parents feel guilty even though they often had had little to do with the development of the disorder. Third, when parents are not involved in treatment, the treatment gains are more likely to diminish over time (Lock et al., 2010). Finally, hospitalization has the potential to be traumatic for both the youth and their parents (Le Grange, n.d.). Thus, whenever possible, the best treatment path incorporates parents in a way that does not assign them primary blame.

What you need to know

In 2008, a systematic review of the existing research revealed that family therapy was the only well-established psychosocial treatment for youth with anorexia (Keel & Haedt, 2008). Seven years later, an updated review by a different author also came to the same conclusion (Lock, 2015). More specifically, the Maudsley Model is a type of family therapy used in many of the studies demonstrating a good outcome. This approach includes: (a) making the whole family aware of the dangers associated with anorexia, (b) assessing the family interactions related to eating, and (c) helping the family change in ways to better facilitate healthy eating (Lock & Le Grange, 2015). Although family members are not blamed as the primary cause of anorexia, they're incorporated because they help make the greatest changes. Interestingly, the Maudsley Model did receive brief mention in the *To the Bone* movie described earlier, but this was only to point out that it didn't work for a young woman in the waiting room.

There are currently no well-established treatments (or even probably efficacious treatments) for youth with other eating disorders such as bulimia nervosa or binge-eating disorder (Lock, 2015). Family therapy and supportive individual therapy are both currently considered to be possibly efficacious for bulimia, and internet-delivered cognitive-behavioral therapy is possibly efficacious for binge-eating disorder. However, the bar for a treatment to be considered possibly efficacious is relatively low (Southam-Gerow & Prinstein, 2014). Thus, more treatment research is especially needed for bulimia and binge-eating disorder.

References

American Psychiatric Association (2013). *Diagnostic and statistical manual of mental disorders: DSM-5.* Washington, DC: American Psychiatric Association.

Bozsik, F., Bennett, B., Stefano, E., Whisenhunt, B., & Hudson, D. (In press). Eating. In S. Hupp (Ed.), *Pseudoscience in child and adolescent psychotherapy: Ineffective, implausible, and potentially harmful treatments.* Cambridge: Cambridge University Press.

Bulik, C. M., Slof-Op't Landt, M. C., Van Furth, E. F., & Sullivan, P. F. (2007). The genetics of anorexia nervosa. *Annual Review of Nutrition, 27,* 263–275.

Curtis, B., Miller, K., Lynn, J. (Producers), & Noxon, M. (Director). (2017). *To the Bone* [Motion Picture]. United States: AMBI Group.

Gull, W. W. (1874). Anorexia nervosa (apepsia hysterica, anorexia hysterica). *Transactions of the Clinical Society, 7,* 22–28.

Harper, G. (1983). Varieties of parenting failure in anorexia nervosa: Protection and parentectomy, revisited. *Journal of the American Academy of Child Psychiatry, 22*(2), 134–139.

Insel, T. (2012). Spotlight on eating disorders. Retrieved from https://www.nimh.nih.gov/about/directors/thomas-insel/blog/2012/spotlight-on-eating-disorders.shtml

Keel, P. K., & Haedt, A. (2008). Evidence-based psychosocial treatments for eating problems and eating disorders. *Journal of Clinical Child & Adolescent Psychology, 37*(1), 39–61.

Le Grange, D. (n.d.). Evidence-based treatment for adolescents with anorexia and bulimia. Keynote address for the Society for Child and Adolescent Psychology (SCCAP): Initiative for Dissemination of Evidence-Based Treatments for Childhood and Adolescent Mental Health Problems. Retrieved from http://effectivechildtherapy.fiu.edu

Le Grange, D., Lock, J., Loeb, K., & Nicholls, D. (2009). Academy for eating disorders position paper: The role of the family in eating disorders. *International Journal of Eating Disorders, 43*(1), 1–5.

Lock, J. (2015). An update on evidence-based psychosocial treatments for eating disorders in children and adolescents. *Journal of Clinical Child & Adolescent Psychology, 44*(5), 707–721.

Lock, J., & Le Grange, D. (2015). *Treatment manual for anorexia nervosa: A family-based approach.* New York, NY: Guilford Press.

Lock, J., Le Grange, D., Agras, W. S., Moye, A., Bryson, S. W., & Jo, B. (2010). Randomized clinical trial comparing family-based treatment with adolescent-focused individual therapy for adolescents with anorexia nervosa. *Archives of General Psychiatry, 67*(10), 1025–1032.

Mazzeo, S. E., & Bulik, C. M. (2009). Environmental and genetic risk factors for eating disorders: What the clinician needs to know. *Child and Adolescent Psychiatric Clinics of North America, 18*(1), 67–82.

Minuchin, S., Baker, L., Rosman, B. L., Liebman, R., Milman, L., & Todd, T. C. (1975). A conceptual model of psychosomatic illness in children: Family organization and family therapy. *Archives of General Psychiatry, 32*(8), 1031–1038.

Minuchin, S., Rosman, B. L., & Baker, L. (1978). *Psychosomatic families: Anorexia nervosa in context*. Cambridge, MA: Harvard University Press.

Silverman, J. A. (1997). Charcot's comments on the therapeutic role of isolation in the treatment of anorexia nervosa. *International Journal of Eating Disorders, 21*(3), 295–298.

Southam-Gerow, M. A., & Prinstein, M. J. (2014). Evidence base updates: The evolution of the evaluation of psychological treatments for children and adolescents. *Journal of Clinical Child & Adolescent Psychology, 43*(1), 1–6.

Wynne-Jones, J. (2006). Pushy parents "to blame for anorexia in sporty teenagers." Retrieved from http://www.telegraph.co.uk/news/uknews/1534571/Pushy-parents-to-blame-for-anorexia-in-sporty-teenagers.html

Myth #5

Technology has made teens better at multitasking

The Sims 4, the popular life simulation video game, takes multitasking to a whole new level. Sims, or players' virtual characters, are able to exercise, talk with other Sims, and watch television, all at the same time. Not impressed? The latest installment of the game allows Sims to simultaneously flirt, give career advice, and use the toilet. Try that at home.

The Sims creates a world enveloped by technology. Where your little pixel person goes, in even the simplest of Sim worlds, there's bound to be technology. Contrast any Sim with Peter Griffin from the crude but popular adult cartoon *Family Guy*. After being told by his friend Quagmire that he's an idiot and "can't even talk and chew gum at the same time," a cutaway reveals Peter lying face down on the sidewalk, apparently chewing gum ("Brian's a Bad Father" from Season 12, Episode 11). His wife calls for him and he replies, "I'm doing something. One thing at a time" (Langford & Sheridan, 2014). Peter is not known for being savvy with technology, unlike his Sim counterparts (watch "Quagmire's Quagmire," from *Family Guy* Season 12, Episode 3, when Peter travels to the Apple Store to help Quagmire purchase a computer only to become entangled by an earbud cord; Chevapravatdumrong & Michels, 2013). Considering these two popular culture amusements, it's easy to understand how one might presume that technology use is associated with effective multitasking.

Some scientists believe that multitasking is, itself, a myth. What appears to be multitasking is actually switching attention between tasks. It's very difficult for the brain to think about two ideas simultaneously or attend to multiple tasks concurrently (Howard, 2006). As neuroscientist John Medina (2008) said, "we are biologically incapable of processing attention-rich inputs simultaneously" (p. 85). Others have suggested that multitasking, such as driving and talking on the phone simultaneously, is one end of a continuum describing time between switching tasks (Salvucci, Taatgen, & Borst, 2009). Listening to a lecture and taking notes is an example of task-switching where the time between tasks might only be seconds. Regardless, there is a general belief that multitasking exists and that it is an important skill, especially in today's technology-rich society (Rose, 2010).

Today's teenagers have grown up not knowing a time without easy access to technology. First-year college students in Western cultures don't understand what it's like to live in a time without cell phones or the internet. Moreover, teenagers are spending much of their time immersed in technology (e.g., smartphone, computer, tablet, television, gaming device). In fact, many young people are spending more time with technology than sleeping. In a 2015 study, teenagers reported using technology almost 9 h per day, minus time spent using technology for school or homework (Common Sense Media, 2015). However, this figure is considerably more than what's been reported in the recent past. According to a 2010 Kaiser Foundation study, kids 8 to 18 years of age spent an average of more than 7.5 h a day, 7 days a week using technology, up from just over 6 h per day in 1999, but considerably lower than the 9 h per day reported by teenagers in the 2015 study (Rideout, Foehr, & Roberts, 2010). And college students are using smartphones just as often. A 2014 study found college women use their cell phones approximately 10 h per day, whereas men reported spending an average of approximately 7.5 h per day using cell phones (Roberts, Yaya, & Manolis, 2014). Not surprisingly, college students' cell phone usage has also increased in recent years. A 2012 study estimated college students used their cell phones approximately 7 h per day (Junco & Cotton, 2012).

While these numbers are staggering, the implications of increased technology usage among young people are interesting. For example, technology among teens is believed to aid in multitasking, a concept that involves quickly switching attention between multiple tasks. A 2006 *Time*

Magazine article proclaimed millennials as "the multitasking generation" (Wallis, 2006). Youth in the story described completing homework while listening to music, checking email while reading, and looking at Facebook while responding to texts—lots of time spent with technology and lots of time spent multitasking with technology.

The misguided belief that teens are good multitaskers because of their use of technology may have something to do with the numbers. Research suggests that media multitasking is commonplace among young people today. For example, a 2010 study found that almost 30% of youth in seventh through twelfth grade reported using two or more media (i.e., listening to music, using a computer or tablet, watching television, reading, playing video games) simultaneously (Rideout et al., 2010). The same study found that between half and three-quarters of adolescents reported media multitasking at least some or most of the time. For example, 66% of youth reported often using a computer and another media form concurrently. Another study found that 81% of 8- to 18-year-olds endorsed spending at least some of their time media multitasking (Foehr, 2006). The study also found that heavy multitaskers (i.e., those reporting multitasking most of the day), which amounted to approximately 15% of the sample, were engaged with technology almost 13 h per day. Given these numbers, there appears to be a relationship between technology use and media multitasking. However, one cannot infer causation (i.e., technology use causes teens to be effective multitaskers) from the available data. Rather, all that can be said is that frequent technology use and heavy media multitasking appear to occur together, which isn't surprising given that most new technologies encourage multitasking (e.g., smartphones allow users to concurrently hold a conversation via text message, track a snowstorm, and play a game of Candy Crush).

Myths are also promoted by the tendency to make meaningful connections between two variables based solely on their similarities. Technology and multitasking are clearly related. Again, smartphones allow users to easily engage in multiple tasks simultaneously (e.g., listen to music while texting a friend). It stands to reason that frequent technology usage would improve multitasking. Experimental research has found that teaching people to perform two tasks concurrently improves performance on those tasks (Cardoso-Leite, Green, & Bavelier, 2015). This isn't surprising, as training and practice improve performance. Researchers in the field of learning agree that "repeating an activity (i.e., training) leads to performance benefits on the trained and possibly similar activities" (Cardoso-Leite et al., 2015, p. 106). The more one does something, the more one becomes proficient at it. Characters in *The Sims* universe are effective multitaskers because they're able to practice multitasking with technology over and over. The logic makes sense, which might help explain why the myth that adolescents' use of technology enhances multitasking is so believable.

However, the truth of the statement that technology use enhances multitasking ability relies on the assumption that multitasking using technology (e.g., media multitasking) does, in fact, lead to improved multitasking. Yet, research suggests that heavy media multitaskers might be less effective at task-switching (e.g., shifting attention between one task and another) than those who rarely media multitask (Strayer & Watson, 2012). In one study, researchers compared heavy and light media multitaskers' performance on tasks requiring subjects to classify letters as vowels or consonants and classify digits as odd or even (Ophir, Nass, & Wagner, 2009). The researchers examined participants' response times during switch trials (trial followed by trial of the other type) and nonswitch trials (trial followed by trial of the same type). Surprisingly, heavy media multitaskers performed worse than light media multitaskers when required to switch tasks. Specifically, the heavy media multitaskers responded slower than light media multitaskers during both trial types and slowed down more during switch trials than the light media multitaskers. Put differently, frequent multitasking with technology did not lead to improved multitasking. Rather, light media multitaskers performed better than heavy media multitaskers when required to switch attention when completing two different tasks. Other research has found that college student subjects identifying themselves as expert multitaskers performed poorly on a laboratory task of attention and recall (Sanbonmatsu, Strayer, Mederios-Ward, & Watson, 2013). The researchers hypothesized that multitasking might result from an individual's inability to "block out distractions and focus on a singular task" (p. 7). This might help explain why some people find it so difficult to ignore text messages while driving.

The myth that technology use has made teens better multitaskers also relies on the assumption that multitasking, as a skill, is desirable. However, there appears to be a number of pitfalls related to multitask-ing. For example, a Forbes.com article from February 2017 titled "Want to be more Productive? Stop Multitasking" reported that multitasking could reduce productivity by as much as 40% (Quast, 2017). Although this figure is only an estimate, much of the research on multitasking suggests it is not something one wants to do very often. Reviews of the literature consistently find that heavy media multitasking negatively affects attention, concentration, academic assignment quality, learning quality, and academic performance (Levine, Waite, & Bowman, 2012; Wallis, 2010). Specific to middle and high school aged students, research indicates frequent media multitaskers do poorly on performance measures of attention, inhibition, and working memory (Baumgartner, Weeda, van der Heijden, & Huizinga, 2014; Cain, Leonard, Gabrieli, & Finn, 2016; Moisala et al., 2016). Furthermore, teenagers who identify themselves as heavy media multitaskers report higher levels of impulsivity and score significantly lower on standardized assessment of academic achievement than light media multitaskers (Cain et al., 2016; Moisala et al., 2016). For example, one study found that statewide academic assessment scores in Math and English Language Arts were negatively correlated with self-reported media multitasking (Cain et al., 2016). Specifically, light media multitaskers performed better than heavy media multitaskers on both tests.

For college students, multitasking during class, especially when social media is used, is also associated with distractibility and poor academic performance (Junco, 2012; McCoy, 2016). For example, one study using survey data from almost 2,000 students from a large university found that frequent Facebook use or text messaging while completing schoolwork was negatively associated with grade point average (GPA; Junco & Cotton, 2012). This isn't surprising as experimental research has found that multitasking negatively affects classroom performance. In one study, researchers provided students in an upper-level communications course with laptops as a "supplement to the lecture, discussion and lab activities" (Hembrooke & Gay, 2003, p. 7). During one particular class, students were randomly assigned to one of two conditions: laptop open or laptop closed during lecture. Those in the laptop open condition began the class period in the lecture and then moved to a lab activity, while those in the laptop closed condition began the class in the lab activity and moved to the lecture. Each group was tested on the lecture's content immediately after the lecture portion of the class. Not surprisingly, the researchers found that students in the laptop open condition scored significantly worse than the laptop-closed group on short answer recall questions. The results were the same two months later when researchers replicated the study but with subjects assigned to the opposite condition. The researchers also found that students using their laptops for course-related purposes (e.g., looking up information relevant to the course) performed as poorly on comprehension questions as those who used their laptops to look up irrelevant information. In a more recent study, researchers found low student engagement during class and poor lecture comprehension when students were intentionally distracted in class by Facebook (Gupta

& Irwin, 2016). Surprisingly, this was true whether the lecture was of high or low interest to students.

Taken altogether, technology does not appear to improve multitasking for the vast majority of individuals. Moreover, research indicates that adolescent media multitasking negatively impacts various aspects of cognitive functioning including attention, concentration, inhibition, and working memory, as well as academic performance. Although most of us are not productive multitaskers, how is it that *The Sims* characters are able to simultaneously talk on the phone, cook a grilled cheese sandwich, and put out a fire? And how can Homer Simpson, after learning to drive with his knees, simultaneously make snow cones, turn on a fog machine, and DJ using a turntable all while driving ("Brake My Wife, Please," from Season 14, Episode 20)? Perhaps they represent what cognitive psychologists David Strayer and Jason Watson call "Supertaskers," or the very small minority of individuals who are highly effective multitaskers (Strayer & Watson, 2012). Most likely it's because they're fictional characters who defy the laws of reality.

What you need to know

There is still a lot to learn about technology and multitasking beyond what's already been studied. For example, research continues to investigate the long-term effects of chronic technology usage and media multitasking on the brains of children and adolescents. Additional research is also needed to help understand differences between heavy and light media multitaskers. While basic and applied research works to answer these questions, there are some points to consider currently when thinking about teenagers, technology, and multitasking.

Not surprisingly, research has offered many advantages to limiting adolescents' screen time. A recent review published in *Pediatrics*, the primary journal of the American Academy of Pediatrics, noted several significant health and developmental risks associated with heavy technology usage (Chassiakos, Radesky, Christakis, Moreno, & Cross, 2016). For example, teenagers' excessive television viewing is correlated with obesity and sleep problems. There is also an inverse relationship between technology usage and academic performance (Rideout et al., 2010). Specifically, heavy technology use is associated with lower grades.

However, research also indicates that there are potential benefits associated with technology usage. For example, online social interactions among teenagers have been found to be mostly positive and neutral

(Underwood, Ehrenreich, More, Solis, & Brinkley, 2015), which might help explain why online social communication among teenagers has been shown to improve the quality of existing relationships (Davis, 2012). In addition, technology used wisely in educational contexts can enhance learning outcomes. For example, a statistical analysis of 20 studies found that the use of technology in middle school literacy programs improved reading comprehension skills (Moran, Ferdig, Pearson, Wardrop, & Blomeyer, 2008).

When it comes to adolescent technology use, most experts in child development, education, and healthcare recommend sensible family practices. For example, the American Psychological Association suggests that parents closely monitor their teen's use of technology and not allow teens to use technology in their bedrooms or other locations where parental monitoring is difficult (da Salvia, 2015). Parents are also encouraged to maintain open lines of communication with their adolescent to explain and discuss media content that might involve adult themes. The American Academic of Pediatrics recommends parents work with their teenagers to develop a Family Media Plan (www.healthychildren.org/MediaUsePlan). The plan can help families and teenagers negotiate screen-free areas of the home (e.g., bedroom, dinner table), device curfews and other times when technology shouldn't be used, and appropriate media content. Parents can also use this resource to help their teenager balance online and offline time, and understand appropriate media manners (e.g., not using their cell phone during mealtimes) and digital citizenship (e.g., being polite to people while online). Ideally, parents should be working with teenagers to ensure the development of healthy technology usage. Behaviors that promote healthy technology usage established during adolescence are likely to remain with the individual into adulthood.

References

Baumgartner, S. E., Weeda, W. D., van der Heijden, L. L., & Huizinga, M. (2014). The relationship between media multitasking and executive function in early adolescence. *Journal of Early Adolescence*, 34, 1120–1144.

Cain, M. S., Leonard, J. A., Gabrieli, J. D. E., & Finn, A. S. (2016). Media multitasking in adolescence. *Psychonomic Bulletin & Review*, 23, 1932–1941.

Cardoso-Leite, P., Green, C. S., & Bavelier, D. (2015). On the impact of new technologies on multitasking. *Developmental Review*, 35, 98–112.

Chassiakos, Y. R., Radesky, J., Christakis, D., Moreno, M. A., & Cross, C. (2016). Children and adolescents and digital media. *Pediatrics*, 138, e1–e18.

Chevapravatdumrong, C. (Writer), & Michels, P. (Director). (2013). Quagmire's quagmire [Television episode]. In S. McFarland (Producer), *Family Guy*. Los Angeles, CA: 20th Century Fox.

Common Sense Media (2015). *Common sense consensus: Media use by teens and tweens*. San Francisco, CA: Author.

Davis, K. (2012). Friendship 2.0: Adolescents' experiences of belonging and self-disclosure online. *Journal of Adolescence, 35*, 1527–1536.

Foehr, U. G. (2006). *Media multitasking among American youth: Prevalence, predictors and pairings*. Menlo Park, CA: Kaiser Family Foundation.

Gupta, N., & Irwin, J. D. (2016). In-class distractions: The role of Facebook and the primary learning task. *Computers in Human Behavior, 55*, 1165–1178.

Hembrooke, H., & Gay, G. (2003). The laptop and the lecture: The effects of multitasking in learning environments. *Journal of Computing in Higher Education, 15*, 46–64.

Howard, P. J. (2006). *The owner's manual for the brain: Everyday applications from mind-brain research*. Austin, TX: Bard Press.

Junco, R. (2012). In-class multitasking and academic performance. *Computers in Human Behavior, 28*, 2236–2243.

Junco, R., & Cotton, S. R. (2012). No A for U: The relationship between multitasking and academic performance. *Computers & Education, 59*, 505–514.

Langford, J. (Writer), & Sheridan, C. (Director). (2014). Brian's a bad father [Television episode]. In S. McFarland (Producer), *Family Guy*. Los Angeles, CA: 20th Century Fox.

Levine, L. E., Waite, B. M., & Bowman, L. L. (2012). Mobile media use, multitasking and distractibility. *International Journal of Cyber Behavior, Psychology, and Learning, 2*, 15–29.

McCoy, B. R. (2016). Digital distractions in the classroom phase II: Student classroom use of digital devices for non-class related purposes. *Journal of Media Education, 7*, 5–32.

Medina, J. (2008). *Brain rules: 12 principles for surviving and thriving at work, home, and school*. Seattle, WA: Pear Press.

Moisala, M., Salmela, V., Hietajarvi, L., Salo, E., Carlson, S., Salonen, O., … Alho, K. (2016). Media multitasking is associated with distractibility and increased prefrontal activity in adolescents and young adults. *NeuroImage, 134*, 113–121.

Moran, J., Ferdig, R. E., Pearson, P. D., Wardrop, J., & Blomeyer, R. L. (2008). Technology and reading performance in middle school grades: A meta-analysis with recommendations for policy and practice. *Journal of Literacy Research, 40*, 6–58.

Ophir, E., Nass, C., & Wagner, A. D. (2009). Cognitive control in medial multitasking. *Psychological and Cognitive Sciences, 106*, 15583–15587.

Quast, L. (2017, February 6). Want to be more productive? Stop multi-tasking. Forbes.com. Retrieved from https://www.forbes.com/sites/lisaquast/2017/02/06/want-to-be-more-productive-stop-multi-tasking/#528c52455a64

Rideout, V. J., Foehr, U. G., & Roberts, D. F. (2010). *Generation M2: Media in the lives of 8- to 18-year-olds*. Menlo Park, CA: Kaiser Family Foundation.

Roberts, J. A., Yaya, L. H. P., & Manolis, C. (2014). The invisible addition: Cell-phone activities and addiction among male and female college students. *Journal of Behavioral Addictions*, 3, 254–265.

Rose, E. (2010). Continuous partial attention: Reconsidering the role of online learning in the age of interruption. *Educational Technology*, 50, 41–46.

da Salvia, J. (2015, June). Children and electronic media: How much is too much? Retrieved from http://www.apa.org/pi/about/newsletter/2015/06/electronic-media.aspx

Salvucci, D. D., Taatgen, N. A., & Borst, J. P. (2009). Toward a unified theory of the multitasking continuum: From concurrent performance to task switching, interruption, and resumption. In D. R. Olsen, Jr., & R. B. Arthur (General Chairs), K. Hinckley, M. R. Morris, S. Hudson, & S. Greenberg (Program Chairs) *Proceedings of the SIGCHI Conference on Human Factors in Computing Systems* (pp. 1819–1828). Boston, MA: Association for Computing Machinery.

Sanbonmatsu, D. M., Strayer, D. L., Medeiros-Ward, N., & Watson, J. M. (2013). Who multi-tasks and why? Multi-tasking ability, perceived multi-tasking ability, impulsivity, and sensation seeking. *PLoS ONE*, 8, e54402.

Strayer, D. L., & Watson, J. M. (2012). Supertaskers and the multitasking brain. *Scientific American Mind*, 23, 22–29.

Underwood, M. K., Ehrenreich, S. E., More, D., Solis, J. S., & Brinkley, D. Y. (2015). The BlackBerry Project: The hidden world of adolescents' text messaging and relations with internalizing symptoms. *Journal of Research on Adolescence*, 25, 101–117.

Wallis, C. (2006, March 27). The multitasking generation. *Time Magazine*. New York, NY: Time.

Wallis, C. (2010). *The impacts of media multitasking on children's learning and development: Report from a research seminar*. New York, NY: The Joan Ganz Cooney Center at Sesame Workshop.

Mini myths for development of the body, brain, and mind

Myth #6 Pubertal "early bloomers" fare better than "late bloomers"

Ten-year-old boys are playing Little League and a wayward ball has been thrown far, far off the field, well behind home plate. Suddenly, a much more mature-looking boy rides by the dugout on his moped. He dismounts, picks up the ball, and throws it all the way to the outfield.

"Who is *he*?" the coach asks.

"He's in our grade," the kids tell him. "I heard he spent two years in 'juvi,'" one offers. "I heard he broke some kid's arm who owed him money." And the coach, in awe, responds "Who cares about that crap, can he play?"

This scene is from a remake of the classic film, *The Bad News Bears* (Linklater, 2005), and illustrates both the myth as well as the nugget of truth behind the myth, which is that, while kids who develop more quickly than others may be envied on the field, their off-field behavior can be troublesome.

And while many parents hold a favorable view of their child experiencing puberty earlier, if they have aspirations for their teen to become the next great athlete, unexpected negative consequences often follow these "early bloomers." This notion has psychologists worried. Many suggest it creates what scientists call "biopsychosocial asynchrony," meaning that children's bodies appear to be ready for sexual debut and accordingly, based on their appearance alone, they may be treated by others with expectations, advances, or assumptions that are commensurate with someone much older. But because their brain development, life experience, and access to social support still reflects that of a typical child years younger than they appear, this is a mismatch that could confer serious risk for a wide range of psychological problems (Rudolph, 2014).

Many studies now suggest that early pubertal development is associated with a greater likelihood of externalizing symptoms, such as aggressive behavior, earlier sexual debut, and substance use (Negriff & Susman, 2011). Among girls, early-onset puberty also is significantly associated with depression and body-dissatisfaction (Ge, Conger, & Elder, 1996).

Research also suggests the most powerful factors predicting negative outcomes may be related to the tendency for those who develop early to begin hanging out with peers who are closer to their apparent age, rather than their actual age. Among girls, this may be especially problematic (Negriff & Susman, 2011). Research suggests that early-blooming girls, who often are the most physically mature compared with any others in their grade, often attract the attention of older boys. Within this older peer group, girls are exposed to opportunities for sexual behavior, substance use, and deviancy that are not present when spending time with their same-aged peers, and this accelerates girls' social maturation at a rate that does not match their psychological readiness (Negriff & Susman, 2011). Research confirms that this early affiliation with risky teens explains much of the association between early puberty and negative outcomes (Negriff & Susman, 2011).

Early bloomers trick us. Based on their physical maturity, their peers, parents, and even they themselves may sometimes feel that they're ready to experience adult-like challenges within the world around them. But we should not let ourselves be fooled, because early-bloomers are children in adolescents' clothing, and they still need the protections and support that we would offer any child their age.

References

Ge, X., Conger, R. D., & Elder, G. H. (1996). Coming of age too early: Pubertal influences on girls' vulnerability to psychological distress. *Child Development*, 67(6), 3386–3400.

Linklater, R. (Director). (2005). *The Bad News Bears*. Los Angeles, CA: Paramount Pictures.

Negriff, S., & Susman, E. J. (2011). Pubertal timing, depression, and externalizing problems: A framework, review, and examination of gender differences. *Journal of Research on Adolescence*, 21(3), 717–746.

Rudolph, K. D. (2014). Puberty as a developmental context of risk for psychopathology. In M. Lewis & K. D. Rudolph (Eds.), *Handbook of developmental psychopathology*.

Myth #7

Teens can study better while listening to music

University professors, who are often required to walk across campus, can become pretty good experts on the behavioral routines of college students. And while it actually *is* relatively common to see college students walking around in pajama pants, there's a more universal fashion trend—headphones. They come in all sizes and colors. Students wear them while walking to class, while laying around waiting for class, and yes—sometimes—while in class. Unfortunately, research has recently found that headphone use is increasingly a cause of death for some, with pedestrian deaths related to headphone use more than doubling from 2004 to 2011 (Lichensetin, Smith, Ambrose, & Moody, 2012).

But most often students wear headphones and listen to music while studying and reading. In fact, research shows that listening to music while studying is actually the norm. For example, research by Johansson and colleagues (Johansson, Holmqvist, Mossberg, & Lindgren, 2012) found that 81% of their college student sample sometimes listened to music while studying. Similarly, 90% of students in a study by Furnham, Trew, and Sneade (1999) reported listening to music while studying. Therefore, it's no surprise that teens (and probably many adults) believe that listening to music helps them study. In fact, data from our own research (Jewell & Hupp, 2018) indicates that an overwhelming majority of college students

(85%) have heard of this myth, and a majority also believe the myth (44–62%). And belief in this myth was even higher, 77%, for the sample of college students in the study by Johansson et al. (2012).

So before looking at the research, let's make sure to clearly understand what the myth is saying—that listening to music helps one study *better* than the alternative to music, which would presumably be silence. To shed some light on this question, a recent study by Dobbs, Furnham, and McClelland (2011) tested the cognitive performance of girls ages 11–18 years old in the following three conditions: silence, pop music, and the background noise typical in an office. Students were assessed on three cognitive performance measures testing abstract reasoning, a popular test of logic and reasoning, and a test of verbal reasoning. Silence was better than noise in all three tasks and better than music in two of the three tasks. In fact, while listening to music students did not perform better than silence on any of the tasks. However, the researchers didn't stop there, going one step further to investigate difference in introverts compared to extraverts. In 1967, Hans Eysenck theorized that extraverts essentially live in a state of understimulation and therefore they seek out external stimuli, while introverts often feel overstimulated in social situations and seek solitude (Eysenck, 1967). Interestingly, a number of researchers have examined how one's level of extraversion may predict whether listening to music harms cognitive performance. So going back to the study by Dobbs et al. (2011), they in fact did find that as students' levels of extraversion increased, the deleterious effects of noise disappeared. So what's the simple answer to the myth? Well, if you are an extreme extravert, listening to music while you study is about the same as studying in silence. But if you are not an extravert, listening to music will hinder your studying, so you can keep the headphones on but just don't turn on the music.

References

Dobbs, S., Furnham, A., & McClelland, A. (2011). The effect of background music and noise on the cognitive test performance of introverts and extraverts. *Applied Cognitive Psychology*, 25(2), 307–313.

Eysenck, H. J. (1967). *The biological basis of personality*. Piscataway, NJ: Transaction Publishers.

Furnham, A., Trew, S., & Sneade, I. (1999). The distracting effects of vocal and instrumental music on the cognitive test performance of introverts and extra-verts. *Personality and Individual Differences*, 27(2), 381–392.

Jewell, J. D., & Hupp, S. D. A. (2018). Prevalence of myths about adolescence [Manuscript in preparation].

Johansson, R., Holmqvist, K., Mossberg, F., & Lindgren, M. (2012). Eye movements and reading comprehension while listening to preferred and non-preferred study music. *Psychology of Music*, 40(3), 339–356.

Lichenstein, R., Smith, D., Ambrose, J., & Moody, L. (2012). Headphone use and pedestrian injury and death in the United States: 2004–2011. *Injury Prevention*, 18(5), 287–290.

Myth #8 The "Freshman 15": College students gain 15 pounds their freshman year

While most would agree that adjusting to college life can be stressful, the myth of the "Freshman 15" certainly adds to that stress. The phrase "Freshman 15" was first coined by Watkins (a college student author) in an article in the popular teen magazine, *Seventeen* (1989). In the article, Watkins refers to the "…'freshman fifteen' syndrome, where students gain about fifteen pounds during their first year of college" (p. 162). However, the article appears to have been referring to the research by Hovell, Mewborn, Randle, and Fowler-Johnson (1985) who found that female college freshmen gained almost 9 pounds on average. These researchers surmised that the cause of the weight gain was related to the high fat and calorie food served in typical dormitory housing. By 1990, just one year after the term "Freshman 15" was used in *Seventeen* magazine (1989), the term exploded in the media—occurring in almost 300 newspaper and university newspaper articles (Brown, 2008). The myth has even made its way into pop culture. In a recent episode of *The Walking Dead*, as a group of bad guys takes over "The Kingdom," the leader says, "We're going to give you just enough to keep you working, but you're probably going to lose the freshman fifteen pretty quick" (Johnson, Kang, & Satrazemis, 2017). And this myth appears to have been given a life of its own, as 71–72% of college students in our own research sample believe the myth to be true (Jewell & Hupp, 2018).

While fear of the "Freshman 15" was taking hold across the US and beyond, this fear was definitely unfounded. A review of an average weight gain in college students by Zagorsky and Smith (2011) found that, of the 20 studies available at the time, the average weight gain was only 3.8 pounds. The authors went on to analyze data from the National Longitudinal Survey of Youth, which consisted of almost 9,000 participants. On average, college freshmen gained a relatively small amount (about 3 pounds for females and 3.5 pounds for males). And what about the fatty dorm food hypothesis? Well, the results are mixed. Males who lived in a dorm gained about a pound more than those who did not, but females actually gained about a pound *less* when they lived in a dorm (Zagorsky & Smith, 2011). Maintaining a healthy diet and exercising regularly are two good habits for all of us. But there appears to be no reason for college freshmen to fear dramatic weight gain. So college freshmen can relax. And if they feel the need to stress out about anything, try studying!

References

Brown, C. (2008). The information trail of the "Freshman 15"—a systematic review of a health myth within the research and popular literature. *Health Information & Libraries Journal*, 25(1), 1–12.

Hovell, M. F., Mewborn, C. R., Randle, Y., & Fowler-Johnson, S. (1985). Risk of excess weight gain in university women: A three-year community controlled analysis. *Addictive Behaviors*, 10(1), 15–28.

Jewell, J. D., & Hupp, S. D. A. (2018). Prevalence of myths about adolescence [Manuscript in Preparation].

Johnson, D. L., Kang, A. (Writers), & Satrazemis, M. E. (Director). (2017). How it's gotta be [Television series episode]. In F. Darabont, G. A. Hurd, D. Alpert, R. Kirkman, C. H. Eglee, G. Mazzara, … D. Huth (Executive Producers), *The Walking Dead*. New York, NY: AMC Studios.

Watkins, T. (1989, August). Fight the Freshman 15. *Seventeen*, 48, 162.

Zagorsky, J. L., & Smith, P. K. (2011). The Freshman 15: A critical time for obesity intervention or media myth? *Social Science Quarterly*, 92(5), 1389–1407.

Myth #9 Horses are helpful in the treatment of eating disorders, autism spectrum, and more

According to Dr. Oz, equine-assisted therapy is one of the "hottest" types of alternative medicine (Rader & Chiaro, 2010). Equine-assisted therapy uses horses in a therapeutic manner to provide intervention for psychological disorders. Dr. Oz further indicated that "These beautiful animals uncover psychological issues. You know why? Because based on what patients project on to them, you can actually help figure out what's going on with people. We use horses to treat depression, anxiety, and autism because they bring out honesty in us" (Rader & Chiaro, 2010). Other issues treated by equine-assisted therapy include eating disorders, substance use, and exposure to trauma, with one website suggesting that "82% of teens showed more improvement in just five sessions of EAP [equine-assisted psychotherapy] than they had in years of traditional therapy" (Corcoran, n.d.).

A recent review article summarized the results of 14 studies that used horses as part of therapeutic treatment for issues such as those described above, and the authors concluded that the research does not support the use of this intervention (Anestis, Anestis, Zawilinski, & Lilienfeld, 2014). Specifically, the "studies failed to provide consistent evidence that [using horses in therapy] is superior to the mere passage of time in the treatment of any mental disorder" (p. 1115). That is, any positive results in the studies were likely the result of initial short-lasting positive experiences with trying something new (i.e., novelty effects), experimenter expectancies, and design flaws. We couldn't find evidence that Dr. Oz has changed his tune about equine-assisted therapy; however, his positive promotion of other ineffective interventions has resulted in a reprimand from a consumer protection committee (Christensen & Wilson, 2014), which seems to be a trot in the right direction.

References

Anestis, M. D., Anestis, J. C., Zawilinski, L. L., Hopkins, T. A., & Lilienfeld, S. O. (2014). Equine-related treatments for mental disorders lack empirical support: A systematic review of empirical investigations. *Journal of Clinical Psychology*, 70(12), 1115–1132.

Christensen, J., & Wilson, J. (2014). Congressional hearing investigates Dr. Oz "miracle" weight loss claims. Retrieved from www.cnn.com

Corcoran, L. (n.d.). Straight from the horse's mouth: Equine assisted psychotherapy. Retrieved from www.bestselfatlanta.com

Rader, S., & Chiaro, A. (Executive Producer). (2010). The top 2 alternative treatments [Television talk show segment]. In *Dr. Oz Show*. Chicago, IL: Harpo Productions.

Myth #10

The onset of puberty is very upsetting to most teens

Puberty is one of the most important biological milestones in adolescence. In fact, many cultures use puberty as a social marker for the beginning of adulthood. However, for a variety of reasons puberty has historically been viewed as a life event that is upsetting for those teens that first experience some parts of puberty, such as menarche or onset of menstruation in females. In fact, in our own research using a college student sample, 46–50% of students agreed that the onset of puberty is very upsetting for most teens (Jewell & Hupp, 2018). Perhaps the most shocking and disturbing media example promoting this myth is a scene from the beginning of the movie *Carrie* (De Palma & Cohen, 1976) where the naïve and uninformed main character (Carrie, played by Sissy Spacek) is taking a shower after PE class in high school and is shocked when she begins menstruating. Interestingly, this same scene was repeated in the 2013 remake (Peirce, Cohen, & Aguirre-Sacasa, 2013) of the 1976 movie.

But in fact, research shows that menarche is not a universally distressing and upsetting event to most teens, as early research on this topic in the United States has contradicted this myth (Ruble & Brooks-Gunn, 1982). For example, Ruble and Brooks-Gunn found that while some teens in their sample (46%) noted that menarche created some annoyance due to having to carry menstrual supplies, there were also a number of positive aspects to menarche such as the fact that it reflects becoming physically mature (noted in 76% of the sample). The authors concluded that "while menarche may be initially disruptive, particularly for early-maturing and unprepared girls, it typically does not seem to be a traumatic experience" (p. 1565). In fact, research has generally found that the experience of menarche is mostly positive when cultures highlight the positive aspects of menarche, avoid stigmatizing the event, and provide information regarding menarche prior to the actual event (for a review see Arnett, 2014). The importance of education and preparation for menarche was also noted in the original Ruble and Brooks-Gunn study. Thus, while some factors may lead to distress when menarche occurs, female teens' experiences can certainly be influenced by a number of factors including preparation as well as how others in society view the event.

References

Arnett, J. J. (2014). *Adolescence and emerging adulthood*. Boston, MA: Pearson.
De Palma, B. (Director), & Cohen, L. (Writer). (1976). *Carrie* [Motion picture on DVD]. USA: Red Bank Films.
Jewell, J. D., & Hupp, S. D. A. (2018). Prevalence of myths about adolescence. [Manuscript in preparation].
Peirce, K. (Director), Cohen, L., & Aguirre-Sacasa, R. (Writers). (2013). *Carrie* [Motion picture]. USA: Metro Goldwyn Mayer.
Ruble, D. N., & Brooks-Gunn, J. (1982). The experience of menarche. *Child Development*, 53(6), 1557–1566.

Myth #11 | Male teens are much less likely than females to be preoccupied with their physical appearance

Consider headlines such as "Female Preoccupation with Physical Appearance" (University of Michigan, 1998), "Fighting Unhealthy Perceptions of Body Image: Why Women Obsess Over Appearance" (Valton, 2017), and "Why Disney Princesses and 'Princess Culture' are Bad for Girls" (Hains, 2016). Headlines such as these represent the stereotype that preoccupation with minor (or imagined) flaws in physical appearance is attributed to females much more so than males. This stereotype is especially pronounced in the teenage years. For example, teens are often depicted in the media critically examining their own facial features or bodies in a mirror. When this preoccupation causes significant emotional distress or impairment, the teen may meet the diagnostic criteria for body dysmorphic disorder (BDD; American Psychiatric Association, 2013). Thus, rates of BDD are a good indication how accurate the stereotype really is. Are male teens really less likely to have this disorder? A recent large prevalence study with a community-based sample of teens, the first of its kind, showed that 1.7% of teen females were likely to meet the criteria for BDD, which was not significantly different from the 1.8% of males meeting these criteria (Schneider, Turner, Mond, & Hudson, 2017). Further, a systematic review summarized eight other studies which examined prevalence rates of BDD with adolescents (including college students) (Veale, Gledhill, Christodoulou, & Hodsoll, 2016). Four of the studies did show slightly higher rates of BDD in females; however, the other four studies showed slightly higher rates of BDD in males. All in all, the rates of BDD in females and males are quite similar. Notably, there is one type of BDD that is considerably more common in males—muscle dysphoria, which involves a preoccupation with a perception of one's own smaller muscle size (American Psychiatric Association, 2013; Campagna & Bowsher, 2016).

References

American Psychiatric Association (2013). *Diagnostic and statistical manual of mental disorders (DSM–5)*. Arlington, VA: Author.

Campagna, J. D., & Bowsher, B. (2016). Prevalence of body dysmorphic disorder and muscle dysmorphia among entry-level military personnel. *Military Medicine*, *181*(5), 494–501.

Hains, R. (2016). Why Disney princesses and 'princess culture' are bad for girls. Retrieved from www.washingtonpost.com

Schneider, S. C., Turner, C. M., Mond, J., & Hudson, J. L. (2017). Prevalence and correlates of body dysmorphic disorder in a community sample of adolescents. *Australian & New Zealand Journal of Psychiatry*, 51(6), 595–603.

University of Michigan (1998). Female preoccupation with physical appearance. Retrieved from www.newswise.com

Valton, M. J. (2017). Fighting unhealthy perceptions of body image: Why women obsess over appearance. Retrieved from www.motherforlife.com

Veale, D., Gledhill, L. J., Christodoulou, P., & Hodsoll, J. (2016). Body dysmorphic disorder in different settings: A systematic review and estimated weighted prevalence. *Body Image*, 18, 168–186.

Myth #12 Most teens hardly ever engage in leisure reading these days

It's true that teens these days are spending more and more time engaging with screens (Common Sense Media, 2013). Televisions, computers, tablets, and phones all compete for a teenager's attention. Has the time yet come when teens have given up on other activities, such as leisure reading, altogether? Probably not. Recent research shows that only 22% of 13-year-olds report engaging in leisure reading only rarely (i.e., "never" or "hardly ever"), with 53% of them engaging in leisure reading at least once a week (National Center for Education Statistics, 2013). Older teenagers reported somewhat less reading. That is, 27% of 17-year-olds rarely read for leisure while 40% of them read for leisure a least once a week. Thus, teens are still reading for leisure at a fairly high rate, even though the same study also reported a gradual decline in the number of teens who read every day from 1984 to 2012. Although, increased screen time might help account for why teens are reading less, another answer might be found with their parents. In a national sample of nearly 8,900 parents of 4-year-olds, 49% indicated that they only read to their children twice a week or less (Kahn, Purtell, Logan, Ansari, & Justice, 2017). Thus, a large percentage of the parents weren't following the recommendation of the American Academy of Pediatrics to engage in daily reading with young children (Council on Early Childhood, 2014). In fact, 23% of the parents reported *never* reading to their 4-year-olds. The good news is that teens these days still do a fair amount of leisure reading on their own; however, the myth that they "hardly ever engage in leisure reading" is one of the myths in this book that could one day become a reality. Thus, one potential way parents can increase the likelihood that their teens engage in leisure reading is to start with them when they're young.

References

Common Sense Media. (2013). Zero to eight: Children's media use in America 2013. Retrieved from www.commonsensemedia.org

Council on Early Childhood (2014). Literacy promotion: An essential component of primary care pediatric practice. Pediatrics. doi:10.1542/peds.2014-1384.

Khan, K. S., Purtell, K. M., Logan, J., Ansari, A., & Justice, L. M. (2017). Association between television viewing and parent-child reading in the early home environment. *Journal of Developmental & Behavioral Pediatrics*, 38(7), 521–527.

National Center for Education Statistics (2013). Trends in academic progress. Retrieved from https://nces.ed.gov

Myth #13   Greek life has a negative effect on college students academically

"Greek Life" in college, or membership in fraternities and sororities, is often maligned in television and film. Movies like *Animal House* (Reitman, Simmons, & Landis, 1978) and *Van Wilder* (D'Amico, Foster, von Alvensleben, & Becker, 2002) epitomize the "party first, go to class later" motto portrayed in these films. But is it true that students who become involved in fraternities and sororities have poor academic performance in college? Several researchers over the years have attempted to answer the question, with mixed results, though most of these studies suffered from methodological flaws (e.g., relying on self-reported grades) or small sample sizes (DeBard, Lake, & Binder, 2006; Pike, 1996, 2000). However, one of the largest studies on this topic found results that would surprise many (DeBard & Sacks, 2011). This study of over 45,000 students from 17 institutions compared students involved in fraternities, sororities, and their same sex counterparts not involved in Greek Life on actual academic records of grade point average, retention, and hours earned. They also controlled for high school grade point average and ACT (formerly, American College Testing) score in their analyses. The researchers found that "students who joined Greek letter organizations in their first year earned significantly higher grade point averages than independent students did" (DeBard & Sacks, 2011, p. 114). Additionally, students in Greek organizations also had higher retention rates to the next year compared to students who were not affiliated with a Greek organization. So while movies about debauched frat boys and sorority girls may sell movie tickets, the truth is actually much more complex.

References

D'Amico, K., Foster, L., von Alvensleben, P. (Producers), & Becker, W. (Director). (2002). *Van Wilder* [Motion picture]. United States: Myriad Pictures.

DeBard, R., & Sacks, C. (2011). Greek membership: The relationship with first-year academic performance. *Journal of College Student Retention: Research, Theory & Practice, 13*(1), 109–126.

DeBard, R., Lake, T., & Binder, R. S. (2006). Greeks and grades: The first-year experience. *NASPA Journal, 43*(1), 56–68.

Pike, G. R. (1996). Limitations of using students' self-reports of academic development as proxies for traditional achievement measures. *Research in Higher Education, 37*(1), 89–114.

Pike, G. R. (2000). The influence of fraternity or sorority membership on students' college experiences and cognitive development. *Research in Higher Education, 41*(1), 117–139.

Reitman, I., Simmons, M. (Producers), & Landis, J. (Director). (1978). *Animal House* [Motion picture]. United States: Universal Studios.

Myth #14 Paying for prep courses is the best way to make large gains on the SAT

Another book in Great Myths of Psychology series, *Great Myths of Education and Learning*, debunks the myth that "coaching produces large gains in college admission test scores" (Holmes, 2016, p. 174). Colleges and universities commonly require students to take college admissions tests, and every year over a million students take the Scholastic Aptitude Test (SAT) alone (College Board, 2016). High school students often pay over $1,000 for prep courses with the hope of making large gains on the college admission tests (Carrins, 2014); however, research shows that large gains are unlikely. Examining only studies with good research designs, a meta-analysis (mathematical synthesis of studies) found that students made only small gains attributable to prep courses (Kulik, Bangert-Drowns, & Kulik, 1984), and other reviews have consistently reported similar results (Becker, 1990). The most recent review found more moderate effects but still concluded that the gains were less than promised by the companies offering up the prep course (Montgomery & Lilly, 2012). Taken together, these studies show that prep courses can help improve SAT scores somewhat, but they do not consistently help students make large gains. Even small gains, however, may be enough to make the difference for some students when it comes to getting into the college of their choosing, and this has led some to question how fair it is for wealthier students to afford the course. Interestingly, the College Board (a nonprofit organization) recently partnered with the Khan Academy® to release a free online SAT practice resource which includes practice tests, study tips, and practice tips (College Board, 2016). This free program has yet to be compared with paid programs, but it has the potential to create more equity in terms of college admission tests.

References

Becker, B. J. (1990). Coaching for the Scholastic Aptitude Test: Further synthesis and appraisal. *Review of Educational Research*, 60(3), 373–417.

Carrins, A. (2014). Another college expense: Preparing for the SAT and ACT. Retrieved from www.nytimes.com

College Board. (2016). The College Board announces surge of students taking new SAT® suite of assessments, creating an opportunity pathway for more than six million students. Retrieved from www.collegeboard.org

Holmes, J. (2016). *Great myths of education and learning*. Malden, MA: Wiley-Blackwell.

Kulik, J. A., Bangert-Drowns, R. L., & Kulik, C. L. C. (1984). Effectiveness of coaching for aptitude tests. *Psychological Bulletin*, 95(2), 179–188.

Montgomery, P., & Lilly, J. (2012). Systematic reviews of the effects of preparatory courses on university entrance examinations in high school-age students. *International Journal of Social Welfare*, 21(1), 3–12.

2 DEVELOPMENT OF THE SELF

Great Myths of Adolescence, First Edition. Jeremy D. Jewell, Michael I. Axelrod, Mitchell J. Prinstein, and Stephen Hupp.
© 2019 John Wiley & Sons Ltd. Published 2019 by John Wiley & Sons Ltd.

Myth #15 Significant mood disruptions in adolescence are inevitable

Imagine a toddler or young school-aged child with his or her friends, and you likely will envision running, jumping, singing, skipping, and laughing. Now imagine how teenagers may act when hanging out with their peers, and the picture changes. The scene is different; adolescents with unkempt hair stare down into their phones, loud music plays in the background, and if anyone speaks at all it is likely to reflect some sarcastic, dystopian, cynical world viewpoint. This is the caricature of teens that so many movies, TV shows, and music videos have depicted. Imagine Ally Sheedy's character in *The Breakfast Club* (Hughes, 1985)—mute, dressed completely in black, and hostile towards anyone who shows an interest in her. Or April in the TV series, *Parks and Recreation* (Daniels, 2009–2015)—consistently moody, disengaged, lazy, and oppositional. Is it any wonder that most people believe that adolescents are perpetually moody?

To be fair, the media are not solely responsible for the myths regarding adolescents' moodiness. This is a stereotype that has been perpetuated by scholars for decades, perhaps even millennia. Over 100 years ago, famed psychologist G. Stanley Hall described adolescence as a period of "rapid fluctuations of mood," and suggested that this developmental stage was best described as a period of "storm and stress" (Hall, 1904). Years later, Anna Freud (Sigmund Freud's daughter) wrote "To be normal during the adolescent period is by itself abnormal" (Freud, 1958). And even Aristotle talked of teens who "are heated by Nature as drunken men by wine" (cited in Arnett, 1999). Not surprisingly then, scientists have been especially interested in whether this myth is true. Are teens really more moody, and are their emotional fluctuations inevitable? The implications of this assumption are quite concerning. If parents, teachers, or even teens themselves believe that this developmental period is characterized by the types of dramatic variations in mood that Hall, Freud, and Aristotle spoke of, it may have an effect on how teens are raised and when they're expected to assume adult responsibilities.

Some researchers have found that these stereotypes are indeed very widespread. In one study, researchers asked teachers and parents to identify descriptors of the adolescent period. A surprisingly large proportion of adults believed that adolescents were best described by terms such as "awkward," "anxious," "depressed," and "emotional." This stereotype proved consequential—parents most likely to believe that adolescence was characterized by moodiness were less likely to respond to their children's needs (Hines & Paulson, 2007). Equally concerning, many researchers fear that stereotypes regarding adolescents' moodiness may discourage adults and teens themselves from addressing serious emotional difficulties that sometimes do arise (Hollenstein & Lougheed, 2013).

Of course, several large bodies of research have attempted to address whether teens indeed are inevitably depressive, "hormonal," or "out of control." The results seem to suggest that these stereotypes are exaggerations to say the least. Studies that have examined the prevalence of adolescent depression have revealed that there is something unique about the adolescent period that is associated with heightened risk. Before the age of 13 years, less than one out of every 20 youth meet diagnostic criteria for a major depressive disorder. However, during the teen years, this rate increases significantly. By the age of 25, one out of every five young women and one out of 10 men has had a depressive episode (Hankin et al., 1998).

Importantly, a diagnosis of depression is substantially different from the type of moodiness that many believe characterize adolescence. To receive a diagnosis, one must persistently experience sadness or irritability for most days over a period of at least 2 weeks. In addition, depression is accompanied by a loss of interest in fun activities, disturbances in sleep, appetite, or sex drive, feelings of hopeless or suicidality, that have made it very difficult to function with friends, at school, or at work (American Psychiatric Association, 2013).

It is true that adolescents are at greater risk than are children for depression. Suicide also reflects a serious issue for adolescents—it is currently a leading cause of death for youth aged 15–24 years (Nock et al., 2013). However, it is critical to note that depression and suicide represent extreme levels of difficulty that do not afflict most, let alone all, adolescents. In fact, the vast majority of adolescents report few or no symptoms of depression and never have suicidal thoughts. However, the increased vulnerability to these serious conditions among some adolescents may have been overgeneralized by many who incorrectly assume that all adolescents experience significant moodiness.

In many cases, adults may believe that adolescents' biological development has rendered them more emotionally labile, or "hormonal." This too has been a topic studied in great depth by researchers. In some studies, scientists have examined whether individual differences in levels of testosterone from teen to teen may be associated with differences in their aggressive behavior. Others have examined whether variability in norepinephrine might predict which teens would be more or less anxious (Hollenstein & Lougheed, 2013). Results have surprisingly revealed that differences in hormone levels are far less strongly related to differences in adolescents' behavior than one might think. Researchers now estimate that hormone levels explain only about 6% of all of the variation in why some teens act differently from others (Hollenstein & Lougheed, 2013).

The surprising result makes sense if you consider that the effects of hormones have a lot to do with the environment in which adolescents live. In other words, it's not our biology alone that influences how we act as much as it is the interaction between our biology and the world around us. For instance, those who have high testosterone levels may be more likely to act aggressively, but only if in a situation where they're threatened, required to compete, or need to defend themselves. This is important because the world in which most adolescents find themselves typically is characterized by a growing ability to act independently in a society where independence is often not offered until years later. Adolescents also often are situated within peer worlds that are increasingly sophisticated with social rules that expand in complexity. The influence of hormones may therefore be especially dependent on what adolescents do in their daily lives, with more severe mood fluctuations resulting only from the perfect storm between biological and environmental risk factors coming together (Hollenstein & Lougheed, 2013).

In addition to the study of moodiness and emotionally labile or "hormonal" behavior, scientists have examined whether it is accurate to consider adolescents emotionally "out of control." Among psychologists, this question has been captured in the study of emotional regulation. Researchers interested in the seemingly dysregulated nature of adolescents' behavior and fluctuating emotions have found some support for this notion when examining brain development. Findings have revealed that the regions of the brain do not all mature simultaneously. Rather, neural networks below the cortex—or the "thinking brain" develop first, and this includes regions associated with emotional expression and the regions associated with the desire to obtain pleasure (Casey & Caudle, 2013). Lagging a few years behind is the prefrontal cortex, allowing for more measured, thoughtful, and deliberated responses to stress or impulses. On the surface, these findings might seem to support that adolescents are brimming with unbridled emotions, without the fully formed capability to regulate them.

What you need to know

Indeed, research suggests that many adolescents do experience emotions more intensely than do children and adults (Aldao, 2013). However, data also suggest that adolescents are adept at regulating their emotions, with the vast majority competent with a wide array of coping skills that developed before adolescence and that continue to be efficacious throughout the teenage years. The psychological literature is rich with research describing a wide array of coping skills that adolescents successfully use in response to diverse life stressors and daily hassles, and for adolescents experiencing clinical depression there is hope. A recent review of research has demonstrated that both cognitive-behavioral therapy (CBT) and interpersonal psychotherapy meet the American Psychological Association's criteria for well-established interventions (Weersing, Jeffreys, Do, Schwartz, & Bolano, 2017) by helping adolescents see how their prior experiences may be changing the way they interpret and respond to social experiences all day.

References

Aldao, A. (2013). The future of emotion regulation research: Capturing context. *Perspectives on Psychological Science, 8*(2), 155–172.

American Psychiatric Association (2013). *Diagnostic and statistical manual of mental disorders (DSM-5)*. Arlington, VA: Author.

Arnett, J. J. (1999). Adolescent storm and stress, reconsidered. *American Psychologist, 54*, 317–326.

Casey, B. J., & Caudle, K. (2013). The teenage brain: Self control. *Current Directions in Psychological Science, 22*(2), 82–87.

Daniels, G. (2009–2015). *Parks and recreation*. Hollywood, CA: National Broadcasting Company.

Freud, A. (1958). Adolescence. In A. Freud, H. Hartmann, & E. Kris (Eds.), *Psychoanalytic study of the child* (pp. 255–278). New York, NY: International Universities Press.

Hall, G. S. (1904). *Adolescence: Its psychology and its relation to physiology, anthropology, sociology, sex, crime, religion, and education*. Englewood Cliffs, NJ: Prentice-Hall.

Hankin, B. L., Abramson, L. Y., Moffitt, T. E., Silva, P. A., McGee, R., & Angell, K. E. (1998). Development of depression from preadolescence to young adulthood: Emerging gender differences in a 10-year longitudinal study. *Journal of Abnormal Psychology, 107*(1), 128.

Hines, A. R., & Paulson, S. E. (2007). Parents' and teachers' perceptions of adolescent storm and stress: Relations with parenting and teaching styles. *Family Therapy, 34*(2), 63–80.

Hollenstein, T., & Lougheed, J. P. (2013). Beyond storm and stress: Typicality, transactions, timing, and temperament to account for adolescent change. *American Psychologist, 68*(6), 444–454.

Hughes, J. (Director). (1985). *The Breakfast Club*. [Motion picture]. Los Angeles, CA: Universal Pictures.

Nock, M. K., Green, J. G., Hwang, I., McLaughlin, K. A., Sampson, N. A., Zaslavsky, A. M., & Kessler, R. C. (2013). Prevalence, correlates, and treatment of lifetime suicidal behavior among adolescents: Results from the National Comorbidity Survey Replication Adolescent Supplement. *JAMA Psychiatry*, 70(3), 300–310.

Weersing, V. R., Jeffreys, M., Do, M. C. T., Schwartz, K. T., & Bolano, C. (2017). Evidence base update of psychosocial treatments for child and adolescent depression. *Journal of Clinical Child & Adolescent Psychology*, 46(1), 11–43.

Myth #16   Teens should have a job in high school to build character

> Get a haircut and get a real job
> Clean your act up and don't be a slob
> Get it together like your big brother Bob
> Why don't you get a haircut and get a real job
>> From the song "Get a haircut" by George Thorogood and the Destroyers (Avery & Birch, 1993)

This myth appears to be one that is highly prevalent with people of all ages. In our study of college students, 81% of students had heard of the myth and between 68% and 81% agreed with it, making it one of the highest endorsed myths in this book (Jewell & Hupp, 2018). Unfortunately, few studies have examined how parents really feel about their teens working. In one of the first studies, Phillips and Sandstrom (1990) randomly chose over 1,500 parents of enrolled ninth graders and found something readers may find surprising: Only 27% of parents indicated that too many teens were working part time while going to school, while the vast majority of parents believed that the current situation was "about right" or that more teens should be employed part time. Mothers and fathers agreed that teens on average should begin working for money at about 13 years old. This age may seem relatively young, yet when respondents were asked about how their own teens' employment has impacted their family environment, they reported few negative effects. For example, over 75% of the sample responded that their child does not spend less time with his or her family. A majority of parents also believed that their teens' employment had positive effects such as their teen being more independent, both financially and otherwise. Moreover, a large majority of mothers and fathers believed that their child's employment had no effect on their grades in school, and employment had no negative impact on their child's attitude towards education. And only 15% of fathers and 18% of mothers believed that the hours their child worked should be changed at all. Somewhat shockingly, while 9–16% of parents wanted their child to work fewer hours, 29–44% of parents actually wished that their child would work more hours! Additionally, only 5–8% of parents wished that their child worked earlier hours on school nights. Thus, this study indicates that parents see their teens' employment experience as almost wholly positive with few negative effects, and in fact many parents wished their child would work longer hours (Phillips & Sandstrom, 1990).

More recently, Runyan, Shulman, Dal Santo, Bowling, & Agans (2009) conducted phone interviews with over 1,000 parents of employed teens ages 14–18. Participants also indicated that their child's employment had virtually no deleterious effects. For example, over 99% of parents believed that their child was learning valuable job skills, while over 90% believed that their child was "less likely to get in trouble than teens who don't work." Additionally, a majority of parents believed that the combined demands of work and school did not make their child tired and most parents believed that their child still had plenty of time to spend with their family. A majority of parents also believed that their teens' employment did not interfere with schoolwork or extracurricular activities. Finally, only 7% of parents believed that their child's employment might make them "more likely to use drugs and alcohol." Regarding hours that teens should be allowed to work, about 45% of parents reported that teens should work less than 16 hours per week, although 16% of parents believed that teens should be allowed to work more than 20 hours per week. Along these lines, over 75% of parents believed that teens ages 16 and above should be allowed to work past 9 or 10 p.m. on a school night (Runyan et al., 2009).

Although this research indicates that parents generally support their teenager having a job during the school year, high school student employment has actually been slowly declining for many years. The United States Bureau of Labor Statistics surveys approximately 60,000 households in their annual Current Population Survey, with the latest data from 2016 indicating that about 19% of teens ages 16–17 and 42% of teens ages 18–19 were employed (Bureau of Labor Statistics, 2017). The most thorough and recent analysis of youth employment by the Bureau of Labor Statistics tracked employment trends from 1985 to 2007 (Morisi, 2008). This report indicates that in 1985, 26% of youth were employed while enrolled in high school, with this rate climbing throughout the 1990s and then declining to the 2007 rate of 24%. This report also found a general trend for a growing percentage of youth enrolled in school and not employed, with 47% of these youth in 1985 climbing to 59% in 2007.

Another report by the Bureau of Labor Statistics (2004) identified in what types of jobs these youth are actually employed. As you might expect, the most common occupations for youth in high school are not that glamorous. The top five occupations are rounded out by cooks, cashiers, stock handlers and baggers, sales workers, and restaurant waiting staff (Bureau of Labor Statistics, 2004). Interestingly, even though youth employment in the United States is declining, it stills stands out as among the highest in industrialized nations. For example, youth employment in Europe and industrialized Asian countries (e.g., Japan) is much lower than in the United States (Steinberg, 1996). The idea that holding a job while in high school would lead to desirable character traits emerged in the 1970s as a product of the President's Science Advisory Committee, which was established to explore public policy change. The committee eventually recommended that all youth hold employment in high school in order to realize benefits that included assistance in transitioning to adulthood as well as the acquisition of important character traits such as increased motivation and organizational skills (for a review see Marsh & Kleitman, 2005). However, researchers some years later found that the evidence actually pointed towards the opposite relationship. Specifically, researchers developed what they termed the "threshold model" when they found that a higher number of hours worked per week in high school led to a number of negative consequences (for a review see Marsh & Kleitman, 2005). This threshold model found that a small number of hours worked per week could potentially hold some positive consequences for the youth while a threshold of hours per week worked, once surpassed, would lead to significantly negative consequences (Marsh & Kleitman, 2005).

So the heart of the myth still remains. Do teenagers need to have a job in high school to "build character"? Of course, the opposite of this myth would be that having a job in high school is somehow harmful to teens. In fact, the latter appears to be for the most part true in that having a job in high school appears to have far more negative than positive outcomes. In one of the most extensive studies on this topic, Marsh and Kleitman (2005) analyzed a longitudinal dataset with a total sample size of over 12,000 high school students to understand how employment in high school impacts teens. The findings of this study may be surprising, especially to parents. For example, the study found that the more hours students worked in tenth and twelfth grades, the more likely was the occurrence of a number of negative outcomes in the twelfth grade and beyond. This included lower grades, lower attendance, lower educational and occupational aspirations, and lower likelihood of college enrollment. The authors also went on to test the previously mentioned "threshold model," which posits that there are few to no negative consequences of youth employment if the hours worked per week remain under a particular threshold (often cited as somewhere between 5 and 20 hours per week). However, the data from this large study found no significant evidence for a threshold effect, and the authors state that "For most Grade 12 outcomes, the negative effects associated with hours worked in Grades 8, 10, and 12 were primarily linear" (p. 349). Finally, the authors point out that the negative outcomes associated with youth employment and number of hours worked was consistent across different ethnicities, levels of parent income, gender, and even the type of job the youth worked. This last point is particularly important as some researchers and policy makers have pointed to youth employment as a possible intervention for minority youth in poverty. However, other studies have also noted that the negative outcomes of youth employment are similar across socioeconomic status (SES) levels. In other words, working has negative outcomes for youth in poverty similar to the outcomes for middle-class youth (Kingston & Rose, 2015). Other studies have also shown a link between number of hours worked and substance abuse. For example, a massive study with over 600,000 participants by Bachman and colleagues (Bachman, Staff, O'Malley, & Freedman-Doan, 2013) found that work intensity was related to a higher prevalence of cigarette use, marijuana use, and heavy drinking.

What you need to know

While a great deal of research shows that working as a teenager is associated with a number of negative outcomes, it is also noteworthy that there have been few studies, if any, that directly tested whether having a job "builds character." However, it is possible that the ambiguity of the statement and the concept of "character" has hindered research on the subject. If parents truly wish to build character in their children, the solution appears to be within the family context rather than sending them to work a job that will have little relevance to their future occupation and leads to a number of negative outcomes. If, in contrast, parents are interested in preparing their children for a future vocation, many have lamented the decline in high school vocational training and point to apprenticeships (similar to those found in some European countries) as a possible solution (for a review, see Aivazova, 2013). In fact, some high profile celebrities have discussed the need for relevant vocational training in high school, such as Mike Rowe from the hit television show *Dirty Jobs* who began the Mike Row WORKS foundation (www.profoundlydisconnected.com).

References

Aivazova, N. (2013, August). Role of apprenticeships in combating youth unemployment in Europe and the United States. *Peterson Institute for International Economics Policy Brief.*

Avery, D., & Birch, B. (1993). Get a haircut. [Recorded by George Thorogood and the Destroyers]. On *Haircut* [CD]. Los Angeles, CA: Capital Records.

Bachman, J. G., Staff, J., O'Malley, P. M., & Freedman-Doan, P. (2013). Adolescent work intensity, school performance, and substance use: Links vary by race/ethnicity and socioeconomic status. *Developmental Psychology, 49*(11), 2125.

Bureau of Labor Statistics. (2004, February 18). Employment of teenagers during the school year and summer [Press release]. Retrieved from https://www.bls.gov/nls/nlsy97r5.pdf

Bureau of Labor Statistics (2017, February 8). Labor force statistics from the Current Population Survey [Data table]. Retrieved from https://www.bls.gov/cps/tables.htm

Jewell, J. D. & Hupp, S. D. A. (2018). Prevalence of myths about adolescence. [Manuscript in preparation].

Kingston, S., & Rose, A. (2015). Do the effects of adolescent employment differ by employment intensity and neighborhood context? *American Journal of Community Psychology, 55*(1–2), 37–47.

Marsh, H. W., & Kleitman, S. (2005). Consequences of employment during high school: Character building, subversion of academic goals, or a threshold? *American Educational Research Journal, 42*(2), 331–369.

Morisi, T. L. (2008). Youth enrollment and employment during the school year. *Monthly Labor Review, 131,* 51–63.

Phillips, S., & Sandstrom, K. L. (1990). Parental attitudes toward youth work. *Youth & Society, 22*(2), 160–183.

Runyan, C. W., Schulman, M., Dal Santo, J., Bowling, J. M., & Agans, R. (2009). Attitudes and beliefs about adolescent work and workplace safety among parents of working adolescents. *Journal of Adolescent Health, 44*(4), 349–355.

Steinberg, L. (1996). *Beyond the classroom.* New York, NY: Simon & Schuster.

Myth #17

Risky behavior in adolescence is inevitable

Ever watch MTV? A programming staple each March used to include a series of shows highlighting adolescents' activities on spring break. Every day, dozens of personal profiles and spotlight stories were offered featuring teens from across the US having fun at whatever south Floridian or Mexican hot spot the channel decided to feature. You may not be surprised to learn that these spring break activities rarely included studying. Nor did they include board games, trivia contests, or read-a-thons. No, when we think about adolescents on spring break, different images come to mind, and that is because most people assume that it is inevitable that adolescents will engage in risk-taking behavior. Not just on spring break, but all the time.

When we think of teens, we may often think of heavy drinking, drug use, risky sexual behavior, and daredevil acts. We imagine that adolescents will get swept away into whatever dare or challenge their friends pose, and they may fall susceptible to whatever dangerous trend they see depicted in the movies. Like the "fight clubs" that erupted all over the country after Brad Pitt and Edward Norton starred in the movie of the same name (Fincher, 1999). Or the outrageously risky stunts performed by Johnny Knoxville on MTV's former *Jackass* series (Jonze, 2000–2007). Hard-core drinking and drug use has been depicted in far too many adolescent movies to count.

Of course, many adolescents are indeed more risky than most adults (Casey & Caudle, 2013). Recent data from the field of developmental neuroscience offer some clues why this may be. A key factor has to do with the hormones that increase production around the time that puberty develops. Long before changes to our bodies, voices, or skin are observable, gonadal hormones begin to circulate throughout our bodies, in much stronger concentrations that at any other point in our development. This process is related to a massive change in how our brains operate (Casey & Caudle, 2013; Somerville, 2013). In fact, our brains change more dramatically in adolescence than at any other time after the first year of life (Somerville, Jones, & Casey, 2010).

Some of these changes in the brain help us engage in more complex thought. We develop myelin, a fatty tissue around our neurons that helps neurochemical signals travel faster and increases the speed and complexity of our thought (see more on the development of the adolescent brain in Chapter 3). We also develop more receptors for neurotransmitters, which allows our brain to receive signals more strongly than in childhood (Somerville et al., 2010). However, one region of the brain, the prefrontal cortex, matures much later in adolescence. Some work suggests that the prefrontal cortex is not fully matured until the age of 25 (Casey & Caudle, 2013). This finding is important, because the prefrontal cortex—a region uniquely well-developed in humans—can act like the brain's brakes. Among many other functions, the prefrontal cortex helps us inhibit our most impulsive urges (Casey & Caudle, 2013). While adolescents might be drawn to the rush that comes from unsecured bungee jumping, for example, adults' developed prefrontal cortex offers pause and consideration of the possible problems that could come from impulsive, dangerous acts. Also, researchers have found that adolescents receive neural-based rewards—neurochemical reactions that feel good—when they engage in risky behavior, and they're especially likely to do so when their peers are nearby (Chein, Albert, O'Brien, Uckert, & Steinberg, 2011).

Thus, it is true that adolescents are more likely than younger children or adults to engage in risk-taking behavior. It also is true that adolescents seem to be especially likely to surround themselves with friends who will further enhance their risk-taking tendencies. Yet, adolescents' biological susceptibility to risky behavior still does not suggest that risk-taking is inevitable. In fact, even when examining mildly or severely risky behaviors, epidemiological data suggest that most adolescents refrain from what is most dangerous. Every 2 years or so, the US Centers for Disease Control (CDC) conducts a nationwide study of about 10,000–15,000 high school students from most every state, urban center, and tribal community in the US (CDC, 2015). All students complete the survey anonymously. They're assured that their responses will remain strictly confidential, and the resulting dataset offers one of the world's most comprehensive assessments of risk-taking prevalence.

Contrary to the inevitability myth, the CDC finds that most adolescents don't engage in many risky-behaviors at all. In 2015, results suggested that less than 11% of adolescents smoke cigarettes—a rate that has decreased steadily from 35% back in 1995. Currently, only 24% vape. Only one out of five students reports that they currently use marijuana, 5.2% use cocaine, 5% use ecstasy, 3% use methamphetamine, and 2.1% use heroin. Since 1995, no more than one out of every four adolescents engages in binge episodic drinking (i.e., five or more drinks within a couple of hours) (CDC, 2015).

Rates of other types of risk-taking also are much lower than popular movies may lead you to believe. Only about one out of every three teenagers is sexually active, about 10–15% have had sex with four or more partners, and less than half of students had sex without a condom. In fact, there's ample evidence suggesting that most adolescents engage in behaviors that substantially reduce risks. About 94% of teens reported that they make sure to wear a seat belt when driving, 80% have refrained from riding with a driver who has drunk alcohol, and almost 60% have never texted while driving (CDC, 2015).

What you need to know

The distinction between myth and reality is quite important when it comes to risk-taking behavior, because research says that most humans, adolescents or adults, tend to be guided by what psychologists call "social norms" (Prentice, 2008). Whether we realize it or not, we constantly scan our environment, determine what seems normal, and engage in behaviors that match our perceived norm. In some cases, this tendency towards conformity is pretty innocuous. Imagine walking into a meeting and noticing that everyone else has taken out their laptops and quietly begun working. For many of us, this offers a cue that it would be OK for us to do the same, and we would be highly likely to take out our computers too. Conversely, if no one had their laptops open, we would be highly unlikely to do so ourselves.

Yet, when it comes to risk-taking behavior, these social norms can have more serious and even devastating consequences. This is because it is harder to observe many risk-taking behaviors; thus we have to estimate how much peers around us may be drinking, smoking, or using a condom during sex (Prentice, 2008). And substantial research has demonstrated that we are remarkably bad at estimating the prevalence of the behaviors of others. Thus, we are following a social norm based on incorrect information.

If adolescents believe that adolescent risky behavior is inevitable, they may be especially likely to engage in risk-taking themselves because they may think that risky behavior fits the social norm of how adolescents "inevitably" act. Perhaps for this reason, some high school and college campuses have taken steps to explicitly contradict this myth by posting data regarding the actual level of risk-taking behavior on their campuses. At one school, posters read "83% of students consume 5 or fewer drinks in a typical week." At another, banners indicated, "Five drinks in a single night is crazy...most of us realize that and don't party insanely. Congratulations, and welcome to the majority" (Prentice, 2008).

Adolescents don't always engage in risk behavior, but many don't realize that they're in good company. That may be because the myth about adolescents' risk-taking tendencies has gotten a little too much airtime in spring, and the other seasons as well.

References

Casey, B. J., & Caudle, K. (2013). The teenage brain: Self control. *Current Directions in Psychological Science, 22*(2), 82–87.

Centers for Disease Control and Prevention. (2015). Youth Risk Behavior Survey Data. Retrieved from www.cdc.gov/yrbs

Chein, J., Albert, D., O'Brien, L., Uckert, K., & Steinberg, L. (2011). Peers increase adolescent risk taking by enhancing activity in the brain's reward circuitry. *Developmental Science, 14*(2), F1–F10.

Fincher, D. (Director). (1999). *Fight Club* [Motion picture]. Los Angeles, CA: Fox 2000 Pictures.

Jonze, S. (2000–2007). *Jackass*. Hollywood, CA: MTV.

Prentice, D. A. (2008). Mobilizing and weakening peer influence as mechanisms for changing behavior. In M. J. Prinstein & K. A. Dodge (Eds.), *Understanding peer influence in children and adolescents*. New York, NY: Guilford Press.

Somerville, L. (2013). The teenage brain: Sensitivity to social evaluation. *Current Directions in Psychological Science, 22*(2), 121–127.

Somerville, L. H., Jones, R. M., & Casey, B. J. (2010). A time of change: Behavioral and neural correlates of adolescent sensitivity to appetitive and aversive environmental cues. *Brain and Cognition, 72*(1), 124–133.

Myth #18 Taking care of an infant simulator doll increases abstinence from sexual activity

In the United States, about 11 out of every 1,000 female teens (ages 15–17) gave birth in 2014 (Hamilton, Martin, Osterman, Curtin, & Matthews, 2015), and the birth rate for same-aged females in the United Kingdom was about 7 out of 1,000 (Office for National Statistics, 2016). Although these numbers are fairly low, they would be much higher if all pregnancies, not just successful births, were included. In fact, the most recent Youth Risk Behavior Surveillance Study (Center for Disease Control, 2016) in the United States asked high school students if they had ever engaged in sexual intercourse, and rates were high for seniors (58%), juniors (50%), sophomores (35%), and even freshmen (24%). In fact, about 4% of these students indicated that they had their first experience with sexual intercourse before the age of 13.

Considering the staggering numbers of teens reporting at least some experience with sexual activity, it's no surprise that schools have become interested in trying to prevent teen pregnancies. "When we started the Baby Think It Over program three years ago, we were averaging three pregnancies per year," expressed a Junior High School teacher, adding "This past school year no pregnancies were reported" (Realityworks, 2004). The Baby Think It Over program mentioned in the testimonial is more recently called the RealCare Baby® program, and it's similar to another competing product called the Ready-Or-Not Tot®. More generically, these products are referred to as infant simulator dolls.

These products look like any other baby doll, but they come with enhanced technology. For example, when a doll cries, the computer inside keeps track of the students' attempts to feed the doll or change its diaper. The dolls are also able to monitor if they're being handled too roughly (e.g., shaken) or exposed to unsafe environments (e.g., cold temperatures). Teachers are also able to set the level of difficulty provided by the doll's temperament. Students typically take care of the doll for several days and nights in a row, and teachers can access the data kept by the dolls in order to give the student feedback and perhaps a grade. Additionally, these dolls are usually embedded within programs that include lessons (e.g., information about infant care) and exercises (e.g., finding out how much diapers cost).

Students who aren't exposed to infant simulator dolls in their schools may also see them on television. In an episode of *Saved By the Bell*, a show about life in high school, Principal Belding coordinates a project because of his concern about teen pregnancy (Eberhard & Barnhart, 1996). "Unfortunately, lots of kids your age are having babies," he says, adding, "I'd like you to learn how much time and responsibility parenthood requires." He then calls in his assistant, Screech, who wheels in several infant simulator dolls. Over the course of a week, the students struggle to take care of the dolls, and they realize that they aren't yet ready for the responsibilities of parenthood. One student, Katie, says, "After this week, we know we're not ready to be good parents." The other students quickly agree.

Other television shows have similarly depicted the effects of caring with less technologically advanced variations of this approach to preventing teen pregnancy. For example, students in the *Hannah Montana* show cared for a flour sack to find out what lessons they could learn from the experience (Green, Lapiduss, & Christiansen, 2007). Similarly, students in *South Park* cared for fragile eggs so they could learn about responsible parenting (Hotz & Parker, 2005). Overall, the media provide ample depictions of students realizing how hard it is to care for a real baby after they have had the experience of caring for a pretend baby.

Perhaps influenced by examples on television shows, the public has a pretty positive impression of infant simulator dolls. In our research, 50–53% of students believed that "Taking care of an infant simulator doll increases abstinence" (Jewell & Hupp, 2018). In a study of parent perceptions of a program using the dolls, 90% of the participants indicated that they would recommend that a friend use an infant simulator doll with their teen (Price, Robinson, Thompson, & Schmalzried, 1999). In another sign of public support for infant simulator dolls, according to the company, the RealCare Baby program is currently being used by two-thirds of school districts in the United States (Realityworks, 2016). Is such wide use of this preventative approach warranted?

There have been several studies of infant simulator dolls, and one of the studies with the best research design came out recently (Brinkman et al., 2016). Researchers in Australia randomized 56 high schools such that half of the schools served as the prevention group with their students receiving the Virtual Infant Program (VIP), centered around infant simulator dolls, and the other half of the schools served as the comparison group with their students receiving their standard health education curriculum. Both groups had over 1,000 female participants (ages 13–15) who were contacted again years later at age 20. During this later time period, 8% of the group that received the VIP program had given birth, and this was compared to 4% of the comparison group that had given birth. The VIP group also had more abortions (9%) than the control group (6%). Taken together, the students who were in the program using infant simulator dolls were significantly *more* likely to get pregnant.

Realityworks, the company that sells the RealCare Baby program, issued a swift response to the study in which they attempted to separate themselves from the doll and curriculum used in the study (Realityworks, 2016). They also critiqued the study design, which is a reasonable thing to do because no study is perfect. However, they have also issued a "Realityworks White Paper" (Wang, n.d.) in which they describe other studies that they claim to be supportive of infant simulator dolls. Compared to the Australian study, the studies included in the Realityworks report have considerably bigger methodological flaws than the Australian study (e.g., Barnett & Hurst, 2004; Out & Lafreniere, 2001; Somers & Fahlman, 2001; Strachan & Gorey, 1997; Tingle, 2002). For example, they include unpublished studies, and they rarely have randomized comparison groups. The studies sometimes show a change in one attitudinal measure (e.g., a feeling of susceptibility to getting pregnant), but they fail to show changes in the majority of the other measures in the studies.

Most importantly, no studies show an actual change in sexual behavior or pregnancy outcome in a direction favorable to infant simulator dolls. In fact, in addition to the Australian study showing that adolescent girls were more likely to get pregnant if they cared for the doll, other research has demonstrated a potentially harmful effect of the dolls. For example, in one study, 12% of students reported wanting to be teen parents *before* caring for an infant simulator doll, and this increased to 15% of the teens wanting to be teen parents *after* caring for the doll. Thus, it is possible that infant simulator dolls are actually harmful rather than helpful. In addition to the potential harm possibly experienced by some teens, the dolls also cost the school a lot of money that could be used for more effective programming.

Many people would be surprised to find out about this research showing that infant simulator dolls are ineffective. There are a few reasons why teachers and parents might assume the dolls work. First, companies are motivated to sell their products, and this leads them to call their products "evidence-based" when they're clearly not evidence-based (Wang, n.d.). Realityworks even went so far as to call their doll "THE MOST EFFECTIVE WAY TO TEACH TEENS ABOUT PARENTING" (Realityworks, 2004). This is not only problematic in terms of promoting an ineffective program, but this practice also dilutes the notion of something being evidence-based and erodes public trust in science. Relatedly, infant simulator dolls do not require too much effort on the part of teachers and parents, and so the dolls may seem like a good option for dealing with the real problem of teen pregnancy. Because a relatively small number of teens actually get pregnant, many parents may attribute this to the doll because of post hoc, ergo propter hoc reasoning. In this type of thinking fallacy, people attribute one event (e.g., caring for an infant simulator doll) for causing a second event (e.g., choosing not to have sex) just because one event happened before the other.

Another reason people may be swayed into using infant simulator dolls is that role-play is a generally effective way to change behavior. Unfortunately, infant simulator dolls do not give teens the chance to role-play the actual skills required to remain abstinent, such as assertiveness, or to practice safer sex, such as using a condom effectively. Finally, infant simulator dolls have the potential to make parenting seem fun because when teens carry an infant simulator doll around their community, they may come to realize that having a baby is a sure way to have positive interactions with other people. Moreover, and here comes a spoiler alert, teens may come to realize that parenting a baby really can be an enjoyable experience!

What you need to know

Unlike infant simulator dolls, comprehensive sex education programs are effective at decreasing rates of teen sexual activity and increasing rates of condom use (Bennett & Assefi, 2005). Comprehensive sex education programs (also called abstinence-*plus* programs) overtly encourage abstinence but they also teach youth about safer sex practices. Abstinence-*only* programs, on the other hand, do not teach youth about safer sex practices. In 2005, the American Psychological Association (APA) issued a resolution in support of comprehensive sex education (APA, 2005). The American Academy of Pediatrics also supports comprehensive sex education (Breuner, Mattson, & Committee on Psychosocial Aspects of Child and Family Health, 2016). In addition to decreasing sexual activity, these organizations cite the ability of comprehensive sex education programs to decrease sexually transmitted infections.

References

American Psychological Association. (2005). Resolution in favor of empirically supported sex education and HIV prevention programs for adolescents. Retrieved from www.apa.org

Barnett, J. E., & Hurst, C. S. (2004). Do adolescents take "baby think it over" seriously? *Adolescence, 39*(153), 65–75.

Bennett, S. E., & Assefi, N. P. (2005). School-based teenage pregnancy prevention programs: A systematic review of randomized controlled trials. *Journal of Adolescent Health, 36*(1), 72–81.

Breuner, C. C., Mattson, G., & Committee on Psychosocial Aspects of Child and Family Health (2016). Sexuality education for children and adolescents. *Pediatrics, 138*(2), e1–e12. doi:10.1542/peds.2016-1348.

Brinkman, S. A., Johnson, S. E., Codde, J. P., Hart, M. B., Straton, J. A., Mittinty, M. N., & Silburn, S. R. (2016). Efficacy of infant simulator programmes to prevent teenage pregnancy: A school-based cluster randomised controlled trial in Western Australia. *The Lancet, 388*(10057), 2264–2271.

Center for Disease Control (2016). Youth risk behavior surveillance study—United States, 2015. Retrieved from www.cdc.gov

Eberhard, L. (Writer), & D. Barnhart (Director). (1996). Baby care [Television series episode]. In P. Engel (Executive producer), *Saved By the Bell: The New Class*. Universal City, CA: NBC Productions.

Green, A., Lapiduss, S. (Writers), & Christiansen, R. S. (Director). (2007). My boyfriend's Jackson and there's gonna be trouble. [Television series episode]. In S. Peterman & M. Poryes (Executive producer), *Hannah Montana*. Studio City, CA: It's a Laugh Productions.

Hamilton, B. E., Martin, J. A., Osterman, M. J. K., Curtin, S. C., & Matthews, T. J. (2015). Births: Final data for 2014. *National Vital Statistics Reports, 64*(12), 1–64.

Hotz, K. (Writer), & Parker, T. (Director). (2005). Follow that egg! [Television series episode]. In T. Parker & M. Stone (Executive producers), *South Park*. Braniff Productions.

Jewell, J. D., & Hupp, S. D. A. (2018). Prevalence of myths about adolescence. [Manuscript in preparation].

Office for National Statistics (2016). Conceptions in England and Wales. Retrieved from www.ons.gov.uk

Out, J. W., & Lafreniere, K. D. (2001). Baby think it over (R): Using role-play to prevent teen pregnancy. *Adolescence, 36*(143), 571.

Price, J. H., Robinson, K. L., Thompson, C., & Schmalzried, H. (1999). Rural parents' perceptions of the baby think it over program. *American Journal of Health Studies, 15*(3), 149–155.

Realityworks (2004). Meet your new teaching assistant. [Print advertisement].

Realityworks (2016). Our response to a recent study. Retrieved from http://www.realityworks.com/products/realcare-baby

Roberts, S. W., & McCowan, R. J. (2004). The effectiveness of infant simulators. *Adolescence, 39*(155), 475–487.

Somers, C. L., & Fahlman, M. M. (2001). Effectiveness of the "baby think it over" teen pregnancy prevention program. *Journal of School Health, 71*(5), 188–195.

Strachan, W., & Gorey, K. M. (1997). Infant simulator lifespace intervention: Pilot investigation of an adolescent pregnancy prevention program. *Child & Adolescent Social Work Journal, 14*(3), 171–180. doi:10.1023/A:1024565502423.

Tingle, L. R. (2002). Evaluation of the North Carolina "baby think it over" project. *Journal of School Health, 72*(5), 178–183.

Wang, M. Q. (n.d.). The RealCare baby program: Evidence of efficacy (A Realityworks White Paper). Retrieved from www.realityworks.com

Myth #19 College placement tests are useless at predicting academic success in college

Every spring the same scenario plays out in most homes across the country. High school seniors eagerly rush to the mailbox (or their email inbox) each afternoon, waiting for decision letters (or emails) from the admissions department of their top picks for college. But a nightmare scenario for these teens is played out in the movie *Orange County* (Gains, Schroeder, & Kasdan, 2002) when lead character Shawn (played by Colin Hanks) opens the letter from the only school he applied to, reading the letter aloud with building hysteria "'We regret to inform you that your application to Stanford University was not accepted.' Wait, what? I didn't get in? I didn't get in?!! I don't get it. I don't understand." Another movie that solely focused on the importance of the SAT (formerly, Scholastic Assessment Test) is *The Perfect Score* (Lee & Robbins, 2004) starring Chris Evans and Scarlett Johansson (both of whom go on to be major stars in the Avengers movie franchise). The trailer of the movie sums up how critical the SAT is stating "Three little letters (SAT). It can define your status. It can change your life. And completely stress you out." The entire plot of the movie revolves around six high school students who repeatedly try, and fail, to steal the answers to the SAT. Films like this clearly communicate why parents and teens consider college placement tests like the ACT (formerly, American College Testing) and SAT tests as the epitome of high stakes testing. Perhaps because of the stressful and anxiety provoking nature of these tests, there has been a significant backlash to the general idea of "high stakes testing." For example, in 2014 teachers and parents supported a boycott of standardized tests required by the State of Illinois and Chicago Public Schools (Ahmed-Ullah & Black, 2014). Similarly, 400 high school students organized a walk out to protest standardized testing in their school (Micucci, 2013).

The primary concern that many teachers, parents, and especially students feel about standardized testing is summed up neatly in the title of Seattle high school teacher Jesse Hagopian's book *More than a Score: The New Uprising against High Stakes Testing* (Hagopian, 2014). The idea that a single test can produce a score that reflects one's academic potential is repugnant to most of us. Many students think that college placement tests somehow attempt to reduce who they are to a single score, replying that "I'm more than a score." This disdain for high stakes college placement tests then leads to similar thoughts undermining the validity of such tests. The myth, as we've stated it, is that college placement tests don't predict college academic success. Given that these college placement tests have only one purpose (to predict college academic success), this is a very damning statement indeed. The prevalence of this belief appears to be widespread as well. In our own polling of undergraduate students, an overwhelming number (84%) had heard of this myth while between 78% and 87% agreed with this myth (Jewell & Hupp, 2018). In fact, of all the myths that we discuss in this book, our college student sample agreed with this myth more than any of the others.

So let's begin with the rather simple task of debunking the myth as it is currently stated, that college placement tests are ineffective at predicting academic success in college. If we consider college placement tests by themselves in isolation, it is clear that they do in fact have a relatively strong correlation with college grade point average (GPA). For example, a study by Shaw and colleagues (Shaw, Kobrin, Patterson, & Mattern, 2012) examined data from 39 four-year universities across the United States with a total sample of almost 40,000 students. This study not only looked at the correlation between SAT scores and college GPA, but separately analyzed these students by major, gender, and ethnicity. The correlation between SAT score and second year college GPA ranged from 0.42 to 0.63 depending on the major of the student, with the average correlation being 0.57. Given that a correlation of 0.5 is considered to be "large" (Cohen, 1988), it is clear that there is a strong correlation between the SAT and college GPA and this relationship is pretty consistent across academic majors. The correlation is also relatively consistent for males and females, as well as for students of various ethnicities (Shaw et al., 2012).

Before we move on, let's make clear exactly what we believe this myth to be. As stated earlier, the myth is that college placement tests are essentially useless because they don't predict college academic success. While we believe that the best research on this topic shows that college placement tests in fact do predict college academic performance, we are not necessarily saying they're *the only* predictor or *the best* predictor of college academic performance. As we will explain, there are many different predictors, some that are perhaps better than these tests.

The results of the study by Shaw discussed so far can answer the simple question of whether college placement tests can predict college GPA *by themselves*. However, a more nuanced question that goes beyond this myth is whether college placement tests are *the only* major predictor of college GPA. And the answer is that in fact there is one other big "heavy hitter" that predicts college GPA pretty well, and is, not surprisingly, student high school GPA. Like the common axiom that the best predictor of future behavior is past behavior, it definitely makes sense that high school GPA would predict college success as well. If we go back to the study by Shaw et al. (2012), they also looked at high school GPA as a predictor of college GPA. And in an eerie coincidence, the average correlation between these two was 0.57—exactly the same as SAT correlation with college GPA!

So clearly both high school GPA *and* college placement tests are pretty good predictors of college GPA. But what if admissions officers looked at both (which they do of course)? Do both scores "bring something to the table" that is unique? In most cases, the answer appears to be yes: They both have something to contribute. To answer this question, Sawyer (2013) undertook a largescale study of 192 colleges and universities with data from over 600,000 students. One of the most basic conclusions of the study was that "In most scenarios, using both high school grades and test scores jointly is better than using either by itself" (p. 108). Another example of how the strategy of using both scores is best comes from a study by Bridgeman, Pollack, and Burton (2008). In this study, the authors look at the issue in a unique way. They wanted to get beyond the more complicated statistics that are sometimes difficult to interpret and find a more meaningful way of looking at the issue. To do so, their study considered a unique set of data where high school students with very similar GPAs had very different SAT scores. Specifically, they compared two groups of students. All of the students had a high school GPA of 3.7 or above, but one group had relatively low scores on the SAT while the other group had very high scores on the SAT. For the lower scoring SAT group, only 16% achieved a college GPA of 3.5 or above, while for the highest scoring SAT group 73% achieved a college GPA of 3.5 or above. Remember that in this sample *all* of the students had a very high GPA in high school. So the large difference in college GPA illustrates that to most accurately predict college GPA, a combination of high school GPA and college placement test scores is usually necessary.

But what is the harm in this myth, anyway? Well, first let's talk about why the myth exists at all. It all comes down to the fact that human beings hate to be "summed up" in a single number. We like to think that we are multifaceted and complex, which human beings certainly are. And we also generally hate to think that we are merely "average" and we tend to overestimate our abilities in a number of areas. Interestingly, even though students don't think that their college placement test score represents their potential very well, they also overestimate their score when recalling it. Specifically, Mayer et al. (2007) found that almost 40% of college students overestimated their SAT scores when recalling them from memory, and the average difference between their actual score and reported score was 25 points. The authors also found that lower achieving students tended to overestimate their self-reported SAT score significantly more than higher achieving students.

What you need to know

So back to the original question—what's the harm in the myth? Well, according to Self-Determination Theory, a prevailing theory on human motivation, we tend to be more motivated towards a goal that is internalized and becomes part of our identity (Deci & Ryan, 2008). So in a nutshell, if we don't believe a test is valid, we may be less likely to study prior to the test and we'll be less motivated to do our best while taking the test. Now this point is particularly important, because a lot of research has found one important predictor of college success that has little to do with an SAT score. And this magical predictor is a personality trait called *conscientiousness*. In fact, a meta-analysis of 80 different studies by Poropat

(2009) found that conscientiousness, which comprises dependability and achievement striving, is as important as intelligence in predicting college GPA. So if you're worried you won't do as well as you want on the SAT or that your score isn't what you'd like it to be, remember that maintaining your motivation and "trying hard" may often be just as important as your innate ability.

References

Ahmed-Ullah, N. S., & Black, L. (2014). Kids caught in tug of war over ISAT. Retrieved from http://articles.chicagotribune.com/2014-03-04/news/ct-chicago-testing-isat-met-20140303_1_isat-selective-schools-spokesman-joel-hood

Bridgeman, B., Pollack, J., & Burton, N. (2008). Predicting grades in college courses: A comparison of multiple regression and percent succeeding approaches. *Journal of College Admission*, 199, 19–25.

Cohen, J. (1988). *Statistical power analysis for the behavior sciences*. Hillsdale, NJ: Erlbaum.

Deci, E. L., & Ryan, R. M. (2008). Self-determination theory: A macrotheory of human motivation, development, and health. *Canadian Psychology*, 49(3), 182.

Gains, H. W., & Schroeder, A. (Producers), & Kasdan, J. (Director). (2002). *Orange County* [Motion picture]. United States: Paramount Pictures.

Hagopian, J. (2014). *More than a score: The new uprising against high-stakes testing*. Chicago, IL: Haymarket Books.

Jewell, J. D., & Hupp, S. D. A. (2018). Prevalence of myths about adolescence. [Manuscript in preparation].

Lee Jr., D. J. (Producer), & Robbins, B. (Director). (2004). *The Perfect Score* [Motion picture]. Hollywood, CA: Paramount Pictures.

Mayer, R. E., Stull, A. T., Campbell, J., Almeroth, K., Bimber, B., Chun, D., & Knight, A. (2007). Overestimation bias in self-reported SAT scores. *Educational Psychology Review*, 19(4), 443–454.

Micucci, J. (2013). How Garfield High defeated the MAP test. Retrieved from http://www.seattlemag.com/article/how-garfield-high-defeated-map-test

Poropat, A. E. (2009). A meta-analysis of the five-factor model of personality and academic performance. *Psychological Bulletin*, 135(2), 322.

Sawyer, R. (2013). Beyond correlations: Usefulness of high school GPA and test scores in making college admissions decisions. *Applied Measurement in Education*, 26(2), 89–112.

Shaw, E. J., Kobrin, J. L., Patterson, B. F., & Mattern, K. D. (2012). *The validity of the SAT® for predicting cumulative grade point average by college major*. Research Report 2012–6. United States: College Board.

Mini myths for development of the self

Myth
#20
College students' lives are full of random hook-ups

In the 2007 hit movie *Superbad* (Apatow et al., 2007), high school seniors Seth and Evan (played by Jonah Hill and Michael Cera), complain about the fact that they're both still virgins and look to their college careers with both hope and dread, which is summed up in the following dialogue:

> EVAN: "Well, you'll have sex in college. Everyone does."
> SETH: "Yes, but the point is to be good at sex by the time you get to college."

This dialogue communicates a very real message to teens and society that college sex is common, frequent, and often casual. Perhaps one of the most famous movies in the college party genre is *Animal House* (Reitman, Simmons, & Landis, 1978) starring John Belushi and Kevin Bacon, with similar movies like *Project X* (Budnick et al., 2012) taking the idea to all new heights with escapades more dramatic than ever before. College students themselves also appear to believe in the myth, as 38% of college students in our own research sample endorsed it (Jewell & Hupp, 2018). And the view of college as being full of random hook-ups is magnified by new smartphone apps such as *Tinder* and *Pure*. These apps can connect you with other users near you who are interested in an amorous exchange and you can decide who to connect with by just swiping left or right on the pictures of people near you. In the words of Pure's website (www.pure.dating), "It's spontaneous. Find someone that lights your spark and play with them right now."

But how true is it that college students frequently have casual sex with random people? According to the 2015 book by researcher Susan Caron titled *The Sex Lives of College Students: A Quarter Century of Attitudes and Behaviors*, the truth may be quite surprising. This book essentially summarizes 25 years of research by the author who gathered the data from a single university in the northeast. And while the data are not nationally representative, the results are based on almost 6,000 college students. Regarding one of the most basic results of the study, 87% of the sample reported ever having sexual intercourse. So while most college students are not "virgins," it may come as a surprise to some that 13% are—with no differences between men and women. The average age of first intercourse was between 16 and 17 years old, with males losing their virginity on average several months later than females. And most important to the myth, college students reported their number of sexual partners (not limited to intercourse and could include oral sex), with the average number of sexual partners being 3–4. Additionally, this number has remained steady over the last 25 years, countering the myth that college students today are having more sex that those in the past (Caron, 2015).

Recent data from the Youth Risk Behavior Survey shows that in fact the percentage of high school students reporting having sexual intercourse before age 13 has dropped from 10.2% in 1991 to 3.9% in 2015 (Centers for Disease Control and Prevention, 2017). Relatedly, the percentage of high school students reporting having had sexual intercourse with four or more different partners has also significantly dropped from 18.7% in 1991 to 11.5% in 2015. Also interesting is the result that 55% of Caron's college sample reported thinking that they have had fewer sexual partners than most people their age, and this trend was similar for those who had actually reported an average number of sexual partners. This result confirms the point made earlier that the media and society in general portray teens and young adults as "sex crazed." But as mentioned in the beginning of this book, this idea is certainly not new, as Aristotle once wrote "Young men have strong passions, and tend to gratify them indiscriminately" (Aristotle, Rhetoric Book II Chapter 12). It is also interesting to note that an active sex life with a variety of different partners can occur at any age, as about 11% of adults around 40 years old reported having two or more sexual partners in the last year (Johnston et al., 2016).

References

Apatow, J., Goldberg, E., Robertson, S., Rogen, S., & Weintraub, D. (Producers), & Mottola, G. (Director). (2007). *Superbad* [Motion picture]. Hollywood, CA: Sony Pictures.

Budnick, S., Ewing, M. P., Heineman, A., Phillips, T., Richards, S., Rona, A., … Nourizadeh, N. (Director). (2012). *Project X* [Motion picture]. Hollywood, CA: Warner Bros.

Caron, S. L. (2015). *The sex lives of college students: A quarter century of attitudes and behaviors*. Orono, ME: Maine College Press.

Centers for Disease Control and Prevention. (2017). Trends in the prevalence of sexual behaviors and HIV testing National YRBS: 1991–2015. Retrieved from https://www.cdc.gov/healthyyouth/data/yrbs/pdf/trends/2015_us_sexual_trend_yrbs.pdf

Jewell, J. D., & Hupp, S. D. A. (2018). Prevalence of myths about adolescence [Manuscript in preparation].

Johnston, L. D., O'Malley, P. M., Bachman, J. G., Schulenberg, J. E., Patrick, M. E., & Miech, R. A. (2016). HIV/AIDS risk and protective behaviors among adults ages 21 to 40 in the U.S.: 2004–2015. Ann Arbor (MI): Institute for Social Research, University of Michigan, for National Institute on Drug Abuse National Institutes of Health.

Reitman, I., & Simmons, M. (Producers), & Landis, J. (Director). (1978). *Animal House* [Motion picture]. Hollywood, CA: Universal Studios.

Myth #21 | Teaching teens about contraception makes them more likely to engage in sexual activity

Some people worry that teaching teens about contraception will increase the likelihood that the teens will engage in sexual activity, perhaps because they're freed from the worry of pregnancy or sexually transmitted infections (STIs). A study involving 1,719 adolescents, however, provided some evidence that this idea is a myth (Kohler, Manhart, & Lafferty, 2008). In the study, teens were classified into three groups: (a) comprehensive sex education, (b) abstinence-only education, or (c) no sex education. Of particular note is the comprehensive sex education group, who were taught that abstinence is the safest way to prevent pregnancies and STIs but who were also taught about contraception such as condom use. The teens who had comprehensive sex education were less likely than both of the other groups to later report having engaged in vaginal intercourse, and this finding directly contradicts the myth. They were also less likely to report pregnancy during adolescence than the other groups. One major limitation of this study is that it did not include random assignment (which one needs in order to draw conclusions regarding causality); however, a review of 13 studies that did use random assignment found similar results (Bennett & Assefi, 2005). In particular, eight of the 13 studies asked teens about their frequency of sexual activity in the last 3 months, and five of the eight studies found that teens engaged in less sexual activity if they received comprehensive sex education (the other the studies showed no difference between groups). In short, the review concluded that comprehensive sex education was not associated with earlier sexual debut or increased frequency of sex. Research such as this has led the American Psychological Association to release a resolution explicitly stating that "comprehensive sexuality education programs that discuss the appropriate use of condoms do not accelerate sexual debut…" (American Psychological Association, 2005). In short, comprehensive sex education is effective for many youth, and it does not make teens more likely to have sex.

References

American Psychological Association. (2005). Resolution in favor of empirically supported sex education and HIV prevention programs for adolescents. Retrieved from www.apa.org

Bennett, S. E., & Assefi, N. P. (2005). School-based teenage pregnancy prevention programs: A systematic review of randomized controlled trials. *Journal of Adolescent Health*, 36(1), 72–81.

Kohler, P. K., Manhart, L. E., & Lafferty, W. E. (2008). Abstinence-only and comprehensive sex education and the initiation of sexual activity and teen pregnancy. *Journal of Adolescent Health*, 42(4), 344–351.

Myth #22 Abstinence-only sex education programs are effective at keeping teens abstinent

Many of the same studies that investigated comprehensive sex education also investigated abstinence-only programs. Abstinence-only programs place primary emphasis on why and how to say "no" to sex. If they do mention contraception, it is for the purpose of emphasizing that contraception is not guaranteed to be effective. In the same study that showed comprehensive sex education was more effective than both no sex education and abstinence-only education, the results also showed that the abstinence-only program was not more effective than no sex education at all (Kohler, Manhart, & Lafferty, 2008). A review of studies on abstinence-only sex education showed that in none of the reported studies was the abstinence-only sex education program effective at decreasing the frequency of sexual activity in teens (Bennett & Assefi, 2005). Further, the American Psychological Association's resolution in support of evidence-based sex education, made the point that "published studies associated with abstinence-only education programs…have failed to find a reduction in sexual behavior," and the resolution also made the point that "virginity pledges, abstinence-only programs, and abstinence until marriage programs have been shown to have the unintended consequences of increasing the probability that adolescents will have unprotected intercourse at the time of first intercourse" (American Psychological Association, 2005). Thus, in addition to being ineffective, abstinence-only programs have the potential to be harmful.

References

American Psychological Association (2005). Resolution in favor of empirically supported sex education and HIV prevention programs for adolescents. Retrieved from www.apa.org

Bennett, S. E., & Assefi, N. P. (2005). School-based teenage pregnancy prevention programs: A systematic review of randomized controlled trials. *Journal of Adolescent Health*, 36(1), 72–81.

Kohler, P. K., Manhart, L. E., & Lafferty, W. E. (2008). Abstinence-only and comprehensive sex education and the initiation of sexual activity and teen pregnancy. *Journal of Adolescent Health*, 42(4), 344–351.

Myth #23

The HPV vaccine increases teen sex

The human papillomavirus (HPV) is a major cause of cervical cancer, and the Center for Disease Control recommends the HPV vaccine for girls and boys at around age 11 or 12 years old (CDC, n.d.-a). This vaccine is one of the few well-documented ways to prevent cancer. Some parents refuse to let their children receive the vaccine for fear that their child will be more likely to engage in sexual activity if they know they're at a lower risk for HPV. That is, a large national survey showed that 61% of pediatricians indicated that "Parents of adolescents are likely to be concerned that vaccination against a sexually transmitted infection may encourage risky sexual behavior," and 11% of the pediatricians even shared this same concern (Daley et al., 2006). However, several studies show that children are *not* more likely to engage in sexual activity once they have received the vaccine. For example, a study using up to 3 years of follow-up compared indicators of sexual activity from a group of 493 girls who had been vaccinated to those of a group of 905 girls who had not received the HPV vaccine (Bednarczyk, Davis, Ault, Orenstein, & Omer, 2012). Objective indicators of sexual activity included pregnancy and sexually transmitted infections, and both groups had a very low rate of both (less than 1%). Other research has also shown that teens are not more likely to report having increased sexual activity following the vaccine (Mayhew et al., 2014; Mullins et al., 2018). Research like this has led the Center for Disease Control to state that "HPV vaccination has not been associated with initiation of sexual activity or sexual risk behaviors or perceptions about sexually transmitted infections" (CDC, n.d.-b).

References

Bednarczyk, R. A., Davis, R., Ault, K., Orenstein, W., & Omer, S. B. (2012). Sexual activity–related outcomes after human papillomavirus vaccination of 11-to 12-year-olds. *Pediatrics, 130*(5), 798–805.

Center for Disease Control. (n.d.-a). HPV vaccine recommendations. Retrieved from www.cdc.gov

Center for Disease Control. (n.d.-b). Human Papillomavirus (HPV) Infection. Retrieved from www.cdc.gov

Daley, M. F., Liddon, N., Crane, L. A., Beaty, B. L., Barrow, J., Babbel, C., ... Berman, S. (2006). A national survey of pediatrician knowledge and attitudes regarding human papillomavirus vaccination. *Pediatrics, 118*(6), 2280–2289.

Mayhew, A., Mullins, T. L. K., Ding, L., Rosenthal, S. L., Zimet, G. D., Morrow, C., & Kahn, J. A. (2014). Risk perceptions and subsequent sexual behaviors after HPV vaccination in adolescents. *Pediatrics, 133*(3), 404–411.

Mullins, T. L. K., Rosenthal, S. L., Zimet, G. D., Ding, L., Morrow, C., Huang, B., & Kahn, J. A. (2018). Human papillomavirus vaccine-related risk perceptions do not predict sexual initiation among young women over 30 months following vaccination. *Journal of Adolescent Health, 62*(2), 164–169.

Myth #24

The millennial generation is lazy

The millennial generation is generally regarded as the generation that was born between 1982 and 2004 in a time when parents were said to be focusing more on their own behavior of parenting (Horovitz, 2012). Some worried that a parenting shift to the "every child wins a prize" mentality has led to the millennial generation being "entitled, narcissistic, and lazy" (Cleary, 2017). Further to this point, fans of the television show *Survivor* will recognize that in the "Millennials vs. Gen X" season, the older Generation X participants held the stereotype that the millennial generation was indeed lazy (Parsons, Burnett, & Probst, 2016). Is this a fair depiction of what is currently the largest generation in the United States? The Pew Research Center has collected data by generation that sheds light on the issue. Millennials were more likely to get an undergraduate college degree (40%) than Generation X (32%), and the difference is even bigger for females (Graf, 2017). Other research has failed to find generational differences in terms of work ethic (Zabel, Biermeier-Hanson, Baltes, Early, & Shepard, 2017). The Pew Research Center, however, has perhaps added one nugget of truth to this myth. That is, the millennial generation is more likely to live at home (15%) than

Generation X (10%) and the several preceding generations (Fry, 2017). This one nugget of truth, though, is hardly enough evidence to characterize a whole generation as lazy and in fact may be related to their increased likelihood of graduating from college. In fact, rising student loan debt has been reported as one of the greatest reasons why millennials are living in their parents' basement rather than buying their own home (Nasiripour, 2017). And by the way, of the final three contestants to last the longest on the *Survivor* island, two of them were millennials. You'll have to look up the winner for yourself.

References

Cleary, B. (2017). Millennials are entitled, narcissistic and lazy—but it's not their fault: Expert claims "every child wins a prize" and social media has left Gen Y unable to deal with the real world. Retrieved from www.dailymail.co.uk

Fry, R. (2017). It's becoming more common for young adults to live at home—and for longer stretches. Retrieved from www.pewresearch.org

Graf, N. (2017). Today's young workers are more likely than ever to have a bachelor's degree. Retrieved from www.pewresearch.org

Horovitz, B. (2012). After Gen X, Millennials, what should next generation be? Retrieved from http://usatoday30.usatoday.com

Nasiripour, S. (2017, July 17). Student debt is a major reason millennials aren't buying homes. Bloomberg. Retrieved from https://www.bloomberg.com/news/articles/2017-07-17/student-debt-is-hurting-millennial-homeownership

Parsons, C., Burnett, M., & Probst, J. (Executive Producers). (2016). *Survivor: Millennials vs. Gen X* [Television series]. Beverly Hills, CA: MGM Television.

Zabel, K. L., Biermeier-Hanson, B. B., Baltes, B. B., Early, B. J., & Shepard, A. (2017). Generational differences in work ethic: Fact or fiction? *Journal of Business and Psychology*, 32(3), 301–315.

Myth #25 High school football players are more likely to become seriously injured than cheerleaders

One only has to look to the media to understand how society perceives football players and cheerleaders differently. Just the titles of top football movies like *The Gridiron Gang* and *The Longest Yard* speak to the toughness and courage of football players. In the 2015 movie *Concussion* (Landesman, 2015), the violence of the sport and potential for injury are central to the plot. One of the most stirring scenes occurs when Dr. Bennet Omalu (played by Will Smith) yells the tagline of the movie "Tell the truth!" to the Pittsburgh Steelers team neurosurgeon Dr. Joseph Maroon (played by Arliss Howard) when he discusses the National Football League's cover-up of concussion in players. In contrast, top cheerleader movies are often comedic and rarely show the danger in the sport, but rather depict cheerleaders as egotistical, self-absorbed, and often sexualized. For example, a dream sequence in the cheerleader movie *Bring It On* (Reed, 2000) shows the cheerleaders singing about themselves "I'm sexy, I'm cute, I'm popular to boot, I'm wicked, great hair, the boys all like to stare...hate us 'cause we're beautiful, well we don't like you either, we're cheerleaders."

But the truth about the sport of cheerleading and its potential for injury may be quite surprising. One of the most comprehensive studies on serious injuries in high school and college sports was conducted recently by the National Center for Catastrophic Sports Injury Research (Kucera, Yau, Thomas, Wolff, & Cantu, 2015). This report collected data from 1982 through 2014 on serious injuries, nonfatal but disabling injuries, and fatalities related to various sports. The report notes that when considering the raw number of catastrophic injuries, high school football players have definitely experienced more injuries, with 1,086 from 1982 to 2014 compared to only 74 experienced by female high school cheerleaders. However, it is critical to understand that there are many more football players than cheerleaders (about 12 times more; Mueller & Cantu, 2011), so in order to calculate risk we need to focus on the rate of injury (what are your odds of being injured), not just the raw number of injuries. Perhaps surprising to many, the researchers found that female high school cheerleaders had 4.2 total catastrophic injuries per 100,000 participants while high school football players had fewer at 3.4 per 100,000 (see Kucera et al., 2015, figure 2). Many of the injuries are likely due to stunts that cheerleaders perform, such as when building a human pyramid, being thrown in the air, or dismounting from a great height. So while cheerleaders may be "popular to boot," it seems that cheerleading is actually a pretty risky sport.

References

Kucera, K. L., Yau, R., Thomas, L.C., Wolff, C., & Cantu, R. (2015). Catastrophic Sports Injury Research 32nd Annual Report Fall 1982 Spring 2014. Retrieved from https://nccsir.unc.edu/files/2013/10/NCCSIR-32nd-Annual-All-Sport-Report-1982_2014.pdf

Landesman, P. (2015). *Concussion* [Motion picture]. Hollywood, CA: Sony Pictures Entertainment.

Mueller, F. O., & Cantu, R. (2011). Catastrophic Sports Injury Research 29th Annual Report Fall 1982 Spring 2011. Retrieved from http://nccsir.unc.edu/files/2014/05/2011Allsport.pdf

Reed, P. (2000). *Bring It On* [Motion picture]. Hollywood, CA: Beacon Communications.

Myth #26 Offenders hide sexual interest when using the internet to initiate sex offenses against teens

By contacting law enforcement agencies, researchers have collected information about people who have used the internet in their attempts to initiate sexual relationships with teens. In one study, 99% of the offenders were male, and 99% of the offenders were older than 18 years old (Wolak, Finkelhor, & Mitchell, 2004). The same study also showed that 90% of their victims were 13–16 years old, and 75% of their victims were female. Although the statistics are disturbing, they're not altogether surprising. However, one statistic in the study might be a bit more surprising to anyone who believes that most adults who commit sex offenses against teens hide their sexual interest during online interactions. That is, the adults hid their sexual interest only 26% of the time. Other research has also shown that adults are often overt in their sexual intentions. For example, they commonly send or solicit sexual pictures (Wolak & Finkelhor, 2013). Sexual predators do commonly deceive teens in regard to their age and physical appearance, but the notion that they usually hide their sexual interest is a myth often propagated in the media (Wolak, Finkelhor, Mitchell, & Ybarra, 2008). Overall, research about the behavior of sexual offenders has important implications in terms of the development of prevention efforts targeting online behavior.

References

Wolak, J., & Finkelhor, D. (2013). Are crimes by online predators different from crimes by sex offenders who know youth in-person? *Journal of Adolescent Health, 53*(6), 736–741.

Wolak, J., Finkelhor, D., & Mitchell, K. (2004). Internet-initiated sex crimes against minors: Implications for prevention based on findings from a national study. *Journal of Adolescent Health, 35*(5), 11–20.

Wolak, J., Finkelhor, D., Mitchell, K. J., & Ybarra, M. L. (2008). Online "predators" and their victims: Myths, realities, and implications for prevention and treatment. *American Psychologist, 63*(2), 111–128.

Conversion therapy effectively turns homosexual teens into straight teens

A *New York Times* article tells the intriguing story of Dr. Robert L. Spitzer, regarded by many as one of the most influential figures in psychiatry (Carey, 2012). Spitzer was a hero to many people identifying as LGBT (lesbian, gay, bisexual, or transgender) for fighting against rivals, such as Dr. Charles W. Socarides. Spitzer helped lead the movement to have the diagnosis of "homosexuality" removed from reprints of the second edition of *Diagnostic and Statistical Manual* (American Psychiatric Association, 1968) in the 1970s. Although, Spitzer's side of the debate ultimately won, Socarides' side was able to force a compromise diagnosis of "sexual orientation disturbance" which was only used for individuals who experienced significant distress related to their homosexuality. Though still a controversial diagnosis, sexual orientation disturbance was less stigmatizing than the diagnosis it replaced, and this change helped elevate Spitzer to become the chair of the task force that developed the next edition of the manual, the DSM-III, published in 1980 (American Psychiatric Association, 1980). This newer edition superficially changed the name of sexual orientation disturbance to "ego-dystonic homosexuality" (i.e., expressed orientation does not match ideal orientation) and the controversy continued until it was ultimately removed altogether in the 1987 revision of the manual (American Psychiatric Association, 1987).

Spitzer's rival, Socarides, also continued to be influential by developing an organization called the National Association for Research and Therapy of Homosexuality (NARTH), which promoted a therapy designed to help people change from homosexual to heterosexual—reparative therapy (also called "conversion therapy"; Carey, 2012; Nicolosi, 1991). Reparative therapy is rooted in psychoanalysis and involves the combined use of counseling (individual or group) with prayer. Other more invasive "sexual reorientation" techniques have also been attempted such as masturbatory reconditioning (e.g., masturbating to photos of the opposite sex) and shock therapy (Cramer, Golom, LoPresto, & Kirkley, 2008; Serovich et al., 2008).

Influenced by positive anecdotal reports of reparative therapy and arguments of his rival, Spitzer conducted a study to see if reparative therapy actually was effective by interviewing 200 participants who reported that they had experienced an increase in heterosexuality in terms of both feelings and behavior due to reparative therapy (Spitzer, 2003). The study was immediately critiqued for being based solely on self-report and for leaving out critical aspects of good research design. Nevertheless, Spitzer's name helped give legitimacy to the treatment approach.

More recently, a team of researchers sought to review all of the existing research on reparative therapy (Cramer et al., 2008). The authors made the following points: (a) there is little research on reparative therapy even though it has been in use for decades, (b) the existing studies are retrospective with weak research designs, and (c) the studies are anecdotal, relying only on self-report. Even worse, many participants in reparative therapy have expressed experiencing harm from the approach. For example, participants commonly attribute the therapy to increased depression and suicidal ideation (Shidlo & Schroeder, 2002).

Taken together, the problematic research has led the Just the Facts Coalition to release a document stating therapies designed to change sexual orientation "have serious potential to harm young people because they present the view that the sexual orientation of lesbian, gay, and bisexual youth is a mental illness or disorder, and they often frame the inability to change one's sexual orientation as a personal and moral failure" (American Psychological Association, 2008, p. 5). This document has been endorsed by 13 major organizations including the American Psychological Association, the National Association of School Psychologists, the American Academy of Pediatrics, and the Interfaith Alliance Foundation. Moreover, reparative therapy is now banned in some states in the US as well as areas in other countries (Griffiths, 2017).

Partly prompted by an individual who reported a negative experience with the treatment as a teenager (Arana, 2012), Spitzer published an apology for his previous positive report about reparative therapy:

> I believe I owe the gay community an apology for my study making unproven claims for the efficacy of reparative therapy. I also apologize to any gay person who wasted time and energy undergoing some form or reparative therapy because they believed that I had proven that reparative therapy works with some "highly motivated" individuals. (Spitzer, 2012, p. 757)

It's rare to see a researcher make such a strong apology, and it's a sign that psychology is moving in an evidence-based direction. That said, reparative therapy continues to be used in the US and other countries (Griffiths, 2017). On a final note, parallels can also be drawn between the evolution of the homosexuality diagnosis and that of gender dysphoria in the current (fifth) edition of DSM (American Psychiatric Association, 2013). Like the diagnosis of ego-dystonic homosexuality in the DSM-III, gender dysphoria is only diagnosed in youth who experience distress. Previously called gender identity disorder, gender dysphoria involves distress based on the incongruence of a youth's gender assigned at birth and the gender that they currently experience. As was the case for ego-dystonic homosexuality, will gender dysphoria eventually be removed from the DSM? Only time will tell.

References

American Psychiatric Association (1968). *Diagnostic and statistical manual of mental disorders: DSM-II*. Washington, DC: Author.

American Psychiatric Association (1980). *Diagnostic and statistical manual of mental disorders: DSM-III*. Washington, DC: Author.

American Psychiatric Association (1987). *Diagnostic and statistical manual of mental disorders: DSM-III-R*. Washington, DC: Author.

American Psychological Association (2008). Just the facts about sexual orientation and youth: A primer for principals, educators, and school personnel. Retrieved from www.apa.org

American Psychiatric Association (2013). *Diagnostic and statistical manual of mental disorders: DSM-5*. Washington, DC: Author.

Arana, G. (2012). My so-called ex-gay life. A deep look at the fringe movement that just lost its only shred of scientific support. Retrieved from www.prospect.org

Carey, B. (2012). Psychiatry giant sorry for backing gay "cure." Retrieved from www.newyorktimes.com

Cramer, R. J., Golom, F. D., LoPresto, C. T., & Kirkley, S. M. (2008). Weighing the evidence: Empirical assessment and ethical implications of conversion therapy. *Ethics & Behavior*, *18*(1), 93–114. doi:10.1080/10508420701713014.

Griffiths, J. (2017). Strapped into chairs and electrocuted: How LGBT Chinese are forced into "conversion" therapy. Retrieved from www.cnn.com

Nicolosi, J. (1991). *Reparative therapy of male homosexuality: A new clinical approach*. Lanham, MD: Jason Aronson.

Serovich, J. M., Craft, S. M., Toviessi, P., Gangamma, R., McDowell, T., & Grafsky, E. L. (2008). A systematic review of the research base on sexual reorientation therapies. *Journal of Marital And Family Therapy*, *34*(2), 227–238. doi:10.1111/j.1752-0606.2008.00065.x

Shidlo, A., & Schroeder, M. (2002). Changing sexual orientation: A consumers' report. *Professional Psychology: Research and Practice*, *33*(3), 249–259. doi:10.1037/0735-7028.33.3.249.

Spitzer, R. L. (2003). Can some gay men and lesbians change their sexual orientation? 200 participants reporting a change from homosexual to heterosexual orientation. *Archives of Sexual Behavior*, *32*(5), 403–417. doi:10.1023/A:1025647527010.

Spitzer, R. L. (2012). Spitzer reassesses his 2003 study of reparative therapy of homosexuality. *Archives of Sexual Behavior*, 41(4), 757. doi:10.1007/s10508-012-9966-y.

Myth #28 Teens underestimate the consequences of risky behavior and adults do not

A great deal of research has been conducted on the "teenage brain," and many of the myths described in this book describe some of that research. Essentially, it appears that teens' brains continue to develop until their early to mid-20s, meaning that when teens are in high school their brains are not fully developed. This finding has led researchers to conclude that teens engage in risky behavior at a greater rate due to the lack of a fully developed brain. However, it would be inaccurate to believe that teens underestimate the consequences of risky behavior, and thus engage in risky behavior, while adults do not. Unfortunately, our own research shows that a majority of college students in our sample (54–63%) do believe this myth (Jewell & Hupp, 2018).

While it is true that teens do engage in risky behavior at a rate greater than adults, it may be surprising for many that adults in other age groups engage in risky behavior at nearly the same rate. For example, in 2008 the National Highway Traffic Safety Administration (NHTSA) reported the age of those involved in fatal traffic accidents in the United States when the driver was legally intoxicated (Pickrell, Li, & KC, 2016). They found that 16% of these drivers were 16–20-year-olds, 28% were 21–24-year-olds, 27% were 25–34-year-olds, and 23% were 35–44-year-olds. Thus, it appears that having a fully matured brain does not make one immune to behaving irresponsibly, because half of these fatal crashes involving a drunk driver were committed by 25–44-year-olds. Similarly, the NHTSA conducted research on handheld cell phone use while driving, which has been found to significantly increase one's risk of being in an automobile accident (Pickrell et al., 2016). While 4.6% of 16–24-year-olds were observed using a handheld cell phone, 4.0% of 25–69-year-olds were also observed engaging in the same behavior— which is a rate that is only 15% less. And regarding drug use there are some interesting trends as well. For example, the United States Centers for Disease Control (CDC) found that in 2014, 7.4% of teens (ages 12–17) and 19.6% of college students (ages 18–25) used marijuana in the last month (Azofeifa et al., 2016). However, the same report found that 8.0% of adults ages 35–44 also used marijuana in the last month. This finding led to the headline by the *Washington Post* that "Middle-aged parents are now more likely to smoke weed than their teenage kids" (Ingraham, 2016). And while the myth that adults always behave much more responsibly than teens still exists, you can see that the true state of affairs on this topic may be becoming more widely known based on a few media examples. For example, the 2016 movie *Bad Moms* is entirely focused on the exploits of three middle-aged mothers who are intent on breaking the stereotype of the perfect PTA soccer mom (Lucas & Moore, 2016). So while adults may possess a fully developed brain, they can certainly act like they don't at times.

References

Azofeifa, A., Mattson, M. E., Schauer, G., McAfee, T., Grant, A., & Lyerla, R. (2016, December). National estimates of marijuana use and related indicators— National survey on drug use and national center for statistics and analysis. Alcohol impaired driving: 2015 data. *Traffic Safety Facts. DOT HS 812 350.* Washington, DC: National Highway Traffic Safety Administration.

Ingraham, C. (2016, September). Middle-aged parents are now more likely to smoke weed than their teenage kids. Washington Post, Retrieved from https:// www.washingtonpost.com/news/wonk/wp/2016/09/02/middle-aged-parents-are-now-more-likely-to-smoke-weed-than-their-teenaged-kids/?utm_term=.2796e78ac918

Jewell, J. D., & Hupp, S. D. A. (2018). Prevalence of myths about adolescence [Manuscript in preparation].

Lucas, J., & Moore, S. (Directors & Writers. (2016). *Bad Moms* [Motion picture on DVD]. Hollywood, CA: STX Entertainment.

Pickrell, T. M., Li, R., & KC, S. (2016, September). Driver electronic device use in 2015, *Traffic Safety Facts Research Note* [Report No. DOT HS 812 326]. Washington, DC: National Highway Traffic Safety Administration.

3 THE SOCIAL ENVIRONMENT

Myth #29 More quality time with teens can make up for less quantity of time

Frankie Heck, mother of three kids on ABC's *The Middle*, a television show about a middle-class family living in middle America, wants her family to spend some quality time together before school begins. Summer for the Hecks involved everyone going their own way—Axl was a bossy lifeguard at the town pool, Sue hung out at the mall, and Brick found

Great Myths of Adolescence, First Edition. Jeremy D. Jewell, Michael I. Axelrod, Mitchell J. Prinstein, and Stephen Hupp.
© 2019 John Wiley & Sons Ltd. Published 2019 by John Wiley & Sons Ltd.

nirvana in a volunteer job at the library. The only quality time the Hecks can afford is camping, which turns out to be a disaster as sleeping bags are forgotten at home, siblings fight, and a bear invades the campground. In the end, however, the family grows closer and the myth that quality time makes up for lack of quantity of time grows. In fact, 62–69% of college students in our own research sample endorsed this myth (Jewell & Hupp, 2018).

The notion of quality time between parents and their kids was likely born out of the collective guilt many parents in the 1970s felt as the number of two-career families increased (Kropp, 2001). A 1977 *Business Week* article entitled "When Mothers are also Managers" noted the small but growing trend of mothers emphasizing quality time over quantity of time in their relationships with their children (The Corporate Woman, 1977). In the article, working mothers, echoing what working fathers had been saying for decades, believed that the quality of time spent with their children trumped the overall amount of time. However, research on the topic has failed to support the claim that quality is more important than quantity when it comes to parents' interactions with their teenagers. For example, quantity of time with parents, by itself, has been found to be a protective factor against adolescent depression (Desha, Micholson, & Ziviani, 2011) and alcohol abuse among adolescent girls (Dickson, Laursen, Stattin, & Kerr, 2015), and the frequency of family dinners has been associated with fewer high-risk behaviors among teenagers (Fulkerson et al., 2006).

Yet, research also indicates that the quality of the time parents spend with their teenager is important. A recent longitudinal study of almost 800 adolescents found that the amount of engaged time spent with parents was associated with fewer behavior problems, including drug use and delinquency (Milkie, Nomaguchi, & Denny, 2015). In the study, engaged time, an indicator of quality time, was defined as the total amount of time the parent spent focused on the adolescent, which was contrasted with accessible time, or the amount of time the adolescent spent with the parent but not directly involved in activities. This distinction is noteworthy, as scholars have attempted to distinguish quality time from quantity of time in the literature (Snyder, 2007). However, such a distinction is often difficult to make, as quality and quantity of time are best conceptualized as interconnected. Quality time is dependent on the quantity of time a parent spends with a child. Moreover, research suggests that children need both "focused times and hang-around times" with their parents (Galinsky, 1999, p. 92).

What you need to know

For parents, it's important to know that some quality time is not an adequate substitute for amount of time and that both quality and quantity of time with parents are fundamental for building strong parent–teen relationships. Adolescence is a time when teens are faced with a number of stresses related to building their identity, their social network, and future academic and vocational plans. Teens need their parents to be regularly available to them and interested in their lives. For more information on how to build positive relationships with teens, see the U.S. National Institutes of Health website at https://newsinhealth.nih.gov/2017/09/positive-parenting.

References

Desha, L. N., Nicholson, J. M., & Ziviani, J. M. (2011). Adolescent depression and time spent with parents and siblings. *Social Indicators Research*, *101*, 233–238.

Dickson, D. J., Laursen, B., Stattin, H., & Kerr, M. (2015). *Pediatrics*, *136*, 617–624.

Fulkerson, J. A., Story, M., Mellin, A., Leffert, N., Neumark-Sztainer, D., & French, S. A. (2006). *Journal of Adolescent Health*, *39*, 337–345.

Galinsky, E. (1999). *Ask the children*. New York, NY: William Morrow.

Jewell, J. D., & Hupp, S. D. A. (2018). Prevalence of myths about adolescence [Manuscript in preparation].

Kropp, P. (2001). *I'll be the parent, you be the child: Encourage excellence, set limits and lighten up*. New York, NY: Fisher Books.

Milkie, M. A., Nomaguchi, K. M., & Denny, K. E. (2015). Does the amount of time mothers spend with children or adolescents matter? *Journal of Marriage and Family*, *77*, 355–372.

Snyder, K. A. (2007). A vocabulary of motives: Understanding how parents define quality time. *Journal of Marriage and Family*, *69*, 320–340.

The Corporate Woman. (1977, April 18). When mothers are also managers. *Business Week*, pp. 155–158.

Myth #30 Successful transition from adolescence to adulthood is achieved through detachment from parents

"She's leaving home after living alone for so many years" (Lennon & McCartney, 1967). That poignant line from The Beatles' *She Leaving Home* was meant to reflect the experience of a teenage girl who runs away from home. The line, however, might just as well illustrate a teenage girl's detachment from her parents. While adolescents are meant to separate from their parents, emotionally and physically, it's not common for teenagers and their parents to sever the attachment relationship that John Lennon and Paul McCartney seemed to be describing in that song.

Developmental theorists and researchers have, for a long time, debated the degree to which detachment from one's parents is a necessary component of the successful transition from adolescence to adulthood (Silverberg & Gondoli, 1996). While some scholars have suggested the parent–adolescent relationship does not matter when considering long-term developmental outcomes (see Harris, 1995), empirical findings suggest a strong parent–adolescent attachment relationship is important for healthy teenage psychosocial development (Moretti & Peled, 2004). Recent research also indicates that, at least in healthy families, the parent–adolescent relationship changes through the process of individuation, or an individual's awareness that they're an independent person, separate from one's parents (McElhaney, Allen, Stephenson, & Hare, 2009). Scholars note that individuation happens when teenagers separate, not detach, from their parents (Steinberg & Silk, 2002). Yet, detachment from parents is still considered by some to be an important developmental outcome that reduces an adolescent's psychological dependence on parents.

It's not surprising people believe that the successful transition from adolescence to adulthood involves some level of detachment from parents. Conceptually, detachment from one's parents and family can be easily mistaken for independence and emotional autonomy, which makes understanding the definition of these terms especially critical. Detachment during adolescence is defined as limited parental support and acceptance, and entails the severing of the parent–teenager relationship, which includes the process of "withdrawing from the family" (Ryan & Lynch, 1989, p. 340). Withdrawing from the family implies a psychological withdrawal that potentially reverses a positive relationship that was built during infancy, toddlerhood, and childhood. Independence and emotional autonomy are notably different from detachment. Independence involves self-reliance and individuation, while emotional autonomy concerns the formation of "more adultlike and less childish close relationships with family members and peers" (Steinberg, 2011, p. 280). The distinction between detachment and concepts of independence and emotional autonomy is important, and such terms should not be used interchangeably (McElhaney et al., 2009).

It's also easy to confuse detachment with disengagement, a concept that has been examined extensively by developmental researchers. Disengagement during adolescence implies a decrease in the amount of time teenagers spend with their parents and family. Research has found that the amount of time adolescents spend with their parents during waking hours decreases substantially between the ages of 10 and 18 years (see Larson, Richards, Moneta, Holmbeck, & Duckett, 1996). So, yes, teenagers spend less time with their parents. However, detachment and disengagement are distinct concepts. Detachment involves the severing of the parent–adolescent relationship and could include disengagement. Disengagement, by itself, is not necessarily bad. Rather, it's an important developmental process that aids in individuation and the development of emotional autonomy. For example, research has also found that adolescents' time spent communicating with parents does not decline, despite a decline in the total time adolescents spent with parents, and, for girls, more of the communication involves interpersonal issues, a marker for relationship quality (see Larson et al., 1996). Terminological confusion (e.g., detachment–autonomy, detachment–disengagement) is a common source of myths in psychology and might help explain how the concept of detachment continues to be viewed by some as an important adolescent developmental outcome.

The misuse of these terms among professionals might also help explain how this myth has persisted. For example, Dr. Carl Pickhardt, a clinical psychologist and author on adolescence and parenting, has suggested in his *Psychology Today* blog that a teenager's detachment from the family is a critical feature of adolescence (Pickhardt, 2013, 2014, 2015). While Dr. Pickhardt might have used the term detachment, these columns concern the development of self-reliance, emotional autonomy, and identity. In one column, he suggested that parents detach from their teens by allowing more independence and self-sufficiency, while, at the same time, remaining closely attached to their teenager (Pickhardt, 2013). Dr. Pickhardt is clearly referring to developmental milestones that contribute to an adolescent's individuation and the process of becoming separate from one's parents, and not detachment as defined above. Similarly, Dr. Heidi Smith Luedtke, psychologist and author of *Detachment Parenting: 33 Ways to Keep Your Cool When Kids Melt Down*, used the term "detachment parenting" broadly to describe strategies for responding to kid's emotions (Luedtke, 2012). Specifically, she recommended detaching emotionally from situations in an effort to remain calm when kids become angry or out of control. However, Luedtke explicitly stated that detachment parenting does not mean severing the attachment relationship between parent and child.

History helps us understand where this myth might have originated. The idea that a successful transition from adolescence to adulthood is achieved through the detachment from parents was initially proposed by psychoanalytic theorists. For example, Anna Freud (1958) maintained that puberty caused a significant disturbance within the family system. Specifically, she believed early adolescence was a developmental period during which repressed intrapsychic conflicts revived sexual impulses from early childhood. The conflicts, which involve unconscious feelings toward the opposite sex parent and ambivalent feelings toward the same sex parent, "are expressed as increased tension among family members, an increase in arguments, and a certain degree of discomfort around the house" (Steinberg, 2011, p. 281). Freud thought that adolescents were pushed to separate themselves emotionally from their parents because of this tension, calling the process detachment. The process involves gradually breaking the parent–child attachment bond that was initially established in infancy and developed through childhood. Freud and other psychoanalytic theorists regarded emotional detachment as a normal adolescent developmental process (Steinberg, 2011). In fact, emotional detachment was seen as part of the storm and stress that Freud said characterized adolescence.

Freud's hypothesis about detachment has failed to hold up to rigorous scientific scrutiny. Research examining family relationships during adolescence and emerging adulthood has found little evidence suggesting high levels of conflict with parents is normal or that detachment from the family is common among teenagers (McElhaney et al., 2009). In fact, most adolescents get along well with their parents, despite increases in arguing, and most adolescents and emerging adults report establishing more intimate relationships with their parents over time (McElhaney et al., 2009). For example, one study investigating emerging adults' transition to college found positive changes in the quality of the adolescent–parent relationship (see Lefkowitz, 2005). Specifically, college students reported communicating more openly with their parents, and having more respect and appreciation for one's parents. Moreover, the degree to which this change was viewed as positive was statistically related to the length of time in college. For example, fourth-year college students reported more positive relationships with parents than those in their first year of college. The author of the study noted that, despite college students' emergent independence, there were "positive perceptions of becoming closer to their parents" (Lefkowitz, 2005, p. 58). For most adolescents and emerging adults, the parent–adolescent relationship becomes stronger not weaker as a result of independence and autonomy.

Not only does the parent–teenager relationship improve over the course of adolescence, contrary to Freud's (1958) assertion that a developmental role of adolescence is detachment from one's parents, research finds that parents are generally "maintained as attachment figures" (individuals with whom a trusting relationship has been forged) during high school and college (McElhaney et al., 2009, p. 372). For example, one study found that adolescents, college students, and young adults selected mothers (over close friends and romantic partners) most often when asked to identify the person who provides the most secure base (i.e., "the person you can count on, will always be there for you, and who would do almost anything for you") (Markiewicz, Lawford, & Doyle, 2006). More recently, a study of approximately 400 adolescents and emerging adults (14–23 years of age) found that biological parents, primarily mothers, were most often recognized as the primary or secondary attachment figure (i.e., "who are the important people in your life?") for both high school and college students (Rosenthal & Kobak, 2010). Interestingly, the study also found self-reported internalizing (e.g., anxiety, depression) and externalizing (e.g., oppositional behavior, conduct problems) problems were associated with high levels of peer attachment and lower levels of parental attachment, especially with fathers. These studies underscore the importance adolescents and young adults place on their relationship with parents. Moreover, attachment models remain stable across early childhood and adolescence. Specifically, teenagers generally remain attached to their primary caregivers, especially mom, despite the changes that occur during adolescence (e.g., decreased time spent with parents, strengthened importance of peer group, emergence of romantic relationships, increased autonomy).

Research has also found that detachment from the family might not produce favorable outcomes for adolescents, as Freud's hypothesis also predicted. In fact, teenagers' detachment from parents predicts rather unfavorable outcomes including suicidality, substance use, and delinquency (Moretti & Peled, 2004). In a study of 13- and 14-year-olds, self-reported levels of detachment were positively associated with self-reported internalizing and externalizing problems (Pace & Zappulla, 2012). In addition, lower levels of detachment are generally associated with positive outcomes. In a study of at-risk ninth and tenth graders, researchers found attachment security, defined as feeling emotionally connected to a parent, was associated with lower overall self-reported internalizing problems, maternal-reported externalizing problems, and peer-reported social rejection and delinquency (Allen, Moore, Kuperminc, & Bell, 1998). A more recent study found that 14-year-olds were more likely to report positive peer relationships when levels of parental attachment were reported as high (Jager, Yuen, Putnick, Hendricks, & Bornstein, 2015). As in other research, the authors also found that parental attachment was positively associated with low levels of self-reported internalizing and externalizing problems. All three sets of authors came to similar conclusions, that the quality of the parent–adolescent relationship matters and that emotional separation from parents does not promote adaptive or healthy adjustment nor is it related to positive outcomes for teenagers. In addition, similar research conducted in Australia, East Asia, and Europe has established the role a strong parent–adolescent relationship plays in developmental outcomes including adjustment, "despite cultural differences in families and social mores" (D'Angela & Omar, 2010, p. 158).

The idea that detachment from parents is important for the successful transition from adolescence to adulthood just hasn't been supported by research. Teenagers tend to get along well with their parents, and strong emotional bonds that develop between teenagers and their parents are related to favorable outcomes. Furthermore, detachment is associated with poor outcomes, including delinquency, substance use, and mental health problems.

Interestingly, television shows featuring teenagers typically depict separation from parents as a primarily physical enterprise. For example, high schooler Greg Brady from *The Brady Bunch*, the 1970s sitcom about a large blended family of six kids, sought independence from his parents and refuge from his brothers and sisters by moving to the attic. Haley Dunphy from *Modern Family*, a contemporary sitcom about the lives of three related families, established some autonomy from her parents by moving to the basement. While each television teenager separated physically from his and her parents, a positive parent–adolescent relationship was maintained despite the physical separation. Greg continued to seek guidance from his parents, and Haley and her parents continued to develop a more adult-like relationship over time. It's obvious from these two television shows and other popular culture references (see Katniss from *The Hunger Games* or Axel and Sue Heck from *The Middle*) that teenagers leave their parents physically and become more autonomous, yet often continue to maintain a strong parent–adolescent attachment relationship following the separation. Perhaps this is one myth Hollywood is intent on busting.

What you need to know

Parents have noted that adolescence is the developmental period that makes them most anxious (Pasley & Gecas, 1984). This is partially due to our culture's portrayal of teenagers as "difficult, oppositional, and moody" (Steinberg & Silk, 2002, p. 103) and, perhaps, the longstanding belief that parent–adolescent conflict intensifies during the teenage years. Again, psychoanalytic theorists postulated that this conflict would be resolved only when the parent–adolescent bond was severed or when the adolescent detached from his or her parents. However, more modern views, supported by research, have noted the importance of maintaining a strong parent–adolescent attachment relationship, while, at the same time, having the adolescent establish appropriate levels of autonomy and self-reliance.

Scholars have suggested that achieving autonomy and retaining a close relationship with parents should not be "placed at opposite ends of the spectrum" (Allen, Hauser, Bell, & O'Connor, 1994, p. 179) but, rather, each considered an important feature that facilitates positive outcomes for adolescents (Moretti & Peled, 2004; Steinberg, 2011). Research suggests that a strong parent–adolescent attachment relationship combined with healthy levels of separation and individuation facilitates positive adolescent development. Specifically, strong parent–adolescent attachment, appropriate levels of separation, and the development of autonomy have been shown to predict positive academic, social, and emotional adjustment to high school and college (Jager et al., 2015; Mattanah, Hancock, & Brand, 2004). In addition, research supports the notion that a strong parent–adolescent attachment relationship assists in the development of autonomy and self-reliance (McElhaney et al., 2009). Individuation doesn't happen unless parents maintain a close and positive relationship with their teenager, and, at the same time, allow their teenager to engage in the healthy process of separation. In fact, research suggests that individuation is facilitated, not hindered, by a strong parent–adolescent attachment relationship (Mattanah et al., 2004).

Research-based parenting practices emphasize a style that combines responsiveness and demandingness. This means positive developmental outcomes are most likely when parents provide warmth and unconditional love, offer acceptance and encourage individuality, and allow for emotional and physical autonomy, while, at the same time, holding their teenager to high standards regarding achievement and behavior, and maintaining a high degree of supervision (Steinberg, 2011). Such a parenting style is likely appropriate for adolescents because it strikes a balance "between restrictiveness and autonomy, giving the adolescent opportunities to develop self-reliance while providing standards, limits, and guidelines that developing individuals need" (Steinberg & Silk, 2002, p. 123). This style of parenting, also known as authoritative parenting, has been associated with positive outcomes involving academic, behavioral, psychological, and social functioning (Steinberg & Silk, 2002). Furthermore, parents who are authoritative are more likely to have responsible, self-sufficient teenagers (Steinberg & Silk, 2002).

Parents should also anticipate a transformation in the parent–adolescent relationship. The most notable change involves the teenager's establishment of autonomy (Steinberg & Silk, 2002). Scholars point out that it might be most appropriate to consider autonomy through a multidimensional lens: emotional (i.e., decreased need for parents to help regulate emotions), behavioral (decreased need for parents to help make and follow through with decisions), and cognitive (decreased need for parents to determine one's thoughts, values, and opinions) (McElhaney et al., 2009). Research indicates that parents who allow autonomy, within reason, are rewarded with teenagers who are responsible and self-reliant (Steinberg & Silk, 2002). Those parents who are overly controlling are more likely to raise teenagers who are poorly adjusted (Steinberg & Silk, 2002). As mentioned previously, a teenager's move toward autonomy doesn't necessarily correspond with detachment from parents. Rather, parents are maintained as important attachment figures despite the teenager's push toward autonomy. Parents are reminded that their presence in their teenager's life remains as important as it did during previous developmental stages (e.g., infancy, toddlerhood, early and late childhood). In the end, what happens to most parent–adolescent relationships might be more akin to a realignment and not detachment (Steinberg & Silk, 2002).

References

Allen, J. P., Hauser, S. T., Bell, K. L., & O'Connor, T. (1994). Longitudinal assessment of autonomy and relatedness in adolescent-family interactions as predictors of adolescent ego development and self-esteem. *Child Development*, 65, 179–194.

Allen, J. P., Moore, C., Kuperminc, G., & Bell, K. (1998). Attachment and adolescent psychosocial functioning. *Child Development*, 69, 1406–1419.

D'Angelo, S., & Omar, H. A. (2010). Parenting adolescents. In E. Bell, & J. Merrick (Eds.), *Rural child health: International aspects* (pp. 157–165). Hauppauge, NY: Nova Science.

Freud, A. (1958). Adolescence. *Psychoanalytic Study of the Child, 13,* 255–278.

Harris, J. R. (1995). Where is the child's environment? A group socialization theory of development. *Psychology Review, 102,* 458–489.

Jager, J., Yuen, C. X., Putnick, D. L., Hendricks, C., & Bornstein, M. H. (2015). Adolescent-peer relationships, separation and detachment from parents, and internalizing and externalizing behaviors: Linkages and interactions. *Journal of Early Adolescence, 35,* 511–537.

Larson, R. W., Richards, M. H., Moneta, G., Holmbeck, G., & Duckett, E. (1996). Changes in adolescents' daily interactions with their families from ages 10 to 18: Disengagement and transformation. *Developmental Psychology, 32,* 744–754.

Lefkowitz, E. S. (n.d.). "Things have gotten better": Developmental changes among emerging adults after the transition to university. *Journal of Adolescent Research, 20,* 40–63.

Lennon, J., & McCartney, P. (1967). She's leaving home. On *Sgt. Pepper's Lonely Hearts Club, Band.* New York, NY: Capitol Records.

Luedtke, H. S. (2012). *Detachment parenting: 33 ways to keep your cool when kids melt down* (Vol. 1). Pennsauken, NJ: Bookbaby.

Markiewicz, D., Lawford, H., & Doyle, A. B. (2006). Developmental differences in adolescents' and young adults' use of mothers, fathers, best friends, and romantic partners to fulfill attachment needs. *Journal of Youth and Adolescence, 35,* 127–140.

Mattanah, J. F., Hancock, G. R., & Brand, B. L. (2004). Parental attachment, separation-individuation, and college student adjustment: A structural equation analysis of mediational effects. *Journal of Counseling Psychology, 51,* 213–225.

McElhaney, K. B., Allen, J. P., Stephenson, J. C., & Hare, A. L. (2009). Attachment and autonomy during adolescence. In R. M. Lerner, & L. Steinberg (Eds.), *Handbook of adolescent psychology* (3rd ed., Vol. 1) (pp. 358–403). New York, NY: Wiley.

Moretti, M. M., & Peled, M. (2004). Adolescent-parent attachment: Bonds that support healthy development. *Pediatrics and Child Health, 9,* 551–555.

Pace, U., & Zappulla, C. (2012). Detachment from parents, problem behaviors, and the moderating role of parental support among Italian adolescents. *Journal of Family Issues, 34,* 768–783.

Pasley, K., & Gecas, V. (1984). Stresses and satisfactions of the parental role. *Personnel and Guidance Journal, 2,* 400–404.

Pickhardt, C. E. (2013, December 9). A detachment theory of parenting adolescents. *PsychologyToday.*Retrievedfromhttps://www.psychologytoday.com/blog/surviving-your-childs-adolescence/201312/detachment-theory-parenting-adolescents

Pickhardt, C. E. (2014, June 30). How detachment ends dependence between parent and adolescent. *Psychology Today.* Retrieved from https://www.psychologytoday.com/blog/surviving-your-childs-adolescence/201406/how-detachment-ends-dependence-between-parent-and

Pickhardt, C. E. (2015, August 10). How detachment changes both adolescent and parents. *Psychology Today*. Retrieved from https://www.psychologytoday.com/blog/surviving-your-childs-adolescence/201508/how-detachment-changes-both-adolescent-and-parents

Rosenthal, N. L., & Kobak, R. (2010). Assessing adolescents' attachment hierarchies: Differences across developmental periods and associations with individual adaptation. *Journal of Research on Adolescence, 20*, 678–706.

Ryan, R. M., & Lynch, J. H. (1989). Emotional autonomy versus detachment: Revisiting the vicissitudes of adolescence and young adulthood. *Child Development, 60*, 340–356.

Silverberg, S. B., & Gondoli, D. M. (1996). Autonomy in adolescence: A contextualized perspective. In G. R. Adams, R. Montemayor, & T. P. Gullotta (Eds.), *Psychosocial development during adolescence: Progress in developmental contextualism* (pp. 12–61). Thousand Oaks, CA: Sage.

Steinberg, L. (2011). *Adolescence* (9th ed.). New York, NY: McGraw-Hill.

Steinberg, L., & Silk, J. S. (2002). Parenting adolescents. In M. H. Bornstein (Ed.), *Handbook of parenting, vol. 1: children and parenting* (pp. 103–133). Mahwah, NJ: Erlbaum.

Myth #31 Popular teens are usually mean

It was a typical day after school when four popular girls met to begin talking about their classmates. They called one fat, another untrustworthy, and used names for others too offensive to print. Every affront was recorded in a "burn book," with a page dedicated to each of their victims, and each time they met, they added to the growing list of eviscerating insults and reputation-destroying rumors. Savage.

This is how we get to know "the Plastics" in the movie, *Mean Girls* (Waters, 2004), and it is just one of so many portrayals of high school popularity. In *The Breakfast Club* (Hughes, 1985), the popular jock harasses the nerds, physically harming one in the locker room, ultimately earning him detention after he is caught. In *The Karate Kid* (Avildsen, 1984), the most popular student uses illegal martial arts moves and inflicts serious injury on a less popular opponent. In *Heathers* (Lehmann, 1988), the popular clique actually murders their less-liked classmates. All of these depictions, and so many more, help to perpetuate the myth that popular teens are mean. In fact, research on college students' beliefs found that 86% of students had heard of this myth while 43% believed the myth (Jewell & Hupp, 2018).

It is hard to trace the origins of this myth, given its ubiquity across generations and cultures. In part, it may have been derived from the common tendency, at least within U.S. culture, for the most athletically oriented students to be selected as most popular within their schools. These jocks' physical dominance may have equated size and power with high peer status, cultivating an inadvertent association between aggression/bullying and popularity (Merten, 2011).

Alternatively, it may be the commonality between humans and other species that also demonstrate clear popularity hierarchies. Ethology research with other types of animals suggests that those who are most visible, have most access to resources, and are most likely to lead a group—in other words, the most popular—tend to use aggressive tactics to achieve and maintain their top status positions. Scientists who study chimpanzees, for instance, revealed that much like among human teenagers, the use of aggression serves to maintain the boundary between who is popular and who is not (Vaughn & Waters, 1981). In both species, those who challenge or attempt to permeate that boundary are subjected to public humiliation to demonstrate negative consequences to others and reify the pecking order.

This myth also may be perpetuated by scientific research. Research reveals that adolescents can use physical or relational aggression either out of an act of frustration, or as a calculated way to increase their status (Price & Dodge, 1989). Studies show that this latter tactic, called "proactive aggression" seems to work, at least in the short-term. Longitudinal studies that follow adolescents' development over time suggest that teens who are proactively aggressive become more popular (Prinstein & Cillessen, 2003).

So, does that mean that popular teens really are mean? Not entirely. There is also research evidence to suggest that, in general, popular teens are not mean at all. In fact, they're rated by their peers as the most likable kids in their grade. This phenomenon reflects the fact that there are actually two very different types of popularity. One type is established as early as preschool, and it is not based on who is "cool," or powerful at all. It simply reflects who is most "likable." Studies beginning in the 1970s and 1980s began to notice just how powerful likability can be when psychological researchers asked children in kindergarten and beyond to nominate from a list of their classmates those that they "liked the most," and those they "liked the least" (Coie, Dodge, & Coppotelli, 1982). Based on the number of nominations each participant received, children could be classified into one of five groups. Children frequently selected as "liked least," and rarely as "liked most" were classified as Rejected; those nominated as "liked most" and "liked least" about as frequently were classified as Controversial; those rarely nominated at all were Neglected; and about half of all children were Average (Coie et al., 1982). The final group included those who were picked far more than their peers as "liked most," and almost never picked as "liked least" at all. Researchers labeled this group the "Populars," but they were not mean at all. In fact, subsequently research revealed that these Populars were kindest to others, best at sharing and problem-solving, and were natural-born leaders (Coie & Dodge, 1983; Newcomb, Bukowski, & Pattee, 1993). They were smart, most likely to solve disputes among their peers, and often remained quiet while others vied for the most attention.

Research suggests that these likable Popular children remain remarkably well-liked not only throughout the school year, but also for many years later, and even as adults (Almquist & Brännström, 2014). This may be because the qualities that lead children to be likable continue to make them well-liked even by new groups of peers they just met. In one study, psychologists revealed that these Popular children were rated by unfamiliar peers as the most-well-liked all over again after only three hours of playtime (Coie & Kupersmidt, 1983). Researchers found that these likable Populars grow up to live happier, healthier, and more successful lives. They are more likely to be hired and promoted at work. They report more satisfying relationships, and are less likely to experience physical health problems than their less likable peers (Gustafsson, Janlert, Theorell, Westerlund, & Hammarström, 2012).

However, research has revealed that adolescents' pubertal development is accompanied by changes in the brain that give rise to a second form of popularity. A neural region within the brain's limbic system, referred to as the ventral striatum, is among the first to develop among young adolescents' brains, and it offers an enhanced interest in getting attention and approval from our peers. That's probably why preteens suddenly become so much more interested in hanging out with their friends and less interested in their parents. This is exactly when a second form of popularity emerges, and rather than reflecting likability, it reflects those who are most likely to get attention from their peers and have the greatest influence over others. Those with this type of popularity—the ones who are often regarded as "cool," are often those who are most physically attractive, and seem to do best at whatever is most valued in their context. In many schools within Western culture, the Populars are those who have culturally ideal body shapes and also are athletically inclined, because these are traits highly valued within our culture more broadly. However, in more religious communities, those most popular may be those most pious. In urban communities they may include those with greatest independence, and so on. Research suggests that this adolescent form of popularity is not related to life-long benefits. In fact, recent work suggests that those who are most "cool," tend to grow up with relationship difficulties, and greater risk for addictions, depression, and anxiety (Allen, Schad, Ouderkerk, & Chango, 2014). Researchers who have examined both of these types of popularity—the type based on likability and the type fostered by our adolescent instincts for attention and power—have found that there is some modest overlap. About 30% of those considered "most popular" as teens actually seem to possess both types of popularity (Parkhurst & Hopmeyer, 1998). They are "cool," and also among the most "well-liked" in school, and they're extremely unlikely to be mean or aggressive to others (LaFontana & Cillessen, 1999).

What you need to know

No one likes to be the victim of a stereotype, and popular teens are no different. While it may seem easy to assume that anyone who is attractive, cool, confident, and popular also is arrogant or mean, it is neither fair nor true. There are many very popular adolescents who have grown up as the kindest, most considerate, and most generous kids in their peer group. They don't deserve derision, in the same way that others wouldn't like assumptions being made about themselves. Beyond prejudice, there's another reason to be careful not to perpetuate the myth about popular teens being mean too. And it has to do with the way that we may be accidentally encouraging others to be aggressive. In one study, adolescents were asked to report all of the qualities they believed were associated with adolescent popularity (LaFontana & Cillessen, 1999). As you might expect, many reported that they felt that the Populars would be obnoxious, self-absorbed, inconsiderate, and yes, aggressive too. Why is that a problem? Because our collective embrace of this myth basically reifies the norms of what it takes to become or remain popular. It is as if we are telling others who strive for popularity that they *should be* mean, and we will reward them for doing so by making them more popular. In other words, the more we perpetuate this social norm, the more we are contributing to a self-fulfilling prophecy—a cycle wherein we believe that Populars are mean, and inadvertently help mean people become more popular. And that's not only bad for high school, it's a bad message for people at any age.

References

Allen, J. P., Schad, M. M., Oudekerk, B., & Chango, J. (2014). What ever happened to the "cool" kids? Long-term sequelae of early adolescent pseudomature behavior. *Child Development, 85*(5), 1866–1880.

Almquist, Y. B., & Brännström, L. (2014). Childhood peer status and the clustering of social, economic, and health-related circumstances in adulthood. *Social Science & Medicine, 105*, 67–75.

Avildsen, J. G. (1984). *The Karate Kid* [Motion picture]. Los Angeles, CA: Columbia Pictures.

Coie, J. D., & Dodge, K. A. (1983). Continuities and changes in children's social status: A five-year longitudinal study. *Merrill-Palmer Quarterly, 29*(3), 261–282.

Coie, J. D., Dodge, K. A., & Coppotelli, H. (1982). Dimensions and types of social status: A cross-age perspective. *Developmental Psychology, 18*(4), 557.

Coie, J. D., & Kupersmidt, J. B. (1983). A behavioral analysis of emerging social status in boys' groups. *Child Development, 54*, 1400–1416.

Gustafsson, P. E., Janlert, U., Theorell, T., Westerlund, H., & Hammarström, A. (2012). Do peer relations in adolescence influence health in adulthood? Peer problems in the school setting and the metabolic syndrome in middle-age. *PLoS One, 7*(6), e39385.

Hughes, J. (Director). (1985). *The Breakfast Club* [Motion picture]. Los Angeles, CA: Universal Pictures.

Jewell, J. D., & Hupp, S. D. A. (2018). Prevalence of myths about adolescence [Manuscript in preparation].

LaFontana, K. M., & Cillessen, A. H. (1999). Children's interpersonal perceptions as a function of sociometric and peer-perceived popularity. *The Journal of Genetic Psychology, 160*(2), 225–242.

Lehmann, M. (Director). (1988). *Heathers* [Motion picture]. Los Angeles, CA: New World Pictures.

Merten, D. E. (2011). Being there awhile: An ethnographic perspective on popularity. Popularity in the peer system, 57–78.

Newcomb, A. F., Bukowski, W. M., & Pattee, L. (1993). Children's peer relations: A meta-analytic review of popular, rejected, neglected, controversial, and average sociometric status. *Psychological Bulletin, 113*, 99–128. doi:10.1037/0033-2909.113.1.99.

Parkhurst, J. T., & Hopmeyer, A. (1998). Sociometric popularity and peer-perceived popularity: Two distinct dimensions of peer status. *The Journal of Early Adolescence, 18*(2), 125–144.

Price, J. M., & Dodge, K. A. (1989). Reactive and proactive aggression in childhood: Relations to peer status and social context dimensions. *Journal of Abnormal Child Psychology, 17*, 455–471.

Prinstein, M. J., & Cillessen, A. H. (2003). Forms and functions of adolescent peer aggression associated with high levels of peer status. *Merrill-Palmer Quarterly, 49*(3), 310–342.

Vaughn, B. E., & Waters, E. (1981). Attention structure, sociometric status, and dominance: Interrelations, behavioral correlates, and relationships to social competence. *Developmental Psychology, 17,* 275–288.

Waters, M. (Director). (2004). *Mean Girls* [Motion picture]. Los Angeles, CA: Paramount.

Myth #32   Peer pressure only causes teens to make bad decisions

In one of the first scenes of *Finding Nemo* (Stanton & Unkrich, 2003), the eponymous young fish is swimming at the edge of the safe coral reef where he, his dad, and all of his friends live. Just a few feet away is the ocean—a vast expanse of mystery, intrigue, and danger. Nemo knows it's too risky to swim into the ocean, but his new friends pressure him. One by one, they each swim out a little farther, eventually calling to Nemo to try and swim even farther from safety than they had. The scene is suspenseful, because everyone who watches it intuitively knows that it is remarkably difficult to resist pressure from peers, and many believe that peers most always want us to do something dangerous or risky.

In *Thirteen* (Hardwicke, 2003), Tracy is pressured by her popular friend Evie towards a world of sex, drugs, and crime. In *Mean Girls* (Waters, 2004), the Plastics influence Cady to spread damaging rumors about her teacher. And on so many TV shows, such as *Pretty Little Liars* (King, 2009), for example, peer pressure is used to turn once innocent, well-adjusted teens into unrecognizable creatures who engage in any number of dangerous, illegal, or even psychiatrically disordered behaviors simply to try and gain favor with those whom they admire. The expectation that peers will lead adolescents to make horrible decisions is so ubiquitous, in fact, it has become that ironic adage that everyone hears before their teenage years: *"would you jump off a bridge just because your friend did?"* In fact, of all the myths discussed in this book, this myth is one of the most prevalent. Research on college students' opinions found that 97% had heard of this myth and 84–88% of students believed the myth to be true (Jewell & Hupp, 2018).

But is there any truth to this myth? Do teens truly pressure each other only towards bad decisions? Like many myths, there is at least some truth here that deserves attention. Some adolescents engage in a remarkable number of dangerous and risky behaviors. In the United States, about one of every four adolescents has used alcohol before the age of 14; 25% have had five drinks in a row before high school graduation; one in five smokes pot before age 14, and 40% of teens report that they did not use a condom the last time they had sex. More than one out of 10 teens say they have fasted in an attempt to look thinner (Centers for Disease Control and Prevention [CDC], 2015). These are all remarkably risky behaviors that strongly predict which teens will become pregnant before graduating high school, grow up to have substance abuse problems, or develop serious eating disorders. And the number one predictor of who will engage in each of these risky behaviors is the extent to which adolescents believe that their best friend engaged in the same behavior (Brechwald & Prinstein, 2011). In other words, it is true that adolescents are indeed strongly influenced by their peers, and many of these influences lead to bad decisions.

However, there is more to the story: the same processes that lead adolescents to be influenced towards bad decisions also can guide teens to good outcomes as well. Peer influence processes help adolescents as much as hurt them. Among psychological researchers, peer influence is known as an effect of two simultaneously occurring processes (Kandel, 1978). First, research suggests that adolescents, like adults, are extremely likely to select friends who are very similar to themselves. At young ages, we tend to pick friends who look like us. For instance, our friends may be the same gender or ethnicity/race as we are. Beginning in middle childhood, however, we tend to look for friends who share the same values and interests, which means that in many cases, we select those peers with whom we already believe we can identify (Hartup, 1996). Second, research suggests that friends socialize with one another to engage in more of the behaviors they have in common. If those behaviors include risk-taking, such as alcohol use, for instance, then two adolescents are likely to goad one another towards more drinking – more than either may have drunk alone (Hawkins, Catalano, & Miller, 1992).

In the movies, this process plays out in the form of peer *pressure*— explicit moments when adolescents cajole one another to do something, sometimes under the threat of social sanctions. But in real life, researchers have learned that these moments of peer pressure rarely occur (Brown, Bakker, Ameringer, & Mahon, 2008). Instead, peer influence happens through a variety of more subtle processes. Usually, these processes occur outside our conscious awareness, so we are being influenced without even knowing it.

One researcher revealed that some peer influence occurs due to the rewarding nature of conversations that friends may have about common attitudes. In this work, investigators videotaped conversations between best friends when they were asked to talk about specific topics, such as planning a party, or their favorite activities. They found that much like MTV's *Beavis and Butthead* (Judge, 1993–2011), there is a very specific way that some adolescents talk about and respond to dangerous behavior. Among some teens, the influence process is so strongly biased towards risky or illegal behavior, the researchers called these friendship interactions "deviancy training" (Dishion, Spracklen, Andrews, & Patterson, 1996). Here's how it worked. First, a teen mentions something benign, such as an idea to bring food to a party. Their friend listens, but doesn't really respond. Then, the teen suggests something deviant, such as sneaking drugs into the party. Among some friendship pairs, this elicits a stronger response, "He he…yeah, awesome (smiles, nods)!" In the presence of this positive feedback, the teen ups the ante a bit and takes their idea a step more extreme, "Yeah, like a whole pound of drugs! We can fill our whole trunk, maybe." The friend piles on too now, "He he, dude, let's get everyone high!"

This may seem to confirm myths and about peer interactions and bad decisions. But research suggests that the same processes also can influence teens to engage in well-adjusted, adaptive behavior. In the same studies, researchers found that some teens used the same pattern of utterances and positive reinforcement to promote kind and prosocial behavior (Piehler & Dishion, 2007). This, too, was a powerful influential factor. For instance, when discussing how they might plan a party, some teens indicated that they might invite some peers who rarely get invited to social events. In these cases, their friends responded by smiling, leaning forward, prompting teens to expand upon their ideas and develop even more inventive ways that they could help others who feel socially marginalized. Much like "deviancy training," results suggested that conversations about socially appropriate behaviors are also shaped and motivated by friends' reinforcement, suggesting that the power of our peers is not restricted only to bad decisions.

Another body of psychological research suggests that peers influence one another not only through positively reinforcing conversations, but also by setting the standard for what seems "normal," at least within a subgroup of highly desired peers (Prentice, 2008). Theories regarding these "social norms" suggest that adolescents are most likely to be influenced when they want to seem more like others, so they emulate the behavior of those most popular. If you have ever seen a commercial or a poster indicating that "*most teens don't drink more than two alcoholic beverages on the weekend,*" then you have seen the effects of this "social norm" research in action. By educating adolescents about the behaviors that characterize the majority of teens, adults have hoped to curb drinking habits among those who think they need to drink excessively to be like everyone else.

Some researchers have attempted to use these same processes to examine whether adolescents can be directed towards prosocial behavior. In one study, researchers designed a fictional online "chat room" that was ostensibly occupied by some of participants' most popular grademates (Choukas-Bradley, Giletta, Cohen, & Prinstein, 2015). The teens who participated in the study were led to believe that they were talking live to those whom they most strongly admired, and while in the chat room, they had the chance to answer a series of multiple choice questions. For each item, participants would first see how their popular peers responded before they offered their own answer. The researchers were able to use this approach to examine when teens would conform to their more popular peers, and which behaviors were most easily influenced. The results suggested that most teens were especially likely to emulate their popular peers when it seemed that they were endorsing positive, healthy behavior. For instance, before they entered the chat room, participants were asked how likely they may be to volunteer for community service or help an unpopular classmate. Most were only modestly interested in either of these prosocial acts when asked alone. But when in the chat room, after seeing that their most popular classmates would be highly likely to engage in each of these behaviors, participants changed their minds. They had been influenced to express interest in both of these altruistic acts, and they remained interested even after logging off the chat room (Choukas-Bradley et al., 2015).

What you need to know

We don't hear much about this kind of social influence, so it may not seem like it happens often. But psychologists have discovered that peers and their influence play a strong role in a host of behaviors that shape how adolescents grow up. Through their interactions with peers, teens learn how to interact socially, how to navigate the most complex social dilemmas, how to develop adaptive romantic relationship behaviors, how to negotiate an increasingly complex technological word of gadgets, social media sites, and apps, and even how to cope with harsh events (Prinstein & Giletta, 2015). Teens owe a lot to their peers, and their lives often are better thanks to their influence.

References

Brechwald, W. A., & Prinstein, M. J. (2011). Beyond homophily: A decade of advances in understanding peer influence processes. *Journal of Research on Adolescence, 21*(1), 166–179.

Brown, B. B., Bakken, J. P., Ameringer, S. W., & Mahon, S. D. (2008). A comprehensive conceptualization of the peer influence process in adolescence. In M. J. Prinstein & K. A. Dodge (Eds.), *Understanding peer influence in children and adolescents*. New York, NY: Guilford Press.

Centers for Disease Control and Prevention [CDC] (2015). Youth Risk Behavior Survey Data, Retrieved from https://www.cdc.gov/yrbs

Choukas-Bradley, S., Giletta, M., Cohen, G. L., & Prinstein, M. J. (2015). Peer influence, peer status, and prosocial behavior: An experimental investigation of peer socialization of adolescents' intentions to volunteer. *Journal of Youth and Adolescence, 44*(12), 2197–2210.

Dishion, T. J., Spracklen, K. M., Andrews, D. W., & Patterson, G. R. (1996). Deviancy training in male adolescent friendships. *Behavior Therapy, 27*(3), 373–390.

Hardwicke, C. (Director). (2003). *Thirteen* [Motion picture]. Los Angeles, CA: Fox Searchlight Pictures.

Hartup, W. W. (1996). The company they keep: Friendships and their developmental significance. *Child Development, 67*(1), 1–13.

Hawkins, J. D., Catalano, R. F., & Miller, J. Y. (1992). Risk and protective factors for alcohol and other drug problems in adolescence and early adulthood: Implications for substance abuse prevention. *Psychological Bulletin, 112*(1), 64.

Jewell, J. D., & Hupp, S. D. A. (2018). Prevalence of myths about adolescence [Manuscript in preparation].

Judge, M. (1993–2011). *Beavis and Butthead*. Hollywood, CA: MTV.

Kandel, D. B. (1978). Homophily, selection, and socialization in adolescent friendships. *American Journal of Sociology, 84*(2), 427–436.

King, I. M. (2009). *Pretty Little Liars*. Hollywood, CA: ABC Family.

Piehler, T. F., & Dishion, T. J. (2007). Interpersonal dynamics within adolescent friendships: Dyadic mutuality, deviant talk, and patterns of antisocial behavior. *Child Development, 78*(5), 1611–1624.

Prentice, D. A. (2008). Mobilizing and weakening peer influence as mechanisms for changing behavior. In M. J. Prinstein & K. A. Dodge (Eds.), *Understanding peer influence in children and adolescents*. New York, NY: Guilford Press.

Prinstein, M. J., & Giletta, M. (2015). Peer relations and developmental psychopathology. In D. Cicchetti (Ed.), *Developmental psychopathology, theory and method* (Vol. 1). New York, NY: Wiley.

Stanton, A., & Unkrich, L. (Directors). (2003). *Finding Nemo* [Motion picture]. Los Angeles, CA: Pixar Animation.

Waters, M. (Director). (2004). *Mean Girls* [Motion picture]. Los Angeles, CA: Paramount.

Boys only use sticks and stones to hurt while girls use words instead

Most of us have heard the old saying that "Sticks and stones may break my bones but words will never hurt me." While we don't know the originator of this saying, we imagine that it could be a teacher who's sick and tired of hearing kids tattle on their classmates for teasing them on the playground. But within this adage we can find the definition of two types of aggression that continues to interest society and researchers. The "sticks and stones" symbolize all types of physical aggression that one person might inflict on another, including punching, kicking, shoving, and so on. In contrast, the purportedly harmless words symbolize a variety of ways that kids (or adults for that matter) belittle, demean, verbally harass, spread rumors about, or socially embarrass their victim. Physical aggression can include hitting, kicking, and similar behaviors, while verbal aggression is typically limited to cursing, threatening, or even relationally aggressive behaviors such as making fun of someone or excluding them. Cyberbullying is generally considered a subcategory of relational aggression as it uses electronic means (texting or social media) to achieve its aims.

So while teachers are often full of wisdom, the idea that "words will never hurt us" has been dramatically refuted by recent high profile cases of cyberbullying. For example, in 2003 13-year-old Ryan Halligan hanged himself after experiencing repeated cyberbullying at the hands of a few classmates (Flowers, n.d.). Though Ryan had been bullied for several years, he appeared to have been pushed over the edge when a popular girl in school whom he liked pretended to be interested in him and then shared their private messages with several of her friends (Cohen-Almagor, 2015). A similarly tragic story unfolded when Emilie Olsen committed suicide in December of 2014. Her parents alleged that she was harassed at school by several classmates who even went so far as to create a social media account called "Emilie Olsen is gay" (Wang, 2016). In response to this, her parents have filed a federal lawsuit against administrators and other employees of the school district alleging that the school was negligent and failed to respond to bullying. Emilie's principal resigned suddenly a few months after the lawsuit was filed (Pitman, 2016).

A recent public opinion poll reflects society's concern over bullying and also paints a broader and more complex view of the topic. For example, in a Harris Poll of adults (Birth, 2016), 60% of those polled agreed that "bullying in schools today is more common than when I was in school." Related to cyberbullying, this poll also found that most adults

(86%) believe "technology has made it easier to bully someone," and 60% of adults ages 18–24 who were polled reported being cyberbullied. But society often views indirect, verbal, or relational, aggression, as mostly used by girls, with boys tending to only use physical aggression to bully. In fact, in our own research 85% of undergraduate students had heard of this myth and 71–77% of them agreed with it (Jewell & Hupp, 2018). Perhaps this is not surprising given the media's portrayal of typical aggression in adolescence. For example, the character Biff (played by Thomas Wilson) in the popular movie *Back to the Future* (Zemeckis, 1985) is the stereotypical teen bully who is physically bigger and more physically aggressive than his classmates. The audience is introduced to Biff when he bullies George McFly (played by Crispin Glover) into doing his homework for him. On the other hand, in television's *Gossip Girl* (Hull, 2010) and the movie *Mean Girls* (Waters, 2004), the titles really do say it all. One famous scene showing a teen girl insulting and bullying another is in the musical *Grease* (Kleiser, 1978) where Rizzo mocks her rival Sandra Dee with the song *Look at Me, I'm Sandra Dee*. Ironically, in the song Rizzo taunts Sandra Dee for being a "Miss goody two shoes" and sings "Elvis, Elvis let me be! Keep that pelvis far from me!"

But the research in this area may surprise many. In 2008, a team of researchers (Card, Stucky, Sawalani, & Little, 2008) reviewed 148 existing studies on the topic of both physical and relational aggression in order to answer a number of questions. The total pooled sample size for this meta-analysis was over 50,000 participants. It is probably not surprising to most that their results indicated that boys were more likely to be physically aggressive than girls—and the effect size, or difference, between boys and girls was relatively large. However, when it came to relational aggression the researchers found that the difference between boys and girls was so small that it was negligible. Thus, boys and girls were highly similar when it came to displaying relational aggression such as teasing, spreading rumors, and other similar behavior. Another interesting result of their review was that physical and relational aggression were strongly correlated. In other words, those youth who bully others tend to do so both physically and relationally. To dive deeper into the causes and consequences of bullying, the authors also looked at how prosocial behavior (the type of social behavior we usually think of as good) is related to physical and social aggression, with surprising findings. As one would expect, physical aggression was related to lower prosocial behavior. In contrast, relational aggression was actually related to higher prosocial behavior! So it seems that people who relationally bully others tend to have greater prosocial skills. It may be similar to the idea that kids who are physically bigger may be more likely to physically bully others. However, while those youth who engage in relational aggression appear to have greater prosocial skills, their strategy of using this prosocial behavior to be relationally aggressive does not seem to help them climb the social ladder. Specifically, the authors also found that increased relational aggression was related to lower peer acceptance (Card et al., 2008). So if the goal of relational aggression is to undermine others in order to increase social status, it appears not to work.

Another meta-analysis was conducted by Barlett and Coyne (2014) and focused more specifically on cyberbullying, a type of relational aggression that includes using social media to insult, spread rumors, and so on. The researchers summarized 109 articles on the topic that sampled over 200,000 total participants. Similar to the previous study by Card et al. (2008), Barlett and Coyne found that boys, not girls, were actually slightly more likely to cyberbully, though this difference was again trivial. Therefore, two large reviews of several hundred studies found that boys tend to be more physically aggressive than girls, but that boys and girls are about equal in their levels of cyberbullying or other forms of relational aggression.

What you need to know

No matter what the gender of the bully or type of bullying, the subject remains a critical one for adolescents. Research has found a number of systemic causes to bullying in schools. Hong and Espelage (2012) found several individual and broader factors that can either put youth at higher risk for bullying or can protect them from it. For instance, these authors point to the middle school and early high school years as when the most bullying occurs; thus, prevention and intervention efforts could be most useful if focused on those grades. A building literature shows that youth identifying as LGBTQ are at a much higher risk of being bullied compared with their heterosexual peers. Similarly, youth who are overweight or obese are also at greater risk of being bullied. Factors within the family also appear to predict whether a child or adolescent will experience bullying. For example, if a child has been neglected or abused he or she is more likely to be bullied by peers. Witnessing domestic violence between parents also increases the risk of the youth engaging in bullying as well as being a victim of bullying. In contrast, stronger relationships with peers as well as greater feelings of school connectedness decrease the likelihood of being bullied (Hong & Espelage, 2012).

Several school-wide programs have been found to be effective for preventing bullying in schools. For example, the United States Substance Abuse and Mental Health Services Administration (SAMHSA) lists several evidence-based programs on the National Registry of Evidence-based Programs and Practices (www.nrepp.samhsa.gov) to prevent bullying in schools, improve peer relations, and increase feelings of school connectedness. Two examples are the Creating a Peaceful School Learning Environment (CAPSLE; Twemlow, Sacco, & Twemlow, 1999) program as well as the Steps to Respect program (Committee for Children, 2001) that have both been found effective at decreasing bullying victimization and improving school climate and peer relationships (Brown, Low, Smith & Haggerty, 2011; Fonagy et al., 2009). But the public's attitude towards programs such as this may be part of the problem. For example, if we return to the Harris Poll previously cited, 61% of polled adults agreed that "overprotecting school age children from bullying could be bad for their ability to stand up for themselves." Additionally, although 74% of adults polled believed that ignoring bullying is a bad strategy, that also means that 26% of adults polled believed it was a *good* strategy. These findings are perhaps disheartening given that we generally rely on parents, teachers, and other adults to teach children and teens what is socially acceptable. So if youth aren't taught these lessons before they grow up, they're unlikely to learn them as adults.

References

Barlett, C., & Coyne, S. M. (2014). A meta-analysis of sex differences in cyber-bullying behavior: The moderating role of age. *Aggressive Behavior*, 40(5), 474–488.

Birth, A. (2016). Bullying in schools: A growing problem? Americans think so. Retrieved from http://www.theharrispoll.com/health-and-life/Bullying-in-Schools-Growing-Problem.html

Brown, E. C., Low, S., Smith, B. H., & Haggerty, K. P. (2011). Outcomes from a school-randomized controlled trial of Steps to Respect: A bullying prevention program. *School Psychology Review*, 40(3), 423–443.

Card, N. A., Stucky, B. D., Sawalani, G. M., & Little, T. D. (2008). Direct and indirect aggression during childhood and adolescence: A meta-analytic review of gender differences, intercorrelations, and relations to maladjustment. *Child Development*, 79(5), 1185–1229.

Cohen-Almagor, R. (2015). *Confronting the internet's dark side: Moral and social responsibility on the free highway*. Cambridge: Cambridge University Press.

Committee for Children (2001). *Steps to respect: A bullying prevention program*. Seattle, WA: Author.

Flowers, J. (n.d.). Cyber-bullying hits community. Retrieved from http://www. addisonindependent.com/node/280

Fonagy, P., Twemlow, S. W., Vernberg, E. M., Nelson, J. M., Dill, E. J., Little, T. D., & Sargent, J. A. (2009). A cluster randomized controlled trial of child-focused psychiatric consultation and a school systems-focused intervention to reduce aggression. *Journal of Child Psychology and Psychiatry, 50*(5), 607–616.

Hong, J. S., & Espelage, D. L. (2012). A review of research on bullying and peer victimization in school: An ecological system analysis. *Aggression and Violent Behavior, 17*(4), 311–322.

Hull, R. (Writer). (2010, October 11). Goodbye, Columbia [Television series episode]. In *Gossip Girl*. New York, NY: The CW.

Jewell, J. D., & Hupp, S. D. A. (2018). Prevalence of myths about adolescence [Manuscript in preparation].

Kleiser, R. (Director). (1978). *Grease* [Motion picture]. Hollywood, CA: Paramount Pictures.

Pitman, M. D. (2016). Failed principal accused in Emilie Olsen lawsuit resigns. Retrieved from http://www.journal-news.com/news/news/local/fairfield-principal-accused-in-emilie-olsen-lawsui/nrPdY

Twemlow, S. W., Sacco, F. C., & Twemlow, S. W. (1999). *Creating a peaceful school learning environment: A training manual for elementary schools*. Agawam, MA: T & S Publishing.

Wang, Y. (2016). After years of alleged bullying, an Ohio teen killed herself. Is her school responsible? Retrieved from https://www.washingtonpost.com/news/morning-mix/wp/2016/05/23/after-years-of-alleged-bullying-an-ohio-teen-killed-herself-is-her-school-district-responsible

Waters, M. (Director). (2004). *Mean girls* [Motion picture]. Hollywood, CA: Paramount Pictures.

Zemeckis, R. (Director). (1985). *Back to the future* [Motion picture]. Hollywood, CA: Universal Pictures.

Mini myths for the social environment

Myth #34   Most teens have a strained relationship with their parents

In the last of the original Harry Potter books, J. K. Rowling gives readers a glimpse of Harry as a married adult with children. And the newest story in this world, *Harry Potter and the Cursed Child* (a stage play), shares the story of Harry's "cursed" 14-year-old son, Albus, living in the shadow of his famous dad. Evidence of their strained relationship peaks when Albus tells Harry, "I just wish you weren't my dad" (Thorne, Rowling, &

Tiffany, 2016, p. 41). Harry responds by saying, "Well, there are times I wish you weren't my son" (Thorne et al., 2016, p. 41), a comment he immediately regrets. Soon thereafter, Albus embarks on a journey that Harry does not approve.

The strained relationship of teenagers with their parents has been common fodder for fiction for many decades. The five different teenagers in the movie *The Breakfast Club* (Tanen & Hughes, 1985) gradually bond over something they realize they have in common. Andrew, "the athlete," hates his father because of the pressure he applies to succeed in sports. Brian, "the brain," doesn't like either of his parents because of the academic pressure they put on him. Claire, "the princess," thinks her parents don't care about her because they use her to get back at each other when arguing. Allison, "the basket case," is ignored by her parents, and John, "the criminal," is physically and emotionally abused by his father.

Along with the adolescent storm-and-stress issues of mood disruptions and risky behavior, there is a third storm-and-stress aspect—like the experience of the members of The Breakfast Club, is the idea that most teenagers have frequent conflict with their parents (Arnett, 1999). Some conflict between adolescents and parents is inevitable, but does this conflict define the relationship for most families?

According to Anna Freud (1946), who was once the teenage daughter to Sigmund Freud, adolescent–parent conflict is inevitable and lasts for years. However, in a review of 17 adolescent–parent conflict studies spanning over 50 years it was concluded that only about 15–20% of these relationships involve serious conflict (Montemayor, 1983). Further, for the majority of the families, there were only a few topics of conflict. In a more recent study about adolescent–parent conflict, 67% of adolescents were found to have a secure relationship with their parents and this finding was consistent with previous research (Dykas, Woodhouse, Ehrlich, & Cassidy, 2010). Overall, although some conflict between adolescents and parents is normal, the majority of adolescents have a positive relationship with their parents.

References

Arnett, J. J. (1999). Adolescent storm and stress, reconsidered. *American Psychologist*, 54(5), 317–326.

Dykas, M. J., Woodhouse, S. S., Ehrlich, K. B., & Cassidy, J. (2010). Do adolescents and parents reconstruct memories about their conflict as a function of adolescent attachment? *Child Development*, 81(5), 1445–1459.

Freud, A. (1946). *The ego and the mechanisms of defence*. New York, NY: International Universities Press.

Montemayor, R. (1983). Parents and adolescents in conflict: All families some of the time and some families most of the time. *The Journal of Early Adolescence*, 3(1–2), 83–103.

Tanen, N. (Producer), & Hughes, J. (Producer & Director). (1985). *The Breakfast Club* [Motion picture]. Hollywood, CA: A&M Films.

Thorne, J., Rowling, J. K., & Tiffany, J. (2016). *Harry Potter and the cursed child: Parts one and two*. New York: Arthur A. Levine Books.

Myth #35 — Asking teens if they have thought about suicide "plants a seed" and makes them more likely to actually attempt suicide

Suicide is the second leading cause of death among adolescents ages 10–24 (Centers for Disease Control and Prevention, 2014). And the problem of teen suicide is only growing. From 1999 to 2014 the rate of suicide tripled for youth ages 10–14 and increased by over 50% for youth ages 15–24 (Curtin, Warner, & Hedegaard, 2016). However, it does appear that teens would be open to discussing suicidal thinking with others as a poll of teens found that most (77%) would turn to a peer for help (Gallup, 1991). As such, it is important that we all be open to discussing the possibility of suicide with friends and family members. However, suicide prevention is hindered when we commonly subscribe to the idea that asking a potential suicide victim about it will actually push him or her to commit suicide—creating the "planting the seed" effect. For example, research by Voracek, Tran, and Sonneck (2008) found that about 20% of college students either agreed or were unsure of the statement "If you ask someone directly 'Do you feel like killing yourself?' it will likely lead that person to make a suicide attempt." Similarly, research by Hjelmeland and Knizek (2004) sampled 1,000 adults in Norway and found that a majority of their sample either agreed or were unsure of whether "There is a risk to evoke suicidal thoughts in a person's mind if you ask about it," with similar results in a sample from adults in China (Lee, Tsang, Li, Phillips, & Kleinman, 2007).

So is it true that asking potentially suicidal persons about their risk for suicide will "push them over the edge?" Some of the best research on the topic says no. Specifically, Gould et al. (2005) gathered a sample of over 2,300 high school students and split them into two groups. Although both groups were asked to complete a set of screening measures, one group's measures included questions about suicide while the other group's did not. Two days later both groups completed questionnaires assessing their levels of distress as well as suicidal ideation. The groups did not differ on their distress or suicidal ideation; thus asking about suicide does not appear to increase distress or suicidal ideation two days later. However, researchers went one step further by identifying students in both groups who were at high risk for suicide due to a number of risk factors including previous suicide attempt. Their results ran opposite to that predicted by the myth. Specifically, high risk students actually were less distressed and suicidal two days later when they were asked about suicide as opposed to those high-risk students who had not been asked about suicide. The findings of this study have broad implications for suicide prevention programs since one of the first steps to implementing such a program is to encourage participants to approach their friends and others who appear at risk for suicide. Additional research is also emerging regarding probably efficacious treatments for self-injurious thoughts and behavior (Glenn, Franklin, & Nock, 2015). For more information on how you can support those around you who may be suicidal, visit the Suicide Prevention Resource Center at www.sprc.org/settings.

References

Centers for Disease Control and Prevention (2014). 10 leading causes of death by age group, United States. Retrieved from https://www.cdc.gov/injury/images/lc-charts/leading_causes_of_death_age_group_2014_1050w760h.gif

Curtin, S. C., Warner, M., & Hedegaard, H. (2016). Increase in suicide in the United States, 1999–2014. *NCHS Data Brief*, *241*, 1–8.

Gallup, G. (1991). *The Gallup survey on teenage suicide*. Princeton, NJ: The George H. Gallup International Institute.

Glenn, C. R., Franklin, J. C., & Nock, M. K. (2015). Evidence-based psychosocial treatments for self-injurious thoughts and behaviors in youth. *Journal of Clinical Child & Adolescent Psychology*, *44*(1), 1–29.

Gould, M. S., Marrocco, F. A., Kleinman, M., Thomas, J. G., Mostkoff, K., Cote, J., & Davies, M. (2005). Evaluating iatrogenic risk of youth suicide screening programs: A randomized controlled trial. *Jama*, *293*(13), 1635–1643.

Hjelmeland, H., & Knizek, B. L. (2004). The general public's views on suicide and suicide prevention, and their perception of participating in a study on attitudes towards suicide. *Archives of Suicide Research*, *8*(4), 345–359.

Lee, S., Tsang, A., Li, X. Y., Phillips, M. R., & Kleinman, A. (2007). Attitudes toward suicide among Chinese people in Hong Kong. *Suicide and Life-Threatening Behavior*, *37*(5), 565–575.

Voracek, M., Tran, U. S., & Sonneck, G. (2008). Psychometric properties of the Revised Facts on Suicide Quiz in Austrian medical and psychology undergraduates. *Death Studies*, *32*(10), 937–950.

Myth #36

Teens only listen to their peers

Adolescents tend to spend less time with their parents than they did as children, and they tend to rely more on their friends for advice on certain topics; however, research shows they don't stop listening to their parents altogether. For example, one study asked teens to indicate who they would turn to for discussion about certain topics, and the teens indicated that they preferred to go to their friends to discuss topics related to sex (Youniss & Smollar, 1986). In contrast, they still reported preferring to go to their parents on topics related to school and their career goals (for more discussion on teens' evolving relationship with their parents, see Chapter 30). Even on the topic of sex, parent communication can influence the sexual attitudes and behaviors of adolescents (Holman & Kellas, 2015; Rogers, 2017). Thus, even on topics when teens prefer to listen to their peers, they still listen to their parents as well, at least to some degree.

References

Holman, A., & Kellas, J. K. (2015). High school adolescents' perceptions of the parent–child sex talk: How communication, relational, and family factors relate to sexual health. *Southern Communication Journal, 80*(5), 388–403. doi :10.1080/1041794X.2015.1081976.

Rogers, A. A. (2017). Parent-adolescent sexual communication and adolescents' sexual behaviors: A conceptual model and systematic review. *Adolescent Research Review, 2*(4), 293–313.

Youniss, J., & Smollar, J. (1986). *Adolescent relations with mothers, fathers, and friends*. Chicago, IL: University of Chicago Press.

Myth #37

When girls are sexually assaulted it is usually by a stranger

In the popular television show *Degrassi: The Next Generation* (Yorke & Earnshaw, 2007), a main character Darcy is "roofied" (given a rape drug) and raped by an unknown assailant at a party. The issue of rape is a critical one: Numerous studies have found that between 20% and 25% of female college undergraduates have reported being sexually assaulted (Krebs, Lindquist, Warner, Fisher, & Martin, 2009a, 2009b). But the truth is that stranger-perpetrated sexual assault is actually fairly rare. For example, a 2000 study using a large federal database of crime victims examined the relationship between sexual assault victims and their offenders (Snyder, 2000). For female sexual assault victims ages 12–17, 24% of offenders were a family member, 66% were an acquaintance, and only 10% were a stranger. The same was found for victims ages 18–24, as 10% of offenders were a family member, 66% were an acquaintance, and only 24% were a stranger. Therefore, a large majority (about two out of three) of sexual assaults are perpetrated by acquaintances, such as neighbors, friends, dating partners, and others that are known to the victim. The harm in this myth is that potential sexual assault victims may feel that if they're surrounded by acquaintances or those who know them well, then they will always be safe from assault. Unfortunately, this appears to not be the case. In fact, the problem of rape on college campuses was highlighted in the film *The Hunting Ground* (Dick, 2015). For more information about how you can stand up to sexual assault on college campuses, visit the website of the nonprofit agency End Rape On Campus at endrapeoncampus.org.

References

Dick, K. (Director). (2015). *The Hunting Ground* [Motion picture]. Hollywood, CA: Chain Camera Pictures.

Krebs, C. P., Lindquist, C. H., Warner, T. A., Fisher, B. S., & Martin, S. L. (2009a). College women's experiences with physically forced, alcohol or drug-enabled, and drug-facilitated sexual assault before and since entering college. *Journal of American College Health, 57,* 639–647.

Krebs, C. P., Lindquist, C. H., Warner, T. D., Fisher, B. S., & Martin, S. L. (2009b). The differential risk factors of physically forced and alcohol or other drug enabled sexual assault among university women. *Violence and Victims, 24,* 302–321.

Snyder, H. N. (2000). *Sexual assault of young children as reported to law enforcement: Victim, incident, and offender characteristics [NIBRS statistical report].* Washington, DC: U.S. Department of Justice.

Yorke, B. (Writer), & Earnshaw, P. (Director). (2007). Standing in the dark: Part 1 [Television series episode]. In L. Schuyler, S. Stohn, & B. Yorke (Producers). *Degrassi: The Next Generation.* Toronto, ON: CTVglobemedia.

Myth #38
Most college students graduate in 4 years

While most parents of college students (especially those providing financial support) would like to believe this myth is true, it is not. In fact, the U.S. Department of Education requires universities to report their graduation rate after 6 years, not 4 years, as graduating in 4 years is relatively rare. In 2015, the average 6-year graduation rate for full time undergraduate students at public institutions in the United States was only 59% (U.S. Department of Education, 2017). And this rate was actually up 1% (from 58%) in 2010. Not surprisingly, the 6-year graduation rate differs significantly according to whether the student attends a private nonprofit institution, where the 6-year graduation rate is slightly higher at 66% or a private for-profit institution, which is at a low 6-year graduation rate of 23% (U.S. Department of Education, 2017).

But what about the specific myth that most college students graduate in 4 years? A recent report by the nonprofit agency Complete College America recently stated that "Current on-time graduation rates suggest that the 'four year degree' and the 'two year degree' have become little more than modern myths for far too many of our students" (Complete College America, 2014, p. 4). This same report found that on average in the United States, only 36% of students attending "flagship" state universities graduated in 4 years. This on-time graduation rate was much lower at "nonflagship" state universities at 19%. The study also reported that "Only 50 of the more than 580 four-year public institutions in America have on-time graduation rates at or above 50 percent for their full-time students" (Complete College America, 2014, p. 5). This report encourages universities to implement more curricula with fewer options for electives, and stronger academic advising to decrease the amount of excess credits accrued and shorten time to graduation.

References

Complete College America. (2014). New report: "4-year" degrees now a myth in American higher education. Retrieved from https://completecollege.org/article/new-report-4-year-degrees-now-a-myth-in-american-higher-education

U.S. Department of Education. (2017). The condition of education 2017 (NCES 2017-144), *Undergraduate Retention and Graduation Rates*. Washington, DC: Author, National Center for Education Statistics.

Myth #39

College is the happiest time of one's life

In the television show *Two and a Half Men* (Season 6, Episode 10), young Jake Harper (played by Angus Jones) is riding with his grandmother Evelyn (played by Holland Taylor) as she attempts to motivate him to go to college (Lorre, Aronsohn, & Melman, 2008). She tells the reluctant Jake that "I've already been to college darling. They were some of the happiest years of my life." However, the fact is that this myth is perpetuated by a whole film genre. In films such as *21 & Over* (Burkle, Colbeck, Felts, Lucas, & Moore, 2013) and *Van Wilder* (D'Amico, Foster, von Alvensleben, & Becker, 2002), the college years are characterized as one long, carefree party. However, the truth is different. Yang (2008) examined how ratings of happiness change as one becomes older in a sample of almost 30,000 adults in the United States. The author found that "the average happiness level bottoms out in early adulthood and increases at an increasing rate as one moves through the life course" (p. 217). In other words, happiness dips slightly throughout the college years and then begins to climb throughout the rest of one's life. Yang (2008) found that this trend remains the same no matter what time period one is born in (1945 vs. 1975 for example). So data from this large-scale study indicates that the college years are perhaps not as carefree as one might have assumed. This is likely because college students often experience a host of stresses that include acclimating to living away from family and high school friends, building student loan debt, and juggling studying and working. In fact, a recent study by Sweet, Nandi, Adam, and McDade (2013) found that higher student loan debt was related to a host of psychological and physical problems, including higher rates of depression as well as higher blood pressure, even when they controlled for preexisting psychological and physical health factors. Other research has found similar effects (Walsemann, Gee, & Gentile, 2015). So to all those college students out there—keep your chin up. As Frank Sinatra once sang, "The best is yet to come."

References

Burkle, R., Colbeck, J., Felts, J. (Producers), Lucas, J., & Moore, S. (Directors). (2013). *21 & over* [Motion picture]. Hollywood, CA: Relativity Media.

D'Amico, K., Foster, L., von Alvensleben, P. (Producers), & Becker, W. (Director). (2002). *Van Wilder* [Motion picture]. Hollywood, CA: Myriad Pictures.

Lorre, C., Aronsohn, L. (Writers), & Melman, J. (Director). (2008). He smelled the ham, he got excited. In L. Aronsohn & S. Beavers, *Two and a half men*. Los Angeles, CA: Columbia Broadcasting System.

Sweet, E., Nandi, A., Adam, E. K., & McDade, T. W. (2013). The high price of debt: Household financial debt and its impact on mental and physical health. *Social Science & Medicine, 91*, 94–100.

Walsemann, K. M., Gee, G. C., & Gentile, D. (2015). Sick of our loans: Student borrowing and the mental health of young adults in the United States. *Social Science & Medicine, 124*, 85–93.

Yang, Y. (2008). Social inequalities in happiness in the United States, 1972 to 2004: An age-period-cohort analysis. *American Sociological Review, 73*(2), 204–226.

4 PROBLEMS IN MODERN SOCIETY

Myth #40 Teens these days are worse behaved than those of previous generations

"Kids these days," is a common theme in many contemporary television sitcoms depicting multigenerational families living under one roof. These shows typically portray grandparents grumbling to parents about the incorrigible teenager and his or her loud music, unscrupulous friends, and poor attitude. Take, for example, Grandma Ruby from the ABC comedy

Great Myths of Adolescence, First Edition. Jeremy D. Jewell, Michael I. Axelrod, Mitchell J. Prinstein, and Stephen Hupp.
© 2019 John Wiley & Sons Ltd. Published 2019 by John Wiley & Sons Ltd.

Black-ish, a sitcom about an upper-middle class African American family. She's regularly moaning about her grandchildren's terrible behavior (in Season 3, Episode 6, *Jack of All Trades,* Ruby attempted to perform an exorcism on one of her granddaughters, whose behavior was equated with demonic possession) and objecting to her son's and daughter-in-law's parenting approach, suggesting they're spoiling the children. In the episode *Richard Youngsta* (Season 3, Episode 19), Ruby takes over the chore of preparing the family's meals after learning each kid ordered take-out for dinner. "Sushi, hamburgers, Chinese—which place delivers good parenting?" Ruby says (Saji & Weng, 2017). In a later scene, Ruby unveils a meal of meatloaf and squash, and proclaims that it's either this or nothing.

Spoiled kids complaining to an overzealous grandparent insistent on teaching her grandchildren a lesson in humility hardly compares to what most adults mean when they say, "kids these days." The phrase seems to imply a significant generational difference in teenager behavior and "adults these days" do not appear to have much good to say about today's adolescents. Public opinion polls regularly find that adults have rather poor opinions of adolescents and their behavior, as they frequently acknowledge viewing teenagers as disrespectful, irresponsible, and even wild (Nichols & Good, 2004). For example, 82% of adults surveyed in a large-scale poll believed teenagers have no sense of right or wrong (Bostrom, 2001). In another large-scale survey, the vast majority of adults viewed contemporary teenagers as more selfish than teens 20 years ago (81% vs. 6%), more materialistic (79% vs. 15%), and more reckless (74% vs. 14%; Bostrom, 2001). In our own research with college students, 51–62% of our sample endorsed this myth as well (Jewell & Hupp, 2018). Characterological flaws are also used to explain poor teenage behavior, as adults see today's teens as lacking morals and values (Nichols & Good, 2004). Other explanations involve the interaction between poor character and society's acquiescing to demanding teenagers. A 2012 article in *ScienceNordic,* a publication that provides news on research from Nordic countries, attempted to offer scientific explanations for teen rudeness (Karkov, 2012). The article stated that research points to a self-centered, egocentric generation, "out of touch with some of the fundamental principles of life because teachers, parents, and social workers are worried about infringing the child's autonomy and integrity" (p. 2). Perhaps Grandma Ruby was on to something when she subtly disparaged her daughter-in-law's parenting practices.

Public opinion data also support the claim that adults believe teenager behavior is worsening. A 2013 survey asked a nationally representative sample of 1,038 American adults whether they believed the teen pregnancy rate has increased, decreased, or remained about the same (The National Campaign to Prevent Teen and Unplanned Pregnancy, 2013). Exactly half believed the rate had increased, while 24% thought the rate had remained the same. Other surveys have found adults consider adolescents morally inferior when compared to teenagers from previous generations (Bostrom, 2001). Some authors suggest society has come to fear young people over time. Researcher, writer, and broadcaster Dr. Tanya Brown used the term *ephebiphobia* to describe this phenomenon, suggesting it might be historically rooted (Brown, 2009). She also noted that it's likely worsening to some extreme point. For example, researchers have found that almost 75% of adults believe that adolescents with poor education, poor job prospects, and questionable values are a more serious threat to the United States than threats from abroad (Farkas, Johnson, Duffett, & Bers, 1997). Evidently "kids these days" is now on par with threats of international terrorism.

The myth that adolescents today are worse behaved than those of previous generations might have something to do with how teenagers are portrayed on television. Teen-focused television shows from the 1950s through the 1980s depicted teenagers working with their parents to solve problems (*The Brady Bunch, The Cosby Show*), families that, despite their monstrous flaws, exemplified the term close-knit (*The Munsters, Addams Family*), and kids having fun in suburban America (*Leave it to Beaver, The Donna Reed Show*). Any behavior problems were minor and rectified by the end of the episode. On *Leave It to Beaver*, a pioneering sitcom about two boys growing up in 1950s suburbia, 7-year-old Beaver Cleaver and his 12-year-old brother Wally smuggled a baby alligator into the house. Although mortified by the prospect of a small reptile living in the bathroom, Mr. Cleaver calmly helped the boys solve the problem by contacting a nearby alligator farm. Alex P. Keaton, the adolescent protagonist in the popular 1980s sitcom *Family Ties* about two former hippies raising three kids in suburbia, turned the family's home into a Bed & Breakfast when his parents left town for the weekend. When mom and dad returned from their brief getaway from the children, Alex and his two sisters equally shared the blame. These problems were innocent and generally harmless, and always ended in lessons learned. Moreover, teenagers in these shows were polite, thoughtful, responsible, and honest with their parents.

Unplanned pregnancy (*Secret Life of the American Teenager*), drugs (*Gossip Girl*), and blackmail (*Pretty Little Liars*) are just some of what today's fictional television teenagers experience. Moreover, how adolescent themes are depicted in today's television shows strikes a contrast to the shows of the 50s through 80s. Teenage sex, for example, is presented more graphically on television today than it was 30 or 40 years ago. As a result, today's television shows featuring teenagers often carry a TV-14 rating, compared to the TV-G ratings obtained by most shows in the 80s. Adults watching shows about teenagers today can't help but believe adolescent behavior is significantly more deviant today than it was when they were teenagers. And reality television hasn't helped. Shows like *16 and Pregnant*, *Teen Mom*, and *Brat Camp* confirm what many adults believe about adolescents, that they're insolent, defiant, promiscuous, irresponsible, and often on drugs.

The myth that contemporary teens are worse behaved than those of previous generations is also promoted by a literature suggesting adolescents are more narcissistic, less empathetic, and take less personal responsibility for things that happen to them (Konrath, O'Brien, & Hsing, 2011; Twenge, Zhang, & Im, 2004). However, the potential overinterpretation of a kernel of truth has likely advanced the belief that today's adolescents are morally corrupt. A study examining narcissism (i.e., the tendency to have an unduly positive and inflated view of oneself; social extraversion but with little interest in establishing close relationships with others; a high degree of attention-seeking behavior with the purpose of obtaining fame; resentment and bitterness over others' successes) across samples of college students between 1979 and 2006, conducted via a statistical analysis of 85 studies and 16,475 subjects, found that recent American teenagers scored significantly higher on the Narcissistic Personality Inventory, a survey designed to measure narcissism, than those from previous generations (Twenge, Konrath, Foster, Campbell, & Bushman, 2008). The authors indicated that these results might help to understand the criticisms by older generations that young people are "self-centered, entitled, arrogant, and/or disrespectful" (p. 875). However, the authors of the study also noted that the implications of their findings should be tempered given research suggesting youth crime rates are down and volunteerism among this population is on the rise. Furthermore, several limitations plague this study. First, using a convenience sample of college students hardly allows for the results to generalize to the majority of young people today (Trzesniewski & Donnellan, 2009). Second, the detected differences in Narcissistic Personality Inventory scores across cohorts (e.g., 1980–1985, 2005–2006) were statistically significant. However, the scores, themselves, do not necessarily represent pathological narcissism nor were the differences in scores between cohorts clinically meaningful. Yes, today's young people report being more narcissistic than previous generations but that narcissism is neither extreme nor very different from the narcissism expressed by previous generations of adolescents. In addition, these findings hardly provide solid empirical evidence that kids today are lazier, or more rude and selfish than their parents or grandparents.

Finally, adult misconceptions about today's teenagers might be associated with the tendency to form generalizations about groups of people based on limited but memorable experiences. This tendency might be explained by the availability heuristic, or the idea that people place more weight on highly salient or psychologically accessible experiences, and the confirmation bias, which suggests individuals seek out evidence to confirm their preexisting beliefs, while ignoring evidence that refutes or weakens their beliefs (Trzesniewski & Donnellan, 2009). In the case of this myth, adults are likely to remember a remarkable incident involving a disrespectful teenager, generalize the teenager's behavior to all teenagers, and ignore or forget instances of respectful teenager behavior.

So, what does the literature say about the behavior of teenagers these days? Starting with more common adolescent behavior problems (e.g., arguing with adults, bullying, defiance, lying, physical aggression, theft), research suggests that kids today are not worse behaved than previous generations. Studies comparing behavior problems from national samples of young people across several decades have revealed similar or lower mean scores across all categories of behavior problems across time. Specifically, parent-, teacher-, and self-reports of behavior problems have declined or remained the same since the late 1970s (see Achenbach, Dumenci, & Rescorla, 2002; Larsson & Brugli, 2011; Tick, van der Ende, & Verhulst, 2008; Vieno et al., 2015). For example, a 10-year comparison, from 1989 to 1999, of behavior problems found mean score declines across all problem behavior categories and all informants (i.e., parent, teacher, and youth) (Achenbach, Dumenci, & Rescorla, 2003). The authors concluded adolescents experienced slightly fewer behavior problems in 1999 than in 1989.

These trends are similar for more serious problems involving delinquency (e.g., carrying or using a weapon, gang involvement, substance abuse). Juvenile arrest rates have steadily declined since the mid- to late-1990s (Desilver, 2016) and longitudinal research has found decreases in adolescent alcohol, cigarette, and illicit drug (e.g., marijuana, ecstasy, cocaine, heroin) use over the last several years (Johnston, O'Malley, Miech, Bachman, & Schulenberg, 2016). For example, decline in substance use was noted between 2014 and 2016 for youth in all three grades surveyed (eighth, tenth, and twelfth). Even rates of reported marijuana usage, which has historically shown increases across all three grade levels, decreased (eighth and tenth) or held steady (twelfth grade). Other markers of problem behavior show declines over time. For example, data suggest school homicide rates have decreased slightly between 1992 and 2010 (Centers for Disease Control and Prevention, n.d.-a) and the percentage of adolescents who are not enrolled in school and have not obtained a high school credential (e.g., diploma, GED certificate) dropped from around 12% in 1990 to 6.5% in 2014 (National Center for Educational Statistics, n.d.-a).

Remember previously cited research indicating that about 75% of American adults believe the teen pregnancy rate either increased or remained the same. These data probably shouldn't come as a surprise given popular culture's portrayal of today's adolescents (see MTV's *16 and Pregnant*). However, national adolescent health data tell a very different story. According to The National Campaign to Prevent Teen and Unwanted Pregnancy (2013), the teen pregnancy rate is down 42% since 1990 and the teen birth rate is down 49% since 1991. Data reported by the U.S. Department of Health and Human Services indicate the teen birth rate has declined from 59.9 births per 1,000 females in 1990 to 24.2 births per 1,000 females in 2014 (Martin, Hamilton, & Ventura, 2015). Furthermore, teen birth rates for white, black, and Hispanic females have dropped dramatically between 2007 and 2014. It seems that a majority of American adults were wrong and that the teen pregnancy epidemic doesn't exist.

What's more, research has also found that today's adolescents are rated higher by teachers and parents on measures of social competence and adaptive functioning (Achenbach et al., 2002, 2003). For example, parents describe today's teenager as more skilled in terms of social relationships with others (e.g., parents, siblings, peers) and teachers rate today's teenagers higher on measures of work ethic, school behavior, and happiness compared with previous generations. In addition, research has found that today's youth engage in healthier behavior (e.g., regularly wear seatbelts and condoms) and volunteer more than youth of previous generations (Centers for Disease Control and Prevention, n.d.-b; Lam, 2012). Finally, happiness, loneliness, time spent watching television, and the importance of religion are just some of the behaviors and attitudes that have shown little or no generational change (Trzesniewski & Donnellan, 2009).

The saying "young people of today think of nothing but themselves" could easily come from the mouth of Grandma Ruby or the many adults who view today's adolescents as insolent, irresponsible, incorrigible, and selfish. Yet, research again tells a different story. Today's adolescents are similarly, or in some cases slightly better, behaved than adolescents from previous generations. Accepting this myth as true and ignoring the relevant research might lead to some unintended negative consequences. For example, believing there are noteworthy generational differences in teenagers' behavior has the potential to cause disconnections between adolescents and adults (e.g., parents, teachers). Adults subscribing to the idea that today's teens are worse behaved than those of previous generations might also misinterpret routine adolescent behavior. While it's normal for teenagers to be occasionally self-centered (Jaffe, 1998), adults should recognize that this isn't necessarily a significant problem for most adolescents and many adolescents balance this self-centeredness with prosocial behaviors involving peers and the community (Steinberg, 2011).

And what about that quote about young people thinking of nothing but themselves? It was attributed to Peter the Hermit, way back in the 11th century. This belief might just be the longest running myth in psychology.

What you need to know

Despite public opinion polls, kids these days are "more than all right" (Parker-Pope, 2012). However, some problems of adolescence have persisted over time. Epidemiological studies have found that approximately 20% of adolescents meet diagnostic criteria for a psychiatric disorder (e.g., Attention Deficit Hyperactivity Disorder, Anxiety Disorders, Mood Disorders) and there are increases in rates of disorders from childhood to adolescence (Costello, Copeland, & Angold, 2011). Put differently, some teens experience significant mental health problems, and adolescence, as a developmental stage, appears to be a critical period in the development of certain disorders.

To address these problems, several researchers recommend taking a population-based approach to mental health (e.g., Doll, Cummings, & Chapla, 2014; Patel, Flisher, Hetrick, & McGorry, 2007). This tactic relies on the integration of mental health prevention and intervention services within community and school settings by using a multileveled system of care. Multilevel systems of care allow for comprehensive services to reach all youth. Universal services, delivered by school staff (e.g., teachers, counselors), are designed "to promote psychological wellness and to prevent disturbances" for all students (Doll et al., 2014, p. 158). Community mental health education, another universal service, is recommended as a means of enhancing the understanding of normal adolescent developmental processes, recognition of signs and symptoms of adolescent mental health issues, and knowledge about evidence-based treatments (Patel et al., 2007). For those adolescents in need of additional intervention, the intensity of treatment increases as a function of the intensity of the problems (Doll et al., 2014). Within this model, a continuum of services is offered with an emphasis on collaboration among organizations and providers, the use of evidence-based prevention programs and interventions, and parent and family involvement in treatment.

References

Achenbach, T. M., Dumenci, L., & Rescorla, L. A. (2002). Ten-year comparisons of problems and competencies for national samples of youth: Self, parent, and teacher report. *Journal of Emotional and Behavioral Disorders, 10*, 194–203.

Achenbach, T. M., Dumenci, L., & Rescorla, L. A. (2003). Are American children's problems still getting worse? A 23-year comparison. *Journal of Abnormal Child Psychology, 31*, 1–11.

Bostrom, M. (2001). The 21st century teen: Public perception and teen reality. Retrieved from http://frameworksinstitute.org/assets/files/PDF/youth_public_perceptions.pdf

Brown, T. (2009, March 16). We see children as pestilent. *The Guardian.* Retrieved from https://www.theguardian.com/education/2009/mar/17/ephebiphobia-young-people-mosquito

Centers for Disease Control and Prevention. (n.d.-a). School-associated violent death study. Retrieved from https://www.cdc.gov/ViolencePrevention/youthviolence/schoolviolence/SAVD.html

Centers for Disease Control and Prevention. (n.d.-b). Youth risk behavior surveillance system (YRBSS) overview. Retrieved from https://www.cdc.gov/healthyyouth/data/yrbs/overview.htm

Costello, E. J., Copeland, W., & Angold, A. (2011). Trends in psychopathology across the adolescent years: What changes when children become adolescents, and when adolescent become adults? *Journal of Child Psychology and Psychiatry, 52*, 1015–1025.

Desilver, D. (2016, January). Dangers that teens and kids face: A look at the data. *Pew Research Center.* Retrieved from http://www.pewresearch.org/fact-tank/2016/01/14/dangers-that-young-people-face-a-look-at-the-data

Doll, B., Cummings, J. A., & Chapla, B. A. (2014). Best practices in population-based school mental health services. In P. Harrison, & A. Thomas (Eds.), *Best practices in school psychology: Systems level services* (pp. 149–163). Bethesda, MD: National Association of School Psychologists.

Farkas, S., Johnson, J., Duffett, A., & Bers, A. (1997). *Kids these days: What Americans really think about the next generation.* New York, NY: Public Agenda.

Jaffe, M. L. (1998). *Adolescence*. New York, NY: Wiley.

Jewell, J. D., & Hupp, S. D. A. (2018). Prevalence of myths about adolescence [Manuscript in preparation].

Johnston, L. D., O'Malley, P. M., Miech, R. A., Bachman, J. G., & Schulenberg, J. E. (2016). *Monitoring the future national survey results on drug use, 1975–2016: Overview, key findings on adolescent drug use*. Ann Arbor, MI: Institute for Social Research, The University of Michigan.

Karkov, R. (2012, March 25). Understanding today's rude teens. *ScienceNordic*. Retrieved from http://sciencenordic.com/understanding-today%E2%80%99s-rude-teens

Konrath, S. H., O'Brien, E. H., & Hsing, C. (2011). Changes in dispositional empathy in American college students over time: A meta-analysis. *Personality and Social Psychology Review*, *15*, 180–198.

Lam, C. M. (2012). Prosocial involvement as a positive youth development construct: A conceptual review. *The Scientific World Journal*. Retrieved from https://www.hindawi.com/journals/tswj/2012/769158

Larsson, B., & Brugli, M. B. (2011). School competence and emotional/behavioral problems among Norwegian school children as rated by teachers on the Teacher Report Form. *Scandinavian Journal of Psychology*, *52*, 553–559.

Martin, J. A., Hamilton, B. E., & Ventura, S. J. (2015). *Births: Final data for 2014*. Hyattsville, MD: National Center for Health Statistics.

National Center for Education Statistics. (n.d.). Fast facts. Retrieved from https://nces.ed.gov/fastfacts/display.asp?id=16

Nichols, S. L., & Good, T. L. (2004). *America's teenagers—myths and realities: Media images, schooling, and the social costs of careless indifference*. Mahwah, NJ: Erlbaum.

Parker-Pope, T. (2012). The kids are more than all right. *The New York Times*. Retrieved from https://well.blogs.nytimes.com/2012/02/02/the-kids-are-more-than-all-right/?_r=0

Patel, V., Flisher, A. J., Hetrick, S., & McGorry, P. (2007). Mental health of young people: A global health challenge. *Lancet*, *369*, 1302–1313.

Saji, P., & Weng, J. (2017). Richard Youngsta [Television series episode]. In M. Petok (Producer), *Black-ish*. Los Angeles, CA: ABC Studios.

Steinberg, L. (2011). *Adolescence* (9th ed.). New York, NY: McGraw-Hill.

The National Campaign to Prevent Teen and Unwanted Pregnancy (2013). *Survey says: The greatest story never told*. Washington, DC: Author.

Tick, N. T., van der Ende, J., & Verhulst, F. C. (2008). Ten-year trends in self-reported emotional and behavioral problems of Dutch adolescents. *Social Psychiatry and Psychiatric Epidemiology*, *43*, 349–355.

Trzesniewski, K. H., & Donnellan, M. D. (2009). Are today's young people really that different from previous generations? A skeptical perspective on "generation me." *The Jury Expert: The Art and Science of Litigation Advocacy*, *21*, 1–11.

Twenge, J. M., Konrath, S., Foster, J. D., Campbell, W. K., & Bushman, B. J. (2008). Egos inflating over time: A cross-temporal meta-analysis of the Narcissistic Personality Inventory. *Journal of Personality*, 76, 875–901.

Twenge, J. M., Zhang, L., & Im, C. (2004). It's beyond my control: A cross-temporal meta-analysis of increasing externality in locus of control, 1960–2002. *Personality and Social Psychology Review*, 8, 308–319.

Vieno, A., Lenzi, M., Gini, G., Pozzoli, T., Cavallo, F., & Santinello, M. (2015). Time trends in bulling behavior in Italy. *Journal of School Health*, 85, 441–445.

Myth #41

School violence is on the rise

Schools are no longer safe places—at least that's what the kids from South Park (Parker, 2015), an animated television series starring four foul-mouthed fourth-graders, would have you believe. "We have to get guns," Kyle says to his friends. "It's the only way for us to be safe." Later, after the boys have secured various firearms, one of them says, "I already feel a lot safer."

Television, movies, and popular music frequently depict schools as dangerous, fearful, and violent places. "Have you seen those high school fights on YouTube?" asks a geeky freshman in the 2008 comedy *Drillbit Taylor* (Apatow, Arnold, Roth, & Brill, 2008). "Kids are brutal," replies his equally geeky friend as the two consider hiring a bodyguard, played by Owen Wilson, for protection. More serious teen television dramas, like *Glee* and *Degrassi*, have devoted episodes (several episodes in *Degrassi's* case) to school gun violence and lyrics like "you better run, better run, outrun my gun" from the 2001 song *Pumped Up Kicks* (Foster, 2009) by Foster the People about a school shooting would have anyone fearing to go to school. And media examples like this have helped make this one of our most endorsed myths, with 73–82% of our college student sample agreeing with it (Jewell & Hupp, 2018).

It's not surprising the boys from South Park perceive their school as unsafe. Research suggests that more American teenagers are reporting feeling unsafe at school now than ever before (Nichols & Good, 2004). And these statistics aren't particular to the United States. In a 2006 study, almost 43% of Canadian teenagers surveyed reported that violence always or often occurs in their school (Joong & Ridler, 2006). Kids aren't the only ones worried about violence in schools. A 2001 study found that half of surveyed American parents believed a shooting could happen in their teenager's school (Gallup, 2001). That's a stunning number. Even Wikipedia reports school violence "has become a serious problem in recent decades" (Wikipedia, n.d.).

The news media hasn't helped. It portrays schools as dangerous and unsafe. Headlines like "Assistant Principal, Guard Tackled Student with Knife" (Johnson, 2014), "Girls Arrested for planning Attack the Teacher Day" (Matyszczyk, 2011), "Kid Brings BB Gun to School to Scare Bullies" (Hibbard, 2012), and "Teen Stabbed to Death, 3 Hurt in Texas School Fight" (Stanglin, 2013) conjure up images of school hallways transformed into gladiator pits where only the strongest survive. High-profile school violence cases, especially those that involve shootings, bring to the spotlight concerns about a school violence epidemic. How can we not believe our schools are overrun with violence after reading about a 15-year-old Birmingham, England boy being stabbed at school by two classmates (Authi, 2016) or two high school students in Virginia who were attacked near their school by a local gang of teenagers (Dellinger, 2017)?

The publicizing of school violence has not been isolated to the media. In the United States, the response to high-profile school violence cases has resulted in government hearings, FBI and Secret Service studies, government agency guidebooks, a U.S. Surgeon General Report and a White House conference (Cornell, n.d.). Governments in Europe and elsewhere (e.g., Australia) regularly convene similar meetings to define the problem and develop state-sponsored intervention programs to address the "rise in school violence" (see Slee, 2003). Local responses to the supposed school violence epidemic have typically involved schools enhancing building security. During the 2013–2014 school year, 93% of school officials reported having controlled access to their buildings and 75% reported using cameras as a security measure, while 11% of students reported being subjected to random metal detector checks (Zhang, Musu-Gillette, & Oudekerk, 2016). Schools have also adopted zero tolerance philosophies, often involving severe and punitive responses to student misbehavior, to ensure student and staff safety (American Psychological Association (APA) Zero Tolerance Task Force, 2008). And all of this has occurred since the 1990 federal Gun-Free School Zones Act that prohibits unauthorized individuals from knowingly possessing a firearm within a designated school zone.

Authors on the subject have also highlighted the frequency and significance of school violence in the US. Johnson and Johnson, in their 1995 book *Reducing School Violence Through Conflict Resolution*, reported the number of violent incidents in schools was increasing (Johnson & Johnson, 1995). They cited a 1994 National League of Cities report that found 33% of member cities indicated school violence had increased markedly between 1990 and 1994 (45% of cities reported that violence in schools had remained the same, 6% indicated school violence had decreased, and 11% said school violence was not a problem in their city). The authors, writing for a general audience but speaking to school administrators and teachers, suggested violence in communities and schools was so common that it might be considered the norm rather than the exception, a perspective that appears consistent with the media's account and popular culture's portrayal of school violence.

To dispel the myth, it might make sense to begin with student homicide rates. While we would all agree that one person killed in school is too many, research indicates school homicides are actually low. One study, using 18,875 homicide incident reports documented in the Federal Bureau of Investigation's National Incident Based Reporting System (NIBRS) between 2005 and 2010, found only 49 homicides (youth or adult), or less than 0.3%, occurred in schools (Nekvasil, Cornell, & Huang, 2015). In contrast, almost 3% of all homicides occurred in restaurants or bars, suggesting a person is almost 10 times more likely to be murdered in these locations than a school. Moreover, a staggering 52% of homicides occurred in the home suggesting people are 173 times less safe at home. Other research suggests that homicides in schools that are specific to students are also rare. During the 2012–2013 school year, only 31 of the 1,186 youth homicides (2.6%) occurred at school (Zhang et al., 2016). Regarding trends, the Centers for Disease Control (n.d.) cited data indicating that between the 1992–1993 and 2009–2010 school years, school-associated youth homicides ranged from a low of 14 in 1999–2000 and 2000–2001 to a high of 34 in 1992–1993. During the first 5 years of reported data (i.e., 1992–1993 to 1996–1997), there were an average of 30 youth homicides at school per year. During the last 5 years (i.e., 2005–2006 to 2009–2010), there were an average of 21 youth homicides at school per year suggesting a slight downward trend. So, when considering the data, there is a consensus that homicides in schools are largely infrequent.

Unfortunately, the number of active shooter incidents (i.e., incidents in which an individual killed or attempted to kill people in a confined and populated area) in schools and the annual total number of casualties as a result of active school shooter incidents has increased in recent years. According to an FBI report, there were no active school shooter incidents between 2007 and 2009 but 10 incidents with 48 casualties between 2010 and 2013 (Blair & Schweit, 2014). Following the Marjory Stoneman Douglas High School trajedy in Parkland, Florida, NBC News compiled a list of school shooting incidents occurring during the first 6 weeks of 2018 and found that there was a total of eight incidents involving 51 casualties (Ruiz, 2018). Taken altogether, data on school shootings over time are unclear. Although trends over a long period of time appear to be relatively stable, more recent data would suggest increases in the number of school shooting incidents and the total number of casualties.

Regarding nonfatal student victimization, youth ages 12–18 are more likely to experience incidents of petty theft, simple assault, and crimes of rape, robbery, and aggravated assault at school versus away from school (33 nonfatal victimizations per 1,000 students at school in 2014 versus 24 per 1,000 students away from school that same year; Zhang et al., 2016). Considering a high school of 2,000 students, there are likely about 66 nonfatal victimizations in one school year, which sounds like a lot. However, most of the crimes reported in schools involve thefts without threat or use of force. Moreover, these reports include attempted and completed thefts, which may account for the high number. For example, in 2013, about 3% of youth ages 12–18 reported being a victim of a crime at school during the previous 6 months, with most reports involving petty theft (Zhang et al., 2016). Regarding serious violent crimes, the rate is about 5 students in 1,000. Regarding fighting at school, about 8% of high school students reported being in a physical altercation with another student while on school property (Kann et al., 2015). Again, while one violent crime in a school is too many, research indicates that violence in schools is infrequent. As with student homicides in schools, nonfatal student victimization has gone down. Data show the number of students ages 12–18 reporting victimization during the previous 6 months dropped from 10% in 1995 to 3% in 2013 (Zhang et al., 2016). Moreover, fewer high school students reported being the victim of theft (from 7% to 2%), violent victimization (from 3% to 1%), or serious violent crimes (from 1% to less than 0.5%; Zhang et al., 2016). These findings are consistent with national data indicating an overall decline in violent crime in the US (Cornell, n.d.).

If schools are, in fact, dangerous and unsafe, we might expect to see high percentages of students reporting being afraid to attend school. However, the data tell a very different story. Students reporting being fearful of attack or harm while at school dropped from 12% in 1995 to 3% in 2013 (Zhang et al., 2016). In addition, approximately 5% of students reported during the 2012–2013 school year avoiding at least one school activity or class or one or more places while at school because of concern about being attacked or harmed (Zhang et al., 2016). These data are consistent with a 2015 national survey of American high school students that found just under 6% of respondents indicated not going to school because they considered school unsafe (Kann et al., 2015).

Consistent with student data, the majority of teachers also report feeling safe at school (Joong & Ridler, 2006).

There are numerous reasons why people are prone to believing school violence is on the rise including the reporting of high-profile cases, especially school shootings, by the media. Popular culture's depiction of schools as violent places where bullies run free also contributes to the myth that school violence is an epidemic. However, there are some other, less obvious, sources of this myth. For example, the availability heuristic might explain why many people vividly remember the parking lot fights from their high school days and most can't forget the news stories about tragic school shootings. People's selective memories ignore all those times they've been in a school building and witnessed civility or, at least, the absence of violence. People tend to remember incidents that support the myth, while overlooking evidence to the contrary (Lilienfeld, Lynn, Ruscio, & Beyerstein, 2010). We are also frequently exposed to biased samples. Schools rarely show up on the front page of *Yahoo! News* because a specific school violence prevention initiative has been effective or that a school has been free of violent incidents for some period of time. Schools are typically featured in the news media because of something negative. This exposure within the news media might lead someone to believe that many schools experience significant problems with violence, rather than recognizing that the majority of schools are safe and secure places for students and teachers. More Americans are saying there is more crime in this country despite data indicating a decrease in violent crime victimization rates (Gallup, 2015). It's not surprising that the same is true for school violence. Finally, myths can be propagated by authority figures. For example, Dewey Cornell (n.d.), writing about school violence myths, began by discussing a school survey describing the top problems in schools in the 1940s including talking, chewing gum, and running in the hallway. The list was contrasted with a survey of school problems from 1980s and 1990s such as drug abuse, teen pregnancy, and violence. The comparison of problems by era was used by politicians and political commentators to highlight the apparent deterioration of America's public schools. Barry O'Neill (1994), a Yale University professor who investigated the sources of the two lists, eventually found the surveys to be a fraud circulated by a Texas oil tycoon in an effort to condemn public education. Sadly, and troublingly, someone from the U.S. Department of Education cited the surveys in a keynote address at a 2001 conference on school safety. Imagine being in the audience that day as an apparent authority on education cited data that were fabricated.

Despite the myth that school violence is on the rise, schools must still work to keep students safe. School security measures, like those described above, and disciplinary policies involving zero tolerance philosophies have become common approaches to maintaining school safety and some might conclude that these approaches are effective because they coincide with decreases in school violence. However, the rates of violent crimes among youth is the lowest it's been in some time and there is a decreasing trend in juvenile arrests. So, it appears the trends in school violence are related to broader trends in youth violence. In addition, 20 years of high-quality research have failed to find heightened school security measures and the use of zero tolerance policies effective at improving school safety. For example, research has found that school security measures involving metal detectors, cameras, and security guards fail to reduce school violence but are associated with higher rates of crime (Nickerson & Martens, 2008; Schreck, Miller, & Gibson, 2003). Moreover, such attempts at keeping students safe have adversely affected perceptions of school safety and factors related to school climate (e.g., relationships between teachers and students; National Association of School Psychologists (NASP), 2013).

Regarding zero tolerance, the APA Zero Tolerance Task Force (2008), following an exhaustive review of the literature, concluded that strict and overly punitive disciplinary policies did not make schools safer. Rather, these disciplinary practices, especially the use of suspension and expulsion for students who violate rules, failed to produce more positive school climate ratings (APA Zero Tolerance Task Force, 2008). Zero tolerance practices were also associated with lower academic achievement and increases in student misbehavior (Skiba & Rausch, 2006; Tobin, Sugai, & Colvin, 1996). Finally, research suggests that zero tolerance philosophies in schools might "create, enhance, or accelerate negative mental health outcomes for youth by creating increases in student alienation, anxiety, rejection, and breaking of healthy adult bonds" (APA Zero Tolerance Task Force, 2008; p. 856).

What you need to know

While instances of school violence are largely uncommon, there are still violence-related school tragedies and concerns about the safety of students and staff in schools. Most school safety experts highlight the importance of prevention, appropriate responses to violence when it occurs, and long-term follow-up that focuses on the health and wellbeing of those involved. For example, NASP recommends schools implement school violence response programs that stress prevention, preparedness, appropriate emergency response, and recovery. Their own program, called the *PREPaRE (Prevent, Reaffirm, Evaluate, Provide and Response, Examine) School Crisis Prevention and Intervention Training Curriculum* (Brock et al., 2009), combines research supported practices with community-school collaboration. *PREPaRE* and other holistic models (e.g., the *Response to School Violence Plan (RSVP)*, Leh, 2016) highlight the importance of implementing comprehensive and preventative school-wide programs that encourage positive student behavior, teach important social skills, and reduce problem behavior through implementation of effective interventions. In addition, these programs emphasize being prepared for emergencies through training and practice, effective emergency response systems (e.g., the National Incident Management System's Incident Command Structure), and appropriate follow-up for those in need of psychological treatment. Finally, school–community partnerships are critical to addressing prevention, response, and follow-up needs. Many programs recommend schools establish relationships with law enforcement personnel, first responders, and community mental health providers, and engage collaboratively in problem-solving and managing school violence incidents.

Experts also agree that prevention programs that improve school climate by improving students' school connectedness and sense of belonging can profoundly impact school discipline and safety (see Osher, Sandler, & Nelson, 2001). Research consistently finds that school alienation is an important factor in the development of juvenile delinquency and school violence (Baker, 1998; Catalono, Haggerty, Oesterle, Fleming, & Hawkins, 2004). *PREPaRE* and *RSVP* underscore the need to support students exhibiting problem behavior or who are identified with psychological disorders (e.g., anxiety, depression) rather than using tactics that punish or ignore. For example, rewarding positive, prosocial behavior via attention and small incentives or rewards has been demonstrated to be a more effective behavior change strategy than exclusively punishing undesirable behavior (see Axelrod, 2017). In addition, effective classroom discipline involving effective instructional practices and classroom management enhances learning and reduces student misbehavior (Jones & Jones, 2004). Schools that are high in academic achievement are typically low in disciplinary referrals and violent incidents.

Rather than implement ineffective zero tolerance policies that remove students entirely from the education system, school officials might consider flexible disciplinary practices that account for individual student circumstances and contextual factors. One-size-fits-all discipline does not appear to work. Administrators and teachers should work together on defining problems and collaborating on whether specific problems are best handled in the classroom or with an office disciplinary referral. Schools are also encouraged to consider a continuum of intervention services for those students who are frequently disruptive or more prone to violent behavior (APA Zero Tolerance Task Force, 2008). For example, alternative schools for at-risk students have higher academic achievement and lower dropout rates than community schools, especially when the alternative school program focuses on students' strengths and resources (see Franklin, Streeter, Kim, & Tripodi, 2007).

If the South Park boys had carefully examined the research on school violence and school violence trends they would have learned schools are actually safe for youth and teachers, rather than the dangerous places depicted in popular culture and the news media. They would have also learned that zero tolerance policies and school security measures, often employed by schools to curb violence, have limited support in the literature. Educators, although perhaps not those in the South Park School District, are fortunate that research has provided guidance regarding effective school safety practices. Maybe in an upcoming episode Kyle will exclaim, "we have to get sensible school discipline policies that promote a positive school climate" rather than "we have to get guns."

References

American Psychologial Association Zero Tolerance Task Force (2008). Are zero tolerance policies effective in the schools? *American Psychologist*, *63*, 852–862.

Apatow, J., Arnold, S., Roth, D. A., & Brill, S. (2008). *Drillbit Taylor* [Motion picture]. Hollywood, CA: Paramount Pictures.

Authi, J. (2016, November 10). Two teenagers arrested after boy stabbed at Erdington school. *Birmingham Mail*. Retrieved from http://www.birminghammail.co.uk/news/midlands-news/two-teenagers-arrested-after-boy-12159378

Axelrod, M. I. (2017). *Behavior analysis for school psychologists*. New York, NY: Routledge.

Baker, J. A. (1998). Are we missing the forest for the trees? Considering the social context of school violence. *Journal of School Psychology*, *36*, 29–44.

Blair, J. P., & Schweit, K. W. (2014). A study of active shooter incidents, 2000–2013. Washington, DC: Texas State University and the Federal Bureau of Investigation, U.S. Department of Justice.

Brock, S. E., Nickerson, A. B., Reeves, M. A., Jimerson, S. R., Lieberman, R. A., & Feinberg, T. A. (2009). *School crisis prevention and intervention: The PREPaRE model*. Bethesda, MD: National Association of School Psychologists.

Catalano, R. F., Haggerty, K. P., Oesterle, S., Fleming, C. B., & Hawkins, J. D. (2004). The importance of bonding to school for health development: Findings from the social development research group. *Journal of School Health, 74*, 252–261.

Centers for Disease Control. (n.d.). School-associated violent death study. Retrieved from https://www.cdc.gov/ViolencePrevention/youthviolence/schoolviolence/SAVD.html

Cornell, D. (n.d.). Myths about school violence. Retrieved from http://curry.virginia.edu/research/projects/violence-in-schools/school-violence-myths

Dellinger, H. (2017, May 7). Court records: Manassas boys attached by South Side gang members after school. *Prince William Times*. Retrieved from http://www.fauquier.com/prince_william_times/news/court-records-manassas-boys-attacked-by-south-side-gang-members/article_c5567824-3317-11e7-82d8-bf179dbb727c.html

Foster, M. (2009). *Pumped up the kicks [Recorded by Foster the People]*. New York, NY: Columbia.

Franklin, C., Streeter, C. L., Kim, J. S., & Tripodi, S. J. (2007). The effectiveness of a solution-focused, public alternative school for dropout prevention and retrieval. *Children & Schools, 29*, 133–144.

Gallup. (2001). Majority of parents think a school shooting could occur in their community. Retrieved from http://www.gallup.com/poll/1936/majority-parents-think-school-shooting-could-occur-their-community.aspx

Gallup. (2015). More Americans say crime is rising in U.S. Retrieved from http://www.gallup.com/poll/186308/americans-say-crime-rising.aspx

Hibbard, L. (2012, April 19). Ohio boy brings BB gun to elementary school to scare bullies. *The Huffington Post*. Retrieved from http://www.huffingtonpost.com/2012/04/19/ohio-school-bb-gun-bullies_n_1438333.html

Jewell, J. D., & Hupp, S. D. A. (2018). Prevalence of myths about adolescence [Manuscript in preparation].

Johnson, D. W., & Johnson, R. T. (1995). *Reducing school violence through conflict resolution*. Alexandria, VA: Association for Supervision and Curriculum Development.

Johnson, J. (2014, April 9). Assistant principal, guard tackled student with knife. *Newser*. Retrieved from http://www.newser.com/story/185097/assistant-principal-guard-tackled-student-with-knife.html

Jones, V., & Jones, L. (2004). *Comprehensive classroom management: Creating communities of support and solving problems* (7th ed.). Boston, MA: Allyn & Bacon.

Joong, P., & Ridler, O. (2006). Teachers' and students' perceptions of school violence and prevention. *Brock Education, 15*, 65–83.

Kann, L., McManus, T., Harris, W. A., Shanklin, S. L., Flint, K. H., Hawkins, J., ... Zaza, S. (2015). Youth risk behavior surveillance—United States, 2015. *MMWR Surveillance Summaries 2016, 65*(SS–06), 1–174.

Leh, J. M. (2016). The RSVP model: Lifting the veil on school violence. In G. A. Crews (Ed.), *Critical examinations of school violence and disturbance in K-12 education* (pp. 234–256). Hershey, PA: IGI Global.

Lilienfeld, S. O., Lynn, S. J., Ruscio, J., & Beyerstein, B. L. (2010). *50 great myths of popular psychology: Shattering widespread misconceptions about human behavior*. Malden, MA: Wiley-Blackwell.

Matyszczyk, C. (2011, January 8). Facebook "attack a teacher day" invite gets girls arrested. c/net. Retrieved from https://www.cnet.com/news/facebook-attack-a-teacher-day-invite-gets-girls-arrested

National Association of School Psychologists (NASP) (2013). *Research on school security: The impact of security measures on students*. Bethesda, MD: Author Retrieved from https://www.nasponline.org/research-and-policy/nasp-research-center/research-summaries/research-summaries-school-safety

Nekvasil, E. K., Cornell, D. G., & Huang, F. L. (2015). Prevalence and offense characteristics of multiple causality homicides: Are schools at higher risk than other locations? *Psychology of Violence, 5*, 236–245.

Nichols, S. L., & Good, T. L. (2004). *America's teenagers—myths and realities: Media images, schooling, and the social costs of careless indifference*. Mahwah, NJ: Erlbaum.

Nickerson, A. B., & Martens, M. P. (2008). School violence: Associations with control, security/enforcement, education/therapeutic approaches, and demographic factors. *School Psychology Review, 37*, 228–243.

O'Neill, B. (1994, March 6). The history of the hoax. *The New York Times Magazine*, pp. 46–49.

Osher, D. M., Sadnler, S., & Nelson, C. L. (2001). The best approach to safety is to fix schools and support children and staff. In R. J. Skiba & G. G. Noam (Eds.), *New directions for youth development: vol. 92 Zero tolerance: Can suspension and expulsion keep schools safe?* (pp. 127–153). San Francisco, CA: Jossey-Bass.

Parker, T. (Writer and Director). (2015). PC principal final justice [Television series episode]. In T. Parker, M. Stone, A. Garefino, V. Chatman, A. Beard, B. Howell, ... G. Martinez (Producers), *South Park*. Los Angeles, CA: Comedy Central Productions.

Ruiz, R. (2018, February 15). At least one a month: Tracking all the school shooting incidents in 2018. *NBC News*. Retrieved from https://www.nbcnews.com/news/us-news/tracking-all-school-shooting-incidents-2018-n844786

Schreck, C. J., Miller, J. M., & Gibson, C. L. (2003). Trouble in the school yard: A study of the risk factors of victimization at school. *Crime & Delinquency, 49*, 460–484.

Skiba, R. J., & Rausch, M. K. (2006). Zero tolerance, suspension, and expulsion: Questions of equity and effectiveness. In C. M. Evertson & C. S. Weinstein

(Eds.), *Handbook of classroom management: Research, practice, and contemporary issues* (pp. 1063–1089). Mahwah, NJ: Erlbaum.

Slee, P. T. (2003). Violence in schools: An Australian commentary. In P. K. Smith (Ed.), *Violence in schools: The response from Europe* (pp. 301–316). London: Routledge.

Stanglin, D. (2013, September 4). One teen dead, 3 injured in Texas school stabbing. *USA Today*. Retrieved from http://www.usatoday.com/story/news/nation/2013/09/04/spring-texas-houston-harris-county-stabbing-spring-high-school-dead/2762649

Tobin, T., Sugai, G., & Colvin, G. (1996). Patterns in middle school discipline records. *Journal of Emotional and Behavior Disorders*, 4, 82–94.

Wikipedia. (n.d.). School violence. Retrieved from https://en.wikipedia.org/wiki/School_violence

Zhang, A., Musu-Gillette, L., & Oudekerk, B. A. (2016). *Indicators of school climate and safety: 2015*. Washington, DC: National Center for Educational Statistics, U.S. Department of Education and Bureau of Justice Statistics, Office of Justice Programs, U.S. Department of Justice.

Myth #42 Boot camps get teens "on the right path"

Similar to "Scared Straight" programs where students are exposed to adult inmates who threaten and berate them to "scare them straight" (see #48), boot camps were created as a way to intervene with delinquent youth and at-risk teens who exhibit disruptive behavior, such as truancy and defiance. Boot camps have also been known as "shock incarceration" and may be administered by state or county agencies, nonprofit agencies, or for-profit agencies. Boot camps differ widely regarding their type of location, daily experience, and therapeutic interventions implemented. However, there are certain characteristics that are often universal to all boot camps. For example, boot camps often have a military-style aspect that may include uniforms for participants. Additionally, physical exercise, such as running and pushups, are often an integral part of the boot camp experience and is thought to provide its own therapeutic benefit. Finally, boot camps facilitators or administrators interact with youth participants similarly to how someone in military basic training would view a military superior. The first therapeutic boot camps appeared in the United States in the early 1980s but quickly spread throughout the nation since then (MacKenzie, Wilson, & Kider, 2001). The popularity of boot camps as well as similar "scared straight" programs burgeoned at about the same time and represent a popularly held "get tough" attitude towards crime, and juvenile crime, especially.

An example of such boot camps is the Juvenile Impact Program (JIP) sponsored by the Los Angeles Police Department, the LAPD describes JIP as a "12 week boot camp style program intended for at-risk youth between the ages of 9 and 16 years old who have discipline and/or behavioral difficulties" (Los Angeles Police Foundation, 2017). And while the LAPD describe the JIP program as having a "proven 80% success rate," it appears that college students also believe the myth that boot camps set kids on the right path. For example, our own research with college students found that 76% of students had heard of this myth and that 48–57% of these college students believed this myth to be true (Jewell & Hupp, 2018).

But while boot camps appear to be quite popular in the public's view, movies and striking news stories have provided a stark depiction of the potential abuses that can also occur within boot camps. For example, a 14-year-old died while attending the Buffalo Soldiers Re-enactors Association camp in July of 2001. News reports (Thomsen, 2001) indicated that youth received a restricted diet that consisted of fruit and a bowl of beans per day, slept in a sleeping bag outdoors, and did not have the support of medical personnel. Other youth had reportedly indicated being kicked and choked by staff. Shockingly, the youth was found to have been vomiting dirt just before his death (Thomsen, 2001). After the death, the camp closed and all 50 of its youth residents were removed by police. However, in an astonishing turn of events, the camp reopened just 2 months later with many of its previous residents returning along with new youth whose parents were aware of the abuse allegations (Janofsky, 2001). And while this tragedy occurred in 2001, the boot camp industry is still alive and well, as documented in an exposé by the *Rolling Stone* magazine, "Life and Death in a Troubled Teen Boot Camp," which follows the alleged abuses that occurred in 2013 in the Tierra Blanca New Mexico boot camp (Hyde, 2015). In fact, alleged abuses, neglect, and torture in boot camps have become so clichéd that two movies have been produced on the topic. For example, the 2008 (aptly titled) film *Boot Camp* (Greenblatt & Duguay, 2008) stars Mila Kunis as a disrespectful and drug-addicted teen who is taken to a boot camp on an island where abuse and sexual assault of participants is commonplace. Other similar films depicting abuses in a boot camp also include *Coldwater* (Bilotta, J. Dorrance, & Grashaw, 2013) as well as the Disney movie *Holes* (Ewing, Phillips, & Davis, 2003), starring Shia LaBeouf.

So while abuse in boot camps has certainly become a national concern, do positive effects from boot camps outweigh the risk of participant abuse? To the contrary, a large body of research shows that boot camps are largely *in*effective. In one of the first reviews of studies on boot camps, MacKenzie et al. (2001) identified 29 unique research studies on the topic, many of them being state or federal technical reports on boot camp programs in their jurisdiction. Interestingly, only nine of these studies had been published in a peer-reviewed journal. From the 29 studies, the authors extracted 44 distinct effect sizes wherein a boot camp group was compared with a "treatment as usual" comparison group of some kind, such as probation. Overall, the authors found that the recidivism rate for the boot camp groups was 49.4% while the comparison groups' average rate was 50%. That is, boot camps were ineffective in decreasing criminal reoffending, and in the words of the researchers, "Thus, overall the evidence suggests that boot camps do not reduce the risk of recidivism relative to other existing criminal justice system forms of punishment and rehabilitation" (pp. 130–131). More specifically, the authors reported that nine studies found the boot camp group to have significantly lower recidivism compared with a comparison group, while eight studies found the boot camp group to have significantly higher recidivism. But most of the studies (27 out of 44) found no significant differences between the groups at all (Mackenzie et al., 2001). These results are also notable given the high quality of the studies, as most used either methodological or statistical means to control for potential confounding variables. Finally, the authors also found that for juvenile boot camps, no program characteristic (e.g., aftercare and drug treatment) reliably predicted greater effectiveness for the boot camp program (MacKenzie et al., 2001).

More recently, Wilson, MacKenzie, and Mitchell (2003) were able to find only three additional studies that had been conducted and published since their earlier review. Although their later review came to very similar conclusions as their original review, they also found one important difference. After the researchers coded for whether a boot camp program appeared to have a strong versus weak treatment focus with an emphasis on counseling, they found a statistically nonsignificant trend for boot camps with a stronger treatment focus to have a lower recidivism rate compared with boot camps with a weaker treatment focus. In the words of the authors, "We did find, however, larger positive effects for boot camp programs that incorporated counseling and, more generally, for programs that had a primary focus on therapeutic programming beyond discipline, physical training, and military drill and ceremony" (Wilson et al., 2003, p. 19). However, it should be noted that this was only a trend that was not statistically significant.

What you need to know

A recent poll by the Pew Charitable Trusts (2014) found that most Americans (75%), whether Republican or Democrat, prefer the juvenile justice system to provide treatment as opposed to incarceration for juvenile offenders. This same poll found that most Americans (89–92%) believed that schools, parents, and local agencies should take primary responsibility for low-level offenses rather than the justice system. Interestingly, what the average American wants is actually supported by research, as many evidence-based treatments exist for at-risk or court-involved youth. These treatments can be implemented in different contexts, such as in the home or out of the home. They can also focus on enhancing emotional coping, improving family dynamics and relationships, or improving cognitive and behavior skills.

One evidence-based treatment that can be implemented out of the home is Multidimensional Treatment Foster Care (MTFC), a special type of foster care that provides interventions not typically found in traditional foster care settings, including behavioral parent training, behavioral consultation and training in the school, and evidence-based psychotherapy. MTFC reduces recidivism and improves emotional and behavioral functioning in participating youth (Chamberlain, Leve, & DeGarmo, 2007; Chamberlain & Reid, 1998).

The Positive Parenting Program (Triple P) is a behavioral parent training program that seeks to improve parent skills in order to positively impact struggling children (Prinz, Sanders, Shapiro, Whitaker, & Lutzker, 2009). Functional Family Therapy is usually provided in the home and can reduce recidivism and other problematic behaviors in youth that are criminally involved (Sexton & Turner, 2010). Other therapy approaches are provided independently to youth, apart from the family, and include Aggression Replacement Training (ART), which teaches youth to cope with anger and build prosocial skills. ART participants enjoy increases in social skills and moral reasoning and decreases in problem behavior after participation (Gundersen & Svartdal, 2006). Similarly, Relaxation Skills Violence Prevention (RSVP) teaches relaxation skills, such as progressive muscle relaxation and guided imagery, which effectively decrease stress and anger and increase coping in court-involved youth placed in detention (Jewell & Elliff, 2013).

Lastly, a number of evidence-based approaches seek to connect the youth to their broader community. For example, Community Based Mentoring is not a specific program but rather an approach that connects at-risk youth to prosocial adults in their community. These programs seek to give at-risk youth positive role models in order for them to improve their social skills and emotional coping. A recent study of one Community Based Mentoring program found that participants improved on a number of variables. For example, participants' alcohol and drug initiation, truancy, parent relationships, peer relationships, and a number of personality variables were all positively impacted by participation in the program (Tierney, Grossman, & Resch, 2000). Thus, while boot camp interventions may be popular but ineffective, there are many interventions that involve the family that have been shown to be highly effective in treating youth with disruptive behavior.

References

Bilotta, J., Dorrance, M. (Executive Producers), & Grashaw, V. (Director). (2013). *Coldwater* [Motion picture]. Hollywood, CA: Flying Pig Productions.

Chamberlain, P., Leve, L. D., & DeGarmo, D. S. (2007). Multidimensional treatment foster care for girls in the juvenile justice system: 2-year follow-up of a randomized clinical trial. *Journal of Consulting and Clinical Psychology*, 75(1), 187–193.

Chamberlain, P., & Reid, J. B. (1998). Comparison of two community alternatives to incarceration for chronic juvenile offenders. *Journal of Consulting and Clinical Psychology*, 66(4), 624–633.

Ewing, M., Phillips, L. (Executive Producers), & Davis, A. (Director). (2003). *Holes* [Motion picture]. Hollywood, CA: Walt Disney Pictures.

Greenblatt, R. (Executive Producer), & Duguay, C. (Director). (2008). *Boot Camp* [Motion picture]. Canada: CD Films.

Gundersen, K., & Svartdal, F. (2006). Aggression replacement training in Norway: Outcome evaluation of 11 Norwegian student projects. *Scandinavian Journal of Educational Research*, 50(1), 63–81.

Hyde, J. (2015, November). Life and death in a troubled teen boot camp. *Rolling Stone*. Retrieved from http://www.rollingstone.com/culture/news/life-and-death-in-a-troubled-teen-boot-camp-20151112

Janofsky, M. (2001, September 7). Arizona boot camp where boy died reopens. *New York Times*. Retrieved from http://www.nytimes.com/2001/09/07/us/arizona-boot-camp-where-boy-died-reopens.html

Jewell, J. D., & Elliff, S. J. (2013). An investigation of the effectiveness of the Relaxation Skills Violence Prevention (RSVP) program with juvenile detainees. *Criminal Justice and Behavior*, 40(2), 203–213.

Jewell, J. D., & Hupp, S. D. A. (2018). Prevalence of myths about adolescence [Manuscript in preparation].

Los Angeles Police Foundation. (2017). Juvenile Impact Program. Retrieved from https://lapolicefoundation.org/programs/juvenile-impact-program

MacKenzie, D. L., Wilson, D. B., & Kider, S. B. (2001). Effects of correctional boot camps on offending. *The Annals of the American Academy of Political and Social Science*, 578(1), 126–143.

Pew Charitable Trusts. (2014). Public opinion on juvenile justice in America. Retrieved from http://www.pewtrusts.org/~/media/assets/2015/08/pspp_juvenile_poll_web.pdf

Prinz, R. J., Sanders, M. R., Shapiro, C. J., Whitaker, D. J., & Lutzker, J. R. (2009). Population-based prevention of child maltreatment: The U.S. Triple P System Population Trial. *Prevention Science*, 10, 1–12.

Sexton, T. L., & Turner, C. W. (2010). The effectiveness of functional family therapy for youth with behavioral problems in a community practice setting. *Journal of Family Psychology*, 24(3), 339–348.

Thomsen, S. (2001, July 3). Boy dies at boot camp. Retrieved from http://abcnews.go.com/US/story?id=92958&page=1

Tierney, J. P., Grossman, J., & Resch, N. L. (2000). *Making a difference: An impact study of big brothers/big sisters*. Philadelphia, PA: Public/Private Ventures.

Wilson, D. B., MacKenzie, D. L., & Mitchell, F. N. (2003). Effects of correctional boot camps on offending. *Campbell Systematic Reviews*, 1(6), 1–45.

Myth #43 Most teens party with drugs or alcohol on weekends

In the movie *Project X* (Budnick et al., 2012), most of the film focuses on a single night when two high school seniors throw a party to raise their social status. In the words of the trailer, "Experience the event that will turn losers into legends." Throughout the movie, several hundred teens attend the house party engaging in all kinds of raucous behavior that includes chugging beer, smoking marijuana, and abusing prescription pills. One kid even swings from a chandelier. As the party progresses, the bad behavior intensifies as one of the upset neighbors uses a flamethrower to set fire to the neighborhood and the SWAT (Special Weapons And Tactics) team shows up in riot gear. This intense movie has been inspired by a whole genre of teen party movies from the 1980s and 1990s that includes *House Party* (Olson & Hudlin, 1990), with rappers Kid'n Play; *Dazed and Confused* (Daniel & Linklater, 1993); and the movie that launched Sean Penn's career—*Fast Times at Ridgemont High* (Erickson & Heckerling, 1982). Most recently, the teens (not the kids), in the first season of the show *Strangers Things* (Duffer & Duffer, 2016), are too preoccupied with drinking to realize one of their friends goes missing. While these types of depictions may generate entertainment, they also create the pernicious idea that teen partying with drugs and alcohol are an every-weekend occurrence. And it seems that this idea is also prevalent among college students. For example, our own research found that 94% of the college student sample had heard of the myth that most teens party with drugs and alcohol on the weekends, and 63–70% of the sample believed the myth (Jewell & Hupp, 2018). Parents are also concerned about their kids' substance abuse risk. For example, a 2015 survey of parents found that 41% worry that their children will "have problems with drugs or alcohol at some point" (Desilver, 2016).

And yet the truth about teens' alcohol and drug use is actually not nearly as sensational as movies and TV portray. Although alcohol and drug use among any age group can be concerning, the statement that most teens use drugs or alcohol on a weekly basis is simply not true. To start, let's consider teen alcohol use. Some of the most relevant data on the topic of teen alcohol and drug use come from the annual Youth Risk Behavior Surveillance (YRBS) study that is completed every year in the United States. The most recent available survey from 2015 was composed of a geographically and ethnically representative sample of over 15,000 students from across the country. A recent summary of teen alcohol use by the Centers for Disease Control and Prevention (2016a) reported data from the National Youth Risk Behavior Survey from 1991 and 2015 for high school students in the United States. Data from 2015 indicated that only about 33% of the sample had consumed alcohol in the last month, and 37% of the sample had never consumed alcohol. Regarding binge drinking, only 18% of the sample in 2015 had consumed more than five drinks at a time in the last month—which hardly qualifies as "most teens" (Centers for Disease Control and Prevention, 2016a). And when you compare the trends in the data for the last 25 years, teen alcohol use is declining significantly. For example, rates of teen binge drinking are almost half what they were in 1991 (31%), and past alcohol use has also significantly declined since its high of 52% in 1995 (Centers for Disease Control and Prevention, 2016a).

But what about college students? Most of them are getting drunk every weekend—right? Well, not really. Again, research shows that only 30% of college-aged adults (18–24 years old) binged on alcohol at least once in the last month (4–5 drinks at a time) (Kanny, Liu, Brewer, & Lu, 2013). This means that the majority of college-age adults (70%) not only didn't binge drink in the last week, but not even in the last month. Interestingly, the rate of binge drinking for adults between 25 and 34 years old was virtually the same as college-aged adults at 29.7%.

When examining illegal drug use, results again show that teen drug use is relatively uncommon. For example, 2015 data from the Centers for

Disease Control and Prevention (2016b) indicate that very few teens have ever used a number of drugs including hallucinogens (6%), cocaine (5%), methamphetamine (3%), and ecstasy (5%). And more good news is that these rates of lifetime use have generally declined over the last 10–20 years. For example, cocaine use has fallen by about half from 2001 (9.4% ever used) to 2015 (5.2% ever used). Similarly, the rates of those teens who ever used meth were three times higher in 2001 (9.8%) compared to 3% in 2015. However, the story on marijuana is a bit different and likely influenced by the national trend towards marijuana, or medical marijuana, legalization. For example, while only 22% of teens report using marijuana in the last month, this rate is significantly higher than in 1991 when it was 15% (Centers for Disease Control and Prevention, 2016b). Still, it's important to again point out that 78% of teens in 2015 did not use marijuana in the last month.

What you need to know

While some myths in this book may be less harmful than others, the current myth has critical implications for actual teen alcohol and drug use because of a concept called "social norms." A social norm is some expectation for what is normal as deemed by a majority, or at least a large portion, of society. So "*most* teens party with drugs or alcohol on weekends" can be considered to be a social norm, especially when 63–70% of our college student sample endorsed this statement. However, people often use what they believe is normal to defend and rationalize their own bad behavior. For example, if a high school student binge drinks Friday and Saturday every week but believes that everyone else their age does the same, they may use this social norm to resist decreasing their binge drinking behavior. When peers bring up their problematic drinking, the teen may rationalize their own behavior by replying "everyone else is doing it so why can't I?"

However, some researchers have found that they can reduce substance use by educating teens and college students on actual alcohol and drug use rates by their peers. These social norms interventions can be employed as a marketing strategy or as an individual intervention. An example of a social norms marketing strategy could be when high school and college administrators put up posters and other marketing materials stating that "82% of high school students have not binged on alcohol in the last month." This type of strategy for an alcohol prevention program can be effective at re-establishing a more accurate and realistic social norm of teen alcohol use based on actual data (for an example of another social norms intervention, refer back to Chapter 17). In fact, a recent randomized clinical trial found that a social norms marketing prevention program is effective at reducing a number of indicators of problematic alcohol use (DeJong et al., 2006). A social norms individual intervention can also be targeted to specific teens who have a problem with alcohol abuse. For example, a computer-based program or face-to-face intervention with a mental health professional can be employed that serves to educate teens on the true rates of teen alcohol use so that they can understand that their alcohol abuse is "not normal" and not shared among most of their peers (for a review of these programs, see Moreira, Smith, & Foxcroft, 2009). In fact, these types of individual interventions have been found to be highly effective at reducing alcohol misuse in college students (Moreira et al., 2009). Moreover, for teens who are actively engaging in substance use, two treatments have been shown to be well-established—ecological family-based treatment and cognitive-behavioral therapy (Hogue, Henderson, Ozechowski, & Robbins, 2014).

So the next time you've had a hard day and want to relax watching a comedy like *Project X*, don't worry—we won't judge you. Just remember that *Project X* is like almost everything else produced in Hollywood—entertaining fiction.

References

Budnick, S., Ewing, M. P., Heineman, A., Phillips, T., Richards, S., Rona, A., & Silver, J. (Producers), & Nourizadeh, N. (Director). (2012). *Project X* [Motion picture]. Hollywood, CA: Warner Bros.

Centers for Disease Control and Prevention. (2016a). Trends in the prevalence of alcohol use. *National YRBS: 1991–2015*. Atlanta, GA: Centers for Disease Control and Prevention.

Centers for Disease Control and Prevention. (2016b). Trends in the prevalence of marijuana, cocaine, and other illegal drug use. *National YRBS: 1991–2015*. Atlanta, GA: Centers for Disease Control and Prevention.

Daniel, S. (Producer), & Linklater, R. (Director). (1993). *Dazed and Confused* [Motion picture]. Hollywood, CA: Gramercy Pictures.

DeJong, W., Schneider, S. K., Towvim, L. G., Murphy, M. J., Doerr, E. E., Simonsen, N. R., … Scribner, R. A. (2006). A multisite randomized trial of social norms marketing campaigns to reduce college student drinking. *Journal of Studies on Alcohol, 67*(6), 868–879.

Desilver, D. (2016, January 14). Dangers that teens and kids face: A look at the data. Retrieved from http://www.pewresearch.org/fact-tank/2016/01/14/dangers-that-young-people-face-a-look-at-the-data

Duffer, M. & Duffer, R. (2016). *Stranger Things* [Television series]. USA: 21 Laps Entertainment.

Erickson, C. (Producer), & Heckerling, A. (Director). (1982). *Fast Times at Ridgemont High* [Motion picture]. Hollywood, CA: Universal Pictures.

Hogue, A., Henderson, C. E., Ozechowski, T. J., & Robbins, M. S. (2014). Evidence base on outpatient behavioral treatments for adolescent substance use: Updates and recommendations 2007–2013. *Journal of Clinical Child & Adolescent Psychology, 43*(5), 695–720.

Jewell, J. D., & Hupp, S. D. A. (2018). Prevalence of myths about adolescence [Manuscript in preparation].

Kanny, D., Liu, Y., Brewer, R. D., & Lu, H. (2013). Binge drinking—United States, 2011. *Morbidity and Mortality Weekly Report Surveillance Summary, 62*(Supplement 3), 77–80.

Moreira, T., Smith, L., & Foxcroft, D. (2009). Social norms interventions to reduce alcohol misuse in university or college students. *Cochrane Database of Systematic Reviews, 3*(CD006748). doi:10.1002/14651858.CD006748.pub2.

Olson, G. (Producer), & Hudlin, R. (Director). (1990). *House Party* [Motion picture]. Hollywood, CA: New Line Cinema.

Myth #44

DARE programs prevent teen drug use

Why doesn't Daren the Lion, the DARE mascot, wear pants to go along with his DARE T-shirt? Wouldn't it seem like common sense to have a drug prevention mascot wear a socially appropriate wardrobe? After some investigative work, we'll actually be able to share the answer to this mystery at the end of this section, and it far exceeds anything we could have imagined (i.e., you'll have to be smarter than the average bear to guess this one). However, before we get to the wardrobe mystery, there's plenty of investigative work to share about DARE itself.

If you were in fifth or sixth grade in the 1990s or beyond, there's a good chance that you experienced the Drug Abuse Resistance Education (DARE) program. If not, you've probably seen its mascot, or T-shirt, or perhaps its logo wrapped around a police car. DARE is so popular that the third Thursday of every April is National DARE Day in the United States, and this day has been supported through several presidential proclamations representing both political parties. This special day is meant to celebrate over three decades since the implementation of the DARE program which has the meaningful goal of preventing drug use with youth.

DARE is a *universal* prevention program, which means that it's offered to all of the children in a particular school grade. That is, it is not a *selected* or *indicated* prevention program that would be just for students who are at greater risk or who are showing early signs of substance use. Police officers visit schools to implement DARE lessons to children in fifth or sixth grade once a week for about 17 weeks. In addition to covering topics such as changing beliefs about drugs, the program has lessons dedicated to teaching assertiveness and healthy ways to manage stress. Additionally, DARE has sought to decrease violence and prevent youth from joining gangs, typically ending with a graduation ceremony and certificate.

The program began in 1983 in Los Angeles, and since then it has really taken off. DARE can currently be found in about 75% of American school districts across all 50 states, and it's taught in over 50 additional countries across the globe (D.A.R.E. America, 2014). In short, millions of children receive DARE each year, and a lot of people believe that it works. In our own research, 40–44% of students agreed with the statement that "D.A.R.E. prevents teen drug use" (Jewell & Hupp, 2018).

From the beginning, the developers of DARE did little to investigate its effectiveness, but when researchers began investigating the program's effects it did not fare very well. In one of the best studies of DARE, researchers randomly assigned elementary schools to an experimental group who received DARE from a police officer, or who were in a comparison group receiving a curriculum of "whatever the health teachers decided to cover concerning drug education in their classes" (Lynam et al., 1999, p. 591). Ten years later, the researchers paid participants to report about their drug use on a questionnaire. Results demonstrated that there were no differences between the DARE group and the comparison group on drug use for alcohol, cigarettes, marijuana, or illicit drugs. Moreover, peer pressure resistance was no better for the DARE group, and self-esteem was significantly *lower* for students who had been in DARE, a finding that the investigators attributed to chance.

Quite a few other studies have demonstrated similar results regarding DARE's effectiveness. One meta-analysis combined the data from 11 studies on DARE (including the 10-year follow-up discussed above) that were published between 1991 and 2002 (West & O'Neal, 2004). The results of this meta-analysis again confirmed that DARE was ineffective at preventing drug use.

Recognizing that DARE was ineffective, the organization attempted to develop a new curriculum, called *Take Charge of Your Life*, for students in seventh grade, with a booster in ninth grade. Shockingly however, research showed that students in the treatment schools actually ended up being *more* likely to use alcohol and cigarettes than students in the comparison group during the follow-up (Sloboda et al., 2009). This version of the program was quickly abandoned after it continued to show weak results (Singh et al., 2011).

Rather than giving up on DARE, and rather than trying to develop another new curriculum, the organization began searching for a program that was already effective. They found a program, called *Keepin' It REAL* (Refuse, Explain, Avoid, & Leave), which comprised ten lessons delivered by teachers of students in seventh grade (Hecht et al., 2003). Largely designed for Latino students, most of the studies demonstrated mixed results of *Keepin' It REAL* with the Latino samples (Hecht, Graham, & Elek, 2006; Marsiglia, Kulis, Wagstaff, Elek, & Dran, 2005; Warren et al., 2006). However, these early studies of *Keepin' It Real* included some limitations. For example, they were all based on self-report and did not include follow-up measurements after the immediate postintervention measurement. However, there were enough initial positive results to prompt DARE to officially adopt the *Keepin' It REAL* program in 2009. It is important to note that the original *Keepin' It REAL* curriculum is not the same curriculum that is used by DARE. That is, developers combined aspects of the program with the original DARE curriculum, and they also created another version for elementary schools, which captured the same market as the original DARE program (Caputi, 2015).

The adoption of *Keepin' It REAL*, which had mixed research support, gave DARE program administrators some confidence, and a recent article in *Scientific American* was even titled, "The New D.A.R.E. Program— This One Works" (Nordrum, 2014). However, it is a bit of a stretch to assert that this "new DARE" works because the new DARE version of *Keepin' REAL* has not been investigated. One big difference between the original version of *Keepin' it REAL* and the DARE version is that the DARE version uses police officers instead of school teachers. Additionally, *Keepin' it REAL* has little evidence of effectiveness beyond the Latino samples in its research. Moreover, when the developers of *Keepin' It REAL* previously attempted to adapt their program for fifth grade, it fared no better than a comparison group (Hecht et al., 2008).

Why has DARE flourished for over three decades despite the program's weak track record when it comes to positive outcomes? One reason is that something really does need to be done about worldwide drug problems. About 6% of all deaths in the world are attributable to harmful alcohol use, and these deaths commonly occur early in the lifespan (World Health Organization, 2015). Tobacco is responsible for about seven million deaths each year, many of which are from exposure to second-hand smoke (World Health Organization, 2017). Other drugs contribute to many other deaths and related health problems across the world. Thus, it is understandable that schools want to do what they can to prevent drug use.

Another reason that DARE is so popular may be that it fits well with one of the sources of psychological myths described by Lilienfeld, Lynn, Ruscio, & Beyerstein (2010). Specifically, DARE feels like an easy answer to the drug problem. For many schools, DARE has consisted of about 17 lessons, and schools don't even need to train their teachers to implement the program because police officers do the job instead. In fact, one study found that building a positive relationship between officers and students was actually the primary reason that many school districts used DARE even though they knew it was ineffective in countering drug use (Birkeland, Murphy-Graham, & Weiss, 2005).

There are a several reasons why it is important to discuss this myth about the effectiveness of DARE. First, DARE costs a lot of money. Second, implementing DARE makes schools feel like they're doing something to prevent drug use that may prevent them from using approaches or programs that are actually effective. Third, at least one study demonstrated that fifth graders who received *Keepin' It REAL* had *more* substance use than students in comparison schools (Elek, Wagstaff, & Hecht, 2010). Finally, DARE has many corporate sponsors, such as Wal-mart and Target, and these sponsors could be using their funds to support projects with better evidence of effectiveness.

As to the mystery about Daren the Lion's pantless wardrobe, Daren was likely greatly influenced by DARE's first mascot who, as hinted earlier, was smarter than the average bear, loved stealing pic-a-nic baskets, and lived in Jellystone Park. Yes, their first mascot was Yogi Bear (also known as "DARE Bear Yogi"), the famous brown bear who usually wore only a white collar, a green tie, and matching hat; however, in his promotional work for DARE he also wore the classic black DARE t-shirt (but still no pants). Thus, the pantless T-shirt look was later extended to Daren the Lion when Yogi ended his Spokesbear duties. If you have five minutes to spare, you could really enhance your day by searching Youtube for "DARE Bear Yogi." This musical animation centers around Yogi's rap with lyrics such as, "DARE teaches kids to never take drugs, then asks the parents to give the kids hugs!" The lyrics end with, "If you want to be rad, get with it, be cool; make sure there's a DARE class in every single school." While rapping along to the theme song from The Flintstones, Yogi is joined by friends such as the Flintstone kids, Shaggy from Scoobie-Doo, Astro from the Jetsons, Captain Caveman, the Pink Panther, and Boo-Boo Bear, only half of whom are wearing pants.

What you need to know

Preventing drug use will always be a challenging goal, and it will likely require more than 17 lessons in a single school year. While DARE has been attempting to target youth in a wider range of school years, DARE America has not been using well-designed studies to support the newest version of their curriculum. One place to stay up-to-date on progress being made to identify effective programs is the Center for the Study and Prevention of Violence. This center uses their Blueprints for Healthy Youth Development website (www.blueprintsprograms.com) to identify programs with solid research support.

Blueprints for Healthy Youth Development has reviewed over 1,400 programs with less than 5% being identified as being effective as defined by one of three levels (Center for the Study and Prevention of Violence, n.d.). First, in order to be a "promising program," at least one well-done study (e.g., with reliable and valid findings) must demonstrate the program works and is ready for other people to start using (e.g., manuals, training). In addition to these requirements, in order to be a "model program," it must have at least two well-done studies demonstrating the program maintains effects for at least 1 year after the conclusion of the program. Finally, in order to be a "model plus program," the program must also include an independent replication from a different team of investigators.

Currently, the only universal prevention program aimed at drug use that meets the criteria for the model plus category is called Life Skills Training (Botvin & Griffin, 2004). This program includes 30 lessons taught over 3 years during middle school (Botvin Life Skills Training, n.d.). It uses behavioral skills training (i.e., modeling, instructions, rehearsal, and feedback) to teach behavioral and cognitive skills related to drug resistance, self-management, and social skills. Quite a few studies have shown positive results for preventing drug use (Botvin & Griffin, 2002).

It is only fair to point out that the research on Life Skills Training has been criticized on some methodological grounds (Gorman, Conde, & Huber, 2007). Also, a different substance use prevention program, called Project Alert (Ellickson, McCaffrey, Ghosh-Dastidar, & Longshore, 2003), was once on the Blueprints list and was later removed when additional research began showing less positive findings (Montgomery, 2014). Thus, the science behind identifying effective programs is always evolving, but hopefully it is gradually moving in the right direction.

On a final note, most of the myths in this book will probably always be myths; however, DARE has the opportunity to keep modifying their program. The day may come when we can say that some latest version of DARE is strongly supported by research. DARE has a good goal; however, the concerning aspect of their story is how widely they entered school districts *before* they figured which strategies were effective.

References

Birkeland, S., Murphy-Graham, E., & Weiss, C. (2005). Good reasons for ignoring good evaluation: The case of the drug abuse resistance education (D.A.R.E.) program. *Evaluation and Program Planning, 28*(3), 247–256. doi:10.1016/j.evalprogplan.2005.04.001.

Botvin, G. J., & Griffin, K. W. (2002). Life skills training as a primary prevention approach for adolescent drug abuse and other problem behaviors. *International Journal of Emergency Mental Health, 4*(1), 41–48.

Botvin, G. J., & Griffin, K. W. (2004). Life skills training: Empirical findings and future directions. *Journal of Primary Prevention, 25*(2), 211–232. doi:10.1023/B:JOPP.0000042391.58573.5b.

Botvin Life Skills Training (n.d.). Program structure. Retrieved from https://www.lifeskillstraining.com/?s=program+structure

Caputi, T. L. (2015). Selling prevention: Using a business framework to analyze the state of prevention and overcome obstacles to expanding substance abuse prevention. *Journal of Global Drug Policy and Practice, 9*(1), 1–24.

Center for the Study and Prevention of Violence (n.d.). Program Criteria. Retrieved from www.blueprintsprograms.com/criteria

D.A.R.E America (2014). D.A.R.E. Empowering Children to Lead Safe and Healthy Lives: 2014 Annual Report. Retrieved from www.dare.org

Elek, E., Wagstaff, D. A., & Hecht, M. L. (2010). Effects of the 5th and 7th grade enhanced versions of the keepin' it REAL substance use prevention curriculum. *Journal of Drug Education, 40*(1), 61–79. doi:10.2190/DE.40.1.e.

Ellickson, P. L., McCaffrey, D. F., Ghosh-Dastidar, B., & Longshore, D. L. (2003). New inroads in preventing adolescent drug use: Results from a large-scale trial of Project ALERT in middle schools. *American Journal of Public Health, 93*(11), 1830–1836. doi:10.2105/AJPH.93.11.1830.

Gorman, D. M., Conde, E., & Huber, J. J. (2007). The creation of evidence in "evidence-based" drug prevention: A critique of the strengthening families program plus life skills training evaluation. *Drug and Alcohol Review, 26*(6), 585–593. doi:10.1080/09595230701613544.

Hecht, M. L., Elek, E., Wagstaff, D. A., Kam, J. A., Marsiglia, F., Dustman, P., … Harthun, M. (2008). Immediate and short-term effects of the 5th grade version of the keepin' it real substance use prevention intervention. *Journal of Drug Education, 38*(3), 225–251. doi:10.2190/DE.38.3.c.

Hecht, M. L., Graham, J. W., & Elek, E. (2006). The drug resistance strategies intervention: Program effects on substance use. *Health Communication*, *20*(3), 267–276. doi:10.1207/s15327027hc2003_6.

Hecht, M. L., Marsiglia, F. F., Elek, E., Wagstaff, D. A., Kulis, S., Dustman, P., & Miller-Day, M. (2003). Culturally grounded substance use prevention: An evaluation of the keepin' it R.E.A.L curriculum. *Prevention Science*, *4*(4), 233–248. doi:10.1023/A:1026016131401.

Jewell, J. D., & Hupp, S. D. A. (2018). Prevalence of myths about adolescence [Manuscript in preparation].

Lilienfeld, S. O., Lynn, S. J., Ruscio, J., & Beyerstein, B. L. (2010). *50 great myths of popular psychology: Shattering widespread misconceptions about human behavior*. Malden, MA: Wiley-Blackwell.

Lynam, D. R., Milich, R., Zimmerman, R., Novak, S. P., Logan, T. K., Martin, C., … Clayton, R. (1999). Project DARE: No effects at 10-year follow-up. *Journal of Consulting and Clinical Psychology*, *67*(4), 590–593. doi:10.1037/11855-008.10.1037/0022-006X.67.4.590.

Marsiglia, F. F., Kulis, S., Wagstaff, D. A., Elek, E., & Dran, D. (2005). Acculturation status and substance use prevention with Mexican and Mexican-American youth. In M. R. De la Rosa, L. K. Holleran, & S. A. Straussner (Eds.), *Substance abusing Latinos: Current research on epidemiology, prevention, and treatment* (pp. 85–111). Binghamton, NY: Haworth Social Work Practice Press.

Montgomery, K. L. (2014). School-based delinquency prevention. In W. T. Church, D. W. Springer, & A. R. Roberts (Eds.), *Juvenile justice sourcebook* (2nd ed.) (pp. 289–312). Oxford: Oxford University Press.

Nordum, A. (2014, September). The new D.A.R.E. program—this one works. *Scientific American*. Retrieved from www.scientificamerican.com

Singh, R. D., Jimerson, S. R., Renshaw, T., Saeki, E., Hart, S. R., Earhart, J., & Stewart, K. (2011). A summary and synthesis of contemporary empirical evidence regarding the effects of the Drug Abuse Resistance Education Program (D.A.R.E.). *Contemporary School Psychology*, *15*, 93–102.

Sloboda, Z., Stephens, R. C., Stephens, P. C., Grey, S. F., Teasdale, B., Hawthorne, R. D., … Marquette, J. F. (2009). The adolescent substance abuse prevention study: A randomized field trial of a universal substance abuse prevention program. *Drug and Alcohol Dependence*, *102*(1–3), 1–10. doi:10.1016/j.drugalcdep.2009.01.015.

Warren, J. R., Hecht, M. L., Wagstaff, D. A., Elek, E., Ndiaye, K., Dustman, P., & Marsiglia, F. F. (2006). Communicating prevention: The effects of the keepin' it REAL classroom videotapes and televised PSAs on middle-school students' substance use. *Journal of Applied Communication Research*, *34*(2), 209–227. doi:10.1080/00909880600574153.

West, S. L., & O'Neal, K. K. (2004). Project DARE outcome effectiveness revisited. *American Journal of Public Health*, *94*(6), 1027–1029. doi:10.2105/AJPH.94.6.1027.

World Health Organization (2015). Alcohol: Fact sheet. Retrieved from www.who.int

World Health Organization (2017). Tobacco: Fact sheet. Retrieved from www.who.int

Myth #45 Listening to heavy metal or rap music makes teens more likely to defy authority

The post-World War II 1950s triggered a new youth culture exemplified by different music (e.g., Elvis Presley and rock'n'roll), dance styles (e.g., the jitterbug), movies and movie stars (e.g., James Dean and *Rebel without a Cause*; Weisbart & Ray, 1955), and language (e.g., slang phrases such as "don't have a cow"). Different from what they experienced as teenagers, parents of the 1950s viewed these new adolescent interests as representing rebellion and defiance of authority. Teenagers and young people in the 50s (e.g., baby boomers) eventually grew up amid the turmoil of the 1960s. They began to question authority more forcefully as demonstrated through protests in favor of civil rights and against the Vietnam War. The music of the times, mainly folk and pop music, reflected a growing sentiment among young people that those in authority were morally corrupt and shouldn't be trusted. In the 1970s, punk music anthems, like "Anarchy in the UK" by the Sex Pistols (Cook, Jones, Lydon, & Matlock, 1976), became the embodiment of mutiny against authority. In the 1980s, community leaders and politicians again suggested that the disturbing qualities of some music, such as heavy metal, was associated with the destruction of morality in America (Kotarba, Merrill, Williams, & Vannini, 2013).

Today, adults continue to maintain a rather negative view of music favored by adolescents, suggesting specifically that heavy metal and rap music are contributing to the moral decay of today's youth. Heavy metal music has long been associated with violent images (Donkin, 2008). This is made clear in the opening lines from the heavy metal band Autopsy's single *Charred Remains*: "Burning from the inside out, bloody foam spews your mouth, smell the putrid stench of flesh, as it burns you to your death" (Reifert, 1989). Hopefully you haven't eaten recently, otherwise reading that might have upset your stomach! Characteristics of heavy metal music, such as loud sounds, emotional vocals, and lyrics containing themes of aggression and loneliness, are said to cause listeners to be angry and engage in delinquency and suicidal behavior (Sharman & Dingle, 2015). Rap and hip-hop music have also come under fire. In recent years, political commentator Bill O'Reilly claimed rap music deified immoral behavior and was responsible for a decline in Christianity (Bump, 2015), and a *Chicago Tribune* article quoted an ex-gang member as saying rap music presented a positive spin on the gangster life rather than speaking about its destructive nature (Turner, 2015). There have also been United States Senate hearings, high-profile court cases, and public campaigns, all designed to draw attention to the negative impact heavy metal and rap music have on young people (Reddick & Beresin, 2002). While these politically driven attempts at ridding the world of heavy metal and rap music have largely failed, what's clear is the strong belief by many that these music genres cause negative developmental outcomes for teenagers.

Inferring causation from correlation is one obvious source of this myth. It's true that research has found links between music genre preferences and adolescent behavior problems. For example, a study of almost 1,000 Dutch adolescents over a 2-year period found a statistically significant relationship between listening to heavy metal or rap music and self-reported externalizing problems such as aggression and delinquency (Selfhout, Delsing, ter Bogt, & Meeus, 2008). However, the researchers themselves admitted that a causal relationship between music preference and adolescent behavior problems could not be drawn based on their design and methodology. All they could confirm from their findings was that teenagers who listened to heavy metal or rap music were more likely to self-report problem behavior. To make this point more salient, the American Academy of Pediatrics wrote in a revised policy statement that research does not exist supporting a cause and effect relationship between sexually explicit music content and problem behavior, despite a correlational link between the two (see Villani, 2001).

So, why might a relationship exist between music preference and behavior problems? Consider the "third variable" problem, which suggests some other variable might explain the relationship between two associated variables (Lilienfeld, Lynn, Ruscio, & Beyerstein, 2010). Clearly, a multitude of other factors must contribute to a teenager's behavior problems; the music one listens to can't be solely responsible for one's behavior. Volumes of research over many years have found that specific genetic (e.g., heritable traits including temperament) and environmental (e.g., parenting practices, peer group membership, academic achievement) variables interact over the course of development to influence behavior (Beauchaine, Gatzke-Kopp, & Gizer, 2017). Specific to the relationship between music preferences and problem behavior, variables involving degree of sensation-seeking and family relationship qualities have also been found to mediate the impact of music on behavior (Schmaltz, 2016).

The myth that heavy metal or rap music makes teenagers more likely to defy authority might also be promoted by the *argumentum ad antiquitatem* fallacy or the appeal to antiquity or tradition (Vaughn & Schick, 1999). According to psychologist Rodney Schmaltz (2016), "for a long time, there has been public concern about the impact of certain types of music on behavior" (p. 1). Specifically, there appears to have been a historical precedent set for associating music favored by teenagers with rebellion, defiance of authority, and immoral behavior. This was clearly the case of music listened to by teenagers in the 1950s, 1960s, and 1970s. For example, Elvis Presley's appearance on *The Ed Sullivan Show* in the 1950s struck fear in many adults, who were concerned about the negative influence he and his gyrating hips might have on young people. What's interesting is that this way of thinking might be traced all the way back to ancient times. For classical Greeks, the relationship between music and life was represented by music as imitation (Barber, 2008). Specifically, to become a good person, one listened to good music. The degree to which a person listened to bad music influenced the degree to which that person became a bad person. As Aristotle is said to have suggested, "if over a long time a person habitually listens to music that rouses ignoble passions, his whole character will be shaped to an ignoble form" (Grout, 1988, pp. 7–8). Perhaps the Elvis of ancient Greece was rousing ignoble passions in Greek youth causing toga-clad parents great stress.

High-profile cases, often sensationalized by the media, have blamed heavy metal and rap music for causing serious harm to its listeners. For example, the heavy metal band Judas Priest was accused in the 1980s of inserting reverse subliminal messages associated with suicide into their songs (Schmaltz, 2016). After two teenagers attempted suicide after listening to Judas Priest music and smoking marijuana, a lawsuit was filed claiming the subliminal messages coming from the music were responsible for the boys' suicidal behavior. Although the case was eventually dismissed, the horrifying images likely lived on in the minds of many and a perception might have developed that heavy metal music can cause suicidal behavior. As noted in the myths that teens today are worse behaved compared to previous generations and school violence is on the rise, a person's tendency to evaluate the likelihood of something based on how easy an example comes to mind is called the availability heuristic (Tversky & Kahneman, 1974). The availability heuristic might be partially responsible for the promotion of this myth as well. Relating the availability heuristic to rap music, images of high-profile rap musicians being tied to gangs and gang violence are likely to come to mind when people consider the relationship between rap music and violent behavior.

While studies supporting a causal link are nonexistent, there is much research examining the relationship between heavy metal or rap music and adolescent defiance and other behavior problems. For example, a 1994 study investigating the relationship between adolescent psychosocial turmoil (measured broadly using self- and parent-report rating scales) and preference for certain music genres found only below average grades to be associated with teenagers who preferred heavy metal or rap music (Took & Weiss, 1994). When the researchers controlled statistically for gender because of unbalanced groups (i.e., significantly more boys than girls endorsed heavy metal or rap as preferred music, and girls generally tend to have fewer behavior problems), variables involving school behavior problems, sexual activity, drug and alcohol use, and delinquency did not predict music genre preferences. In an earlier study, researchers found no relationship between a preference for or commitment to heavy metal or rap music and middle school students' academic or behavioral functioning (Epstein, Pratto, & Skipper, 1990). Amid claims about the dangers of listening to heavy metal and rap music, the study's authors suggested a "need for a re-evaluation of the public perception toward rock music" (Epstein et al., 1990, p. 391). More recently, researchers, using experimental methods, found that listening to extreme music (e.g., heavy metal, punk) did not cause angry listeners to become angrier (Sharman & Dingle, 2015). Moreover, listening to extreme music corresponded with listeners' physiological arousal resulting in increases in positive emotions. This finding matched subjects' report that listening to extreme music improves their mood. Although the authors admitted additional research to understand these findings is needed, they concluded "the results refute the notion that extreme music causes anger" (Sharman & Dingle, 2015, p. 282).

However, research does indicate a relationship between listening to heavy metal or rap music and adolescent problem behavior. That is, there are studies demonstrating statistically significant correlations between preference for heavy metal or rap music and problems associated with delinquency, social behavior, anxiety, and depression. For example, a Dutch study found that musical taste predicted externalizing (e.g., aggression, noncompliance, attention problems) and internalizing (anxiety, depression) problems of students ages 12–16 years (Mulder, ter Bogt, Raaijmakers, & Vollebergh, 2007). That is, preference for certain music types was associated with psychosocial problems. Specifically, those who reported listening to urban (e.g., rap/hip-hop, soul, reggae) or rock music (i.e., heavy metal, punk, grunge) were more likely to self-report externalizing problems (e.g., defiance, physical aggression). Those who reported listening to rock music were also more likely to self-report internalizing problems (anxiety, depression). However, the effects were quite small and none of the group averages was in the clinical range (i.e., representing noteworthy problems). Taken together, the study indicated that preference for certain music genres, like heavy metal or rap, was only slightly associated with problem behavior and the problems were unlikely to be clinically significant (i.e., problems that warrant professional attention). Interestingly, students who reported preferring classical or jazz music also reported high levels of withdrawn behavior. While the researchers attempted to explain this finding by suggesting this group was likely represented by students on the outside of adolescent peer culture because of their musical preference, the results point to complexities in studying relationships between musical taste and behavior.

A more recent study investigating the relationship between early adolescent music preferences and behavior problems reported that early preferences for heavy metal or rap music predicted current and later behavior problems (ter Bogt, Keijsers, & Meeus, 2013). Yet, while the correlations were statistically significant, the relationships were small to moderate. For example, the correlation between preference for heavy metal music and behavior problems at 12 years of age was 0.25. However, the effect size indicated that just over 6% of the differences in behavior problems among teenagers in the study can be predicted from the relationship between preference for heavy metal music and self-reported behavior problems. This also means that almost 94% of the differences in behavior problems among teenagers in the study cannot be explained by this relationship. Variables other than music genre preference, such as academic problems, peer group affiliation, or level of parental supervision, are likely to be better predictive variables for adolescent behavior problems. More to the point of the myth that heavy metal or rap music makes adolescents defy authority, correlation never means causation.

To summarize, there is no evidence to establish a causal link between listening to heavy metal or rap music and adolescent behavior problems. More specifically, there is no evidence that these music genres make teenagers defy authority. And despite recent studies identifying statistically significant correlations between music genre preference and externalizing and internalizing problems, the identified relationships are small to moderate. Moreover, the identified problems are hardly concern for professional intervention. Finally, the relationship between heavy metal or rap music and problem behavior is likely accounted for by other variables, including genetic predispositions and negative parenting practices. Put slightly differently, it's unlikely one single variable, music genre preference, is responsible for an adolescent's defiance of authority.

What you need to know

Parents should not be completely alarmed that their adolescent listens to or prefers heavy metal or rap music. Not surprisingly, generational differences exist in music genre preference, and young people today appear to favor music that is not liked by their parents or grandparents. These generational differences are most notable when considering heavy metal or rap music (Lizardo & Skiles, 2015). Moreover, fewer young people in America express a distaste for rap music than other mainstream music genres (e.g., country) and fewer young and middle-aged Americans dislike heavy metal music today than 25 years ago (Lizardo & Skiles, 2015). Taken altogether, it's likely that the typical modern-day adolescent listens to heavy metal or rap music, and there might not be anything wrong with that. For example, a study published in 2017 found that listening to music, regardless of genre, had no impact on either ethical or health and safety risk choices made by college students (Enstrom & Schmaltz, 2017).

Parents and other adults, however, should be aware of those adolescents who listen regularly to music containing disturbing themes (e.g., violence, sexual exploitation, suicide). While, again, there is no evidence supporting a causal link between music genre preference and problem behavior, there could be reason for concern when exposure to deviant media content coincides with a history of aggression, defiant behavior, delinquency, and depression. Some research has found that excessive exposure to media violence, including violence portrayed in music, "increases acceptance of violence as an appropriate means of solving problems and achieving one's goals" (American Academy of Pediatrics, 2009, p. 1496), although exposure to violent media content, by itself, might not be associated with aggressive behavior (see Ferguson, 2015a). In fact, research examining societal trends over time found violent videogame use was strongly associated with reduced youth violence rates, not increased youth violence rates (Ferguson, 2015b). However, at the individual level, substantial exposure to certain media content may contribute to negative developmental outcomes and encourage deviant peer group membership (ter Bogt et al., 2013). Research suggests that individual risk factors, such as a history of aggressive behavior, can contribute significantly to the prediction of violence for teens who report a preference for violent media content (see Boxer, Huesmann, Bushman, O'Brien, & Moceri, 2009). Finally, according to the American Academy of Child and Adolescent Psychiatry (2008), preference for certain music content isn't necessarily dangerous "for a teenager whose life is balanced and healthy" (p. 1). However, parents should consider a referral to a qualified professional if their teenager experiences noteworthy changes in behavior (e.g., aggression, isolation, mood, substance abuse).

References

American Academy of Child and Adolescent Psychiatry. (2008). Facts for families: The influence of music and music videos. Retrieved from https://www.aacap.org/App_Themes/AACAP/docs/facts_for_families/40_the_influence_of_music_and_music_videos.pdf

American Academy of Pediatrics (2009). Policy statement—Media violence. *Pediatrics, 124*, 1495–1503.

Barber, J. (2008). *The road from Eden: Studies in Christianity and culture.* Bethesda, MD: Academic Press.

Beauchaine, T. P., Gatzke-Kopp, L., & Gizer, I. R. (2017). Genetic, environmental, and epigenetic influences on behavior. In T. P. Beauchaine & S. P. Hinshaw (Eds.), *Child and adolescent psychopathology* (3rd ed.) (pp. 68–109). Hoboken, NJ: Wiley.

ter Bogt, T. F. M., Keijsers, L., & Meeus, W. H. J. (2013). Early adolescent music preferences and minor delinquency. *Pediatrics, 131*, e380–e389.

Boxer, P., Huesmann, L. R., Bushman, B. J., O'Brien, M., & Moceri, D. (2009). The role of violent media preference in cumulative developmental risk for violence and general aggression. *Journal of Youth and Adolescence, 38*, 417–428.

Bump, P. (2015, May 13). Bill O'Reilly blames rap music for the decline of organized religion. *The Washington Post.* Retrieved from https://www.washingtonpost.com/news/the-fix/wp/2015/05/13/bill-oreilly-blames-rap-music-for-the-decline-of-organized-religion-that-makes-no-sense/?utm_term=.0f0704e42451

Cook, P., Jones, S., Lydon, J., & Matlock, G. (1976). Anarchy in the U.K. [Recorded by the Sex Pistols]. London: EMI.

Donkin, J. (2008, May 12). Heavy metal and violence: More than a myth? *CNN entertainment.* Retrieved from http://www.cnn.com/2008/SHOWBIZ/Music/05/09/metal.violence/index.html

Enstrom, R., & Schmaltz, R. (2017). A walk on the wild side: The impact of music on risk-taking likelihood. *Frontiers in Psychology, 8*, 759–763.

Epstein, J. S., Pratto, D. J., & Skipper, J. K. (1990). Teenagers, behavioral problems, and preferences for heavy metal and rap music: A case study of a southern middle school. *Deviant Behavior, 11*, 381–394.

Ferguson, C. J. (2015a). Do angry birds make for angry children? A meta-analysis of video game influences on children's and adolescents' aggression, mental health, prosocial behavior, and academic performance. *Perspectives on Psychological Science, 10*, 646–666.

Ferguson, C. J. (2015b). Does movie or video game violence predict societal violence? It depends on what you look at and when. *Journal of Communication, 65*, 193–212.

Grout, D. (1988). *A history of western music.* New York, NY: W.W. Norton.

Kotarba, J. A., Merrill, B., Williams, J. P., & Vannini, P. (2013). *Understanding society through popular music* (2nd ed.). New York, NY: Routledge.

Lilienfeld, S. O., Lynn, S. J., Ruscio, J., & Beyerstein, B. L. (2010). *50 great myths of popular psychology: Shattering widespread misconceptions about human behavior.* Malden, MA: Wiley-Blackwell.

Lizardo, O., & Skiles, S. (2015). Musical taste and patterns of symbolic exclusion in the United States 1993–2012: Generational dynamics of differentiation and continuity. *Poetics, 53*, 9–21.

Mulder, J., ter Bogt, T., Raaijmakers, Q., & Vollebergh, W. (2007). Music task groups and problem behavior. *Journal of Youth and Adolescence, 36*, 313–324.

Reddick, B. H., & Beresin, E. V. (2002). Rebellious rhapsody: Metal, rap, community, and individuation. *Academic Psychiatry, 26*, 51–59.

Reifert, C. (1989). *Charred remains [Recorded by Autopsy].* On *Severed survival* [CD]. Richmond, CA: Peaceville Records.

Schmaltz, R. M. (2016). Bang your head: Using heavy metal music to promote scientific thinking in the classroom. *Frontiers in Psychology, 7*, 146–149.

Selfhout, M. H. W., Delsing, M. J. M. H., ter Bogt, T. F. M., & Meeus, W. H. J. (2008). Heavy metal and hip-hop style preference and externalizing problem behavior: A two-wave longitudinal study. *Youth & Society, 39*, 435–452.

Sharman, L., & Dingle, G. A. (2015). Extreme metal music and anger processing. *Frontiers in Human Neuroscience, 9*, 272–283.

Took, K. J., & Weiss, D. S. (1994). The relationship between heavy metal and rap music and adolescent turmoil: Real or artifact? *Adolescence, 29*, 613–623.

Turner, D. W. (2015, November 5). Ex-gang member talks about rap music's influence. *The Chicago Tribune.* Retrieved from http://www.chicagotribune.com/news/columnists/ct-rap-music-gang-influence-turner-20151105-column.html

Tversky, A., & Kahneman, D. (1974). Judgment under uncertainty: Heuristics and biases. *Science (New Series), 185*, 1124–1131.

Villani, S. (2001). Impact of media on children and adolescents: A 10-year review of the research. *Journal of the American Academy of Child and Adolescent Psychiatry, 40*, 392–401.

Vaughn, L., & Schick, T. (1999). *How to think about weird things: Critical thinking for a new age.* Mountain View, CA: Mayfield.

Weisbart, D., & Ray, N. (1955). *Rebel without a cause* [Motion picture]. Hollywood, CA: Warner Brothers.

Mini myths for problems in modern society

Myth #46

Teens have the highest suicide rate

Teen suicide has increasingly garnered media attention in recent years. News headlines such as "Suicide Rate Triples Among Girls" in *U.S. News and World Report* (Leonard, 2016) have fueled panic among many adults and likely has led to the myth that teens have the highest suicide rate. This myth is widely believed as well, with about 70% of college students agreeing with it (Jewell & Hupp, 2018). And while the previously mentioned headline by *U.S. News and World Report* is technically accurate, it is also somewhat misleading. The report it refers to is from the Center for Disease Control and Prevention (Curtin, Warner, & Hedegaard, 2016), which states that suicide in girls from ages of 5 to 14 tripled from 0.5 to 1.5 cases per 100,000 from 1999 to 2014. However, the truth is that this age group actually has the lowest suicide rate of any age group for females. The highest rate of suicide for females occurs in 45–64-year-olds, whose rate is 9.8 cases per 100,000 compared to the adolescent (ages 15–24) rate, which is 4.6 cases per 100,000. Thus, females in middle age are more than twice as likely to commit suicide than female teens. For males this trend is similar as the rate of suicide is 18.2 cases per 100,000 for boys ages 15–24 while the highest suicide rate for males occurs at 75 years and older at 38.8 cases per 100,000, which is again 113% higher than male teens.

There is one group of adolescents, however, that does appear to have a substantially higher risk of suicidal ideation and attempts. Specifically, lesbian and gay youth have a significantly higher likelihood of suicide attempts compared with their heterosexual peers (Eisenberg & Resnick, 2006; Haas et al., 2010; Russell & Joyner, 2001). Researchers have hypothesized that this increase in suicidality in this population is likely related to the stigma of homosexuality and increased rates of bullying in these youth. Thus, while suicide in adolescence may not be higher than most other age groups, suicidality is particularly problematic in certain more vulnerable adolescent populations and deserves resources aimed at screening and treatment. The U.S. Substance Abuse and Mental Health Services Administration (SAMHSA) offers a free resource titled Preventing Suicide: A Toolkit for High Schools that can be obtained at http://store.samhsa.gov/product/Preventing-Suicide-A-Toolkit-for-High-Schools/SMA12-4669. Or if you or someone you know is considering suicide, call the National Suicide Prevention Lifeline at 1-800-273-8255.

References

Curtin, S. C., Warner, M., & Hedegaard, H. (2016). Increase in suicide in the United States, 1999–2014. NCHS Data Brief, (241), 1–8.

Eisenberg, M. E., & Resnick, M. D. (2006). Suicidality among gay, lesbian and bisexual youth: The role of protective factors. *Journal of Adolescent Health*, 39(5), 662–668.

Haas, A. P., Eliason, M., Mays, V. M., Mathy, R. M., Cochran, S. D., D'Augeli, A. R., … Russell, S. T. (2010). Suicide and suicide risk in lesbian, gay, bisexual, and transgender populations: Review and recommendations. *Journal of Homosexuality*, 58(1), 10–51.

Jewell, J. D., & Hupp, S. D. A. (2018). Prevalence of myths about adolescence [Manuscript in preparation].

Leonard, K. (2016, April 22). Suicide rate triples among girls. Retrieved from http://www.usnews.com/news/articles/2016-04-22/cdc-suicide-deaths-on-the-rise-among-teen-girls-and-middle-aged-men

Russell, S. T., & Joyner, K. (2001). Adolescent sexual orientation and suicide risk: Evidence from a national study. *American Journal of Public Health*, 91(8), 1276–1281.

Myth #47 Goggles mimicking drunkenness help prevent impaired driving

In an episode of his show, Dr. Phil wore a special type of goggles, called Fatal Vision goggles, and attempted to walk along a straight line (Winfrey & McGraw, 2010). The talk show host quickly veered off course, demonstrating that the goggles were a good representation of what it's like to be intoxicated. Similar demonstrations are commonly provided across the globe with these same goggles in schools and on college campuses, and many people believe they're effective at preventing impaired driving. Our research shows that 49–54% of students believed that "'Drunk goggles' are an effective component to drinking and driving prevention programs" (Jewell & Hupp, 2018).

The goggles alter the wearer's perceptual field such that it's challenging to see exactly what is in front of them, and the goggles do a good job of making the wearer feel off-balance. In addition to trying sobriety tasks while wearing the goggles, participants in programs using the goggles also often watch videos of testimonials from the family of victims of impaired-driving accidents. In prevention programming efforts, many implementers also have participants wear the goggles while playing sports (e.g., volleyball), games (e.g., musical chairs), or even while driving a golf cart or the Fatal Vision Roadster, a pedal car that's also sold by the same company (Innocorp, ltd, n.d.-a). https://fatalvision.com/fatal-vision-roadster-pedal-kart.html

According to the company that sells the goggles, "This internationally popular evidence-based prevention tool is used to educate people of all ages about the consequences of alcohol misuse and abuse" (Innocorp, ltd, n.d.-b). However, skepticism is always warranted when a company says their product is "evidence-based" because anyone can use the term. In fact, the product was widely being used before any well-designed research had been conducted.

Once research was conducted, Fatal Vision goggles did not fare so well. The first randomized control study demonstrated that college students who participated in an activity while wearing the goggles did become less accepting of impaired driving immediately following the program as compared with a comparison group (Jewell, Hupp, & Luttrell, 2004). However, many programs that use the goggles only have a small percentage of participants wear the goggles (e.g., during an assembly), and the rest of the students simply observe. In this study, the students who were simply onlookers did not experience a significant change in attitudes relative to the comparison group.

It was a second study by the same research team, however, that delivered two more damaging blows to Fatal Vision goggles (Jewell & Hupp, 2005). First, the study examined attitudes 4 weeks later and demonstrated that the immediate attitude change dissipated within 4 weeks. Second, this study examined self-reported impaired driving *behavior* in addition to *attitudes*. The participants in the Fatal Vision groups did *not* engage in less risky behavior related to impaired driving. In short, no well-designed studies have demonstrated that Fatal Vision goggles decreased impaired driving.

References

Innocorp, ltd (n.d.-a). Fatal Vision® Roadster—Pedal Kart (only). Retrieved from https://fatalvision.com

Innocorp, ltd (n.d.-b). Fatal Vision® Community Event Pack. Retrieved from https://fatalvision.com

Jewell, J. D., & Hupp, S. D. A. (2005). Examining the effects of Fatal Vision goggles on changing attitudes and behaviors related to drinking and driving. *Journal of Primary Prevention*, 26(6), 553–565.

Jewell, J. D., & Hupp, S. D. A. (2018). Prevalence of myths about adolescence [Manuscript in preparation].

Jewell, J. D., Hupp, S. D. A., & Luttrell, G. (2004). The effectiveness of Fatal Vision goggles: Disentangling experiential versus onlooker effects. *Journal of Alcohol and Drug Education*, 48(3), 63–85.

Winfrey, O., & McGraw, P. (Executive Producers). (2010). Moms who drink [Television talk show episode]. *Dr. Phil*. Chicago, IL: Harpo Productions.

Myth #48

Teens can be "scared straight"

In the Academy-award winning 1978 documentary *Scared Straight!*, producer Andrew Shapiro (1978) tells the story of the Lifers group (a group of prisoners serving long-term sentences). This group supposedly presents the stark realities of prison to young teenage boys and girls who are at risk for incarceration. As the title of the documentary implies, the experience is meant to scare the youth away from committing crimes. However, while the simple explanation of this intervention might seem both intuitive and relatively harmless, the actual practice of "Scared Straight programs" is definitely scary!

So-called Scared Straight programs began proliferating throughout the United States shortly after the release of the documentary. In programs such as this, youth are subjected to constant harassment, belittling, and threats of physical and sexual abuse by the incredibly intimidating adult inmates. The vulgar and profanity-laced tirades are shocking to view, and one would assume that while the intervention may be unpleasant for the youth, at least it will keep them out of trouble. In fact, according to our own research with college students, this myth is widely endorsed with 45–65% of the sample believing the myth is true (Jewell & Hupp, 2018). Unfortunately, a number of rigorous scientific studies have found that Scared Straight programs not only don't work, but they actually are quite harmful. Specifically, a 2005 review of the nine studies on the topic of Scared Straight programs found that participants were actually 1.6–1.7 times *more* likely to reoffend compared to a group of youth who had never participated in the program (Petrosino, Turpin-Petrosino, & Buehler, 2005). So while advocates of Scared Straight programs might think they're incredible programs, they're right—incredibly harmful. In fact, it is hard to imagine any other program that creates such negative consequences in its participants in such a short amount of time given that the program usually lasts only a single day. And the unintended consequences of Scared Straight programs appears to have caught the attention of the federal government as well. Specifically, two high-ranking federal administrators for the U.S. Department of Justice have stated that the implementation of these programs by a state facility may jeopardize that state's federal funding, as Scared Straight programs violate federal law that prohibits any minor from being within "sight and sound" of adult inmates (Robinson & Slowikowski, 2011). For interested readers, the book *Great Myths of Child Development* (Hupp & Jewell, 2015) dives even deeper into this myth (and for more information on boot camps, which are in some ways similar to Scared Straight, refer to #42 of this volume).

References

Hupp, S., & Jewell, J. (2015). *Great myths of child development*. Malden, MA: Wiley.

Jewell, J. D., & Hupp, S. D. A. (2018). Prevalence of myths about adolescence [Manuscript in preparation].

Petrosino, A., Turpin-Petrosino, C., & Buehler, J. (2005). Scared Straight and other juvenile awareness programs for preventing juvenile delinquency. *The Scientific Review of Mental Health Practice*, 4(1), 48–54.

Robinson, L., & Slowikowski, J. (2011, January 31). Scary—and ineffective. Retrieved from http://articles.baltimoresun.com/2011-01-31/news/bs-ed-scared-straight-20110131_1_straight-type-programs-straight-program-youths

Shapiro, A. (Producer). (1978). *Scared Straight!* [Documentary]. USA: New Video Group.

Myth #49 Sexting is only a teen problem

It seems that sexting, often defined as sending or receiving sexual content or photos by phone, has been around as long as modern cell phones. However, sexting is usually portrayed as mostly limited to teens. For example, in a Season 1 episode of *Glee* (Brennan & D'Elia, 2009) Puck is caught sexting another girl (Santana) in school by his girlfriend (and soon-to-be-mother of his child), Quinn. Santana taunts Quinn by telling her to "Check his cell phone 'cause my sexts are too hot to erase." Teens seem to get the majority of the blame for sexting, as 77–80% of college students in our own research believed this myth to be true (Jewell & Hupp, 2018). On rare occasions, adult sexting has also caught the eye of the media. For example, former New York Congressman Anthony Weiner was famously caught sexting several women, eventually leading to his resignation from

Congress. However, a recent review of the research on sexting has shed new light on the subject. Klettke, Hallford, and Mellor (2014) reviewed 31 studies on the prevalence of sexting in youth (middle school and high school students under 18 years old) and adults (usually defined as persons over 18 though often college students). They found that the average prevalence rate for teen sexting ranged from 10% to 15% while sexting in adult samples was about three times higher, ranging from 33% to 53% (see also Dake, Price, Maziarz, & Ward, 2012). So not only do adults sext, they seem to do so two to three times more than teens!

References

Brennan, I. (Writer), & D'Elia, B. (Director). (2009). Hairography [Television series episode]. In A. M. Woodall, M. Norvick, & K. Silverstein (Producers), *Glee*. Los Angeles, CA: Paramount Studios.

Dake, J. A., Price, J. H., Maziarz, L., & Ward, B. (2012). Prevalence and correlates of sexting behavior in adolescents. *American Journal of Sexuality Education*, 7(1), 1–15.

Jewell, J. D., & Hupp, S. D. A. (2017). Prevalence of myths about adolescence [Manuscript in preparation].

Klettke, B., Hallford, D. J., & Mellor, D. J. (2014). Sexting prevalence and correlates: A systematic literature review. *Clinical Psychology Review*, 34(1), 44–53.

Myth #50   Traditional High School Driver education courses have a strong record of making teens safe drivers

For teenagers in the United States, car crashes are the leading cause of death, and 16–19-year-olds have considerably more crashes when compared to every other age group (Center for Disease Control, n.d.). Teenagers are particularly vulnerable to experiencing a crash soon after receiving their driver's license. Considering the fact that many teens already receive some type of formalized driver's education course, it seems as if these courses aren't helping teens be as safe as we would hope. A review of nine studies looking at traditional high school driver education programs concluded that these programs are not effective at helping teens become safe drivers (Vernick et al., 1999). A more recent review also concluded that "School based driver education leads to early licensing and may increase road crashes" (Roberts & Kwan, 2001, p. 2). One approach that seems more promising is the use of combining a driver education course with a more graduated licensing system in which teens go through different phases such as: (i) a year-long learning phase, (ii) an intermediate phase with driving restrictions, and (iii) full licensure (Shell, Newman, Córdova-Cazar, & Heese, 2015). However, there is little research on this approach, and the existing research does not include randomized control trials. Considering the fact that teens currently have almost three times as many fatal crashes as adults, we still have a long way to go to find the best way to keep our roads safe for everyone.

References

Center for Disease Control (n.d.). Teen drivers: Get the facts. Retrieved from www.cdc.gov

Roberts, I. G., & Kwan, I. (2001). School-based driver education for the prevention of traffic crashes. *The Cochrane Library*, *3*, 1–14.

Shell, D. F., Newman, I. M., Córdova-Cazar, A. L., & Heese, J. M. (2015). Driver education and teen crashes and traffic violations in the first two years of driving in a graduated licensing system. *Accident Analysis and Prevention*, *82*, 45–52. doi:10.1016/j.aap.2015.05.011.

Vernick, J. S., Li, G., Ogaitis, S., MacKenzie, E. J., Baker, S. P., & Gielen, A. C. (1999). Effects of high school driver education on motor vehicle crashes, violations, and licensure. *American Journal of Preventive Medicine*, *16*(1), 40–46.

INDEX

Great Myths of Adolescence, First Edition. Jeremy D. Jewell, Michael I. Axelrod,
Mitchell J. Prinstein, and Stephen Hupp.
© 2019 John Wiley & Sons Ltd. Published 2019 by John Wiley & Sons Ltd.

Rowling, J.K., 121
Ruble, D. N., 53
Runyan, C. W., 65

Sandstrom, K. L., 64
SATs *see* Scholastic Aptitude Tests (SATs)
Saved By the Bell (sitcom), 73
Sawyer, R., 79
Scared Straight programs, myths regarding, 149, 176–177
Schmaltz, Rodney, 167
Scholastic Aptitude Tests (SATs)
  and prediction of academic success at college, 77–81
  prep course myth, 57–58
Science Advisory Committee, US, 66
ScienceNordic, 131
Self-Determination Theory, 80
self-development, myths of, 60–95
  abstinence-only sex education programs effective, 85–86
  college placement tests useless at predicting academic success, 77–81
  conversion therapy turning homosexual teens straight, 91–94
  high school football players more likely to become seriously injured, 88–90
  HPV vaccine increases sexual activity, 86–87
  infant simulator doll increasing abstinence from sexual activity, 72–77
  jobs as character-building, 64–68
  laziness of millennial generation, 26, 87–88
  mini myths, 82–95
  offenders hiding sexual interest when initiating sex offenses online against teens, 90

random hook-ups undertaken by students, 82–84
risky behavior inevitable, 68–72
significant mood disruptions inevitable, 60–64
teaching about contraception increases sexual activity, 84–85
underestimation of consequences of risky behavior by teens, 94–95
sex education programs, 75
Sex Lives of College Students, The (Caron), 82
sexting only a teen problem myth, 5, 177–178
sexual activity myths
  abstinence-only sex education programs effective, 85–86
  conversion therapy turning homosexual teens straight, 91–94
  HPV vaccine increases sexual activity, 86–87
  infant simulator doll increasing abstinence, 72–77
  offenders hiding sexual interest when initiating sex offenses online against teens, 90
  random hook-ups undertaken by students, 82–84
  sexual assault usually by a stranger, 125–126
  teaching about contraception increases sexual activity, 84–85
sexual orientation disturbance, 91
sexually transmitted infections (STIs), 84
Shapiro, Andrew, 176
Shaw, E. J., 79
silence, working in, 49
Sims, The, 38, 40, 43
sleep patterns, 10